Destination Collaboration 1

DESTINATION COLLABORATION 1

A Complete Research Focused Curriculum Guidebook to Educate 21st Century Learners in Grades 3–5

Danielle N. DuPuis and Lori M. Carter

LIBRARIES UNLIMITED

AN IMPRINT OF ABC-CLIO, LLC
Santa Barbara, California • Denver, Colorado • Oxford, England

Copyright 2011 by Danielle N. DuPuis and Lori M. Carter

Library of Congress Cataloging-in-Publication Data

DuPuis, Danielle N.

   Destination collaboration 1 : a complete research focused curriculum guidebook to educate 21st century learners in grades 3-5 / Danielle N. DuPuis and Lori M. Carter.

        p. cm.

   Includes bibliographical references and index.

   ISBN 978-1-59884-581-5 (acid-free paper) — ISBN 978-1-59884-582-2 (ebook)   1. Information literacy—Study and teaching (Elementary)   2. Electronic information literacy—Study and teaching (Elementary)   3. School librarian participation in curriculum planning.   4. Library orientation for school children.   I. Carter, Lori M.   II. Title.

   ZA3075.D87 2011

   372.13'0281—dc22   2010035225

ISBN: 978-1-59884-581-5
EISBN: 978-1-59884-582-2

15   14   13   12   11   1   2   3   4   5

This book is also available on the World Wide Web as an eBook.
Visit www.abc-clio.com for details.

Libraries Unlimited
An Imprint of ABC-CLIO, LLC

ABC-CLIO, LLC
130 Cremona Drive, P.O. Box 1911
Santa Barbara, California 93116-1911

This book is printed on acid-free paper ∞

Manufactured in the United States of America

Excerpts from *Standards for the 21st-Century Learner* by the American Association of School Librarians, a division of the American Library Association, copyright © 2007 American Library Association. Available for download at www.ala.org/aasl/standards. Used with permission.

National Educational Technology Standards for Students, Second Edition, © 2007, ISTE ® (International Society for Technology in Education), Reprinted with permission. www.iste.org. All rights reserved.

Standards for the English Language Art, by the International Reading Association and the National Council of Teachers of English, Copyright 1996 by the International Reading Association and the National Council of Teachers of English. Reprinted with permission.

Contents

3RD-GRADE LESSONS
Lesson 1: You're Invited!

Lesson 2: Welcome to Our State

4TH-GRADE LESSONS
Lesson 1: Take Note!

Lesson 2: Digging into the Past

Lesson 3: Understanding the Past

5TH-GRADE LESSONS

Lesson 1: Get a Clue about Copyright©

Lesson 2: Plagiarism or Not?

Lesson 3: Archiving Information

3RD-GRADE LESSONS
Lesson 1: PAC Scramble

Lesson 2: Locked in the Library

Lesson 3: Mouse Tracks

4TH-GRADE LESSONS
Lesson 1: Branching Out

Lesson 2: Best Book Buds

5TH-GRADE LESSONS

Lesson 1: Unlocking Information

Lesson 2: Finding the Key

3RD-GRADE LESSONS

Lesson 1: Plant an Idea

Lesson 2: Get the Dirt on Plants

4TH-GRADE LESSONS

Lesson 1: Information Metamorphosis

Lesson 2: Inviting All Butterflies!

5TH-GRADE LESSONS
Lesson 1: Going Green

Lesson 2: A Greener Planet

3RD-GRADE LESSONS

Lesson 1: Web Basics

Lesson 2: Searching for Internet Safety

4TH-GRADE LESSONS
Lesson 1: Digital Netiquette

Lesson 2: Online Communication

5TH-GRADE LESSONS
Lesson 1: Practical Communication

Lesson 2: Effective Communication

Acknowledgments

We would like to thank Shellie Elson from National Council of Teachers of English (NCTE), Chi Yang from National Council for the Social Studies (NCSS), Barbara Murphy from National Academies Press, Marian Olivas from National Center for History in the Schools, Tina Wells from International Society for Technology in Education (ISTE), and Alison Cline from American Association of School Librarians (AASL). Thank you so much for taking the time to communicate with us and for giving us permission to use the national standards in our books.

The lessons in this book were created by following the backward design model. Thank you to Grant Wiggins and Jay McTighe for writing *Understanding by Design* to better explain this process.

A big thank you goes out to our teacher and colleague Dr. Ann Weeks. Thank you for encouraging us to write this book, and for your support along the way.

We'd also like to thank Sharon Coatney, our editor and guiding light during the last year of our three-year journey in writing the *Destination Collaboration* books. We really appreciate your guidance and support!

Our acknowledgments wouldn't be complete without mentioning and thanking our families, who have "put up" with us these last few years as we worked evenings and weekends on *Destination Collaboration*.

Danielle dedicates this book in loving memory of her grandfather, who continues to serve as her inspiration.

Lori dedicates this book in loving memory of her father, who always "believed in doing it 'till you get it right," and her mother, who still provides much love and support. She also dedicates this book to her husband, Rick Carter, with much love for his constant support. And to their children, Lindsey, Kelley, Chelsea, Rita, Jason, and Brianna: thank you for understanding the amount of effort involved in writing a book.

Permissions

As with any valuable educational resource, it is of great assistance to other educators to see how the standards are applied for use in student instruction. The various national standards reprinted in this book have been done so within the guidelines of permissible use as associated with each organization. Following is a list of the each organization with a link to each organizations Web site. Use these Web sites as a resource when creating your own collaborative cross-curricular lesson plans.

Excerpted from *Standards for the 21st-Century Learner* by the American Association of School Librarians, a division of the American Library Association, copyright © 2007 American Library Association. Available for download at www.ala.org/aasl/standards. Used with permission.

Curriculum Standards for Social Studies © National Council for the Social Studies. Reprinted by permission. http://www.socialstudies.org/.

Standards for the English Language Arts, by the International Reading Association and the National Council of Teachers of English, Copyright 1996 by the International Reading Association and the National Council of Teachers of English. Reprinted with permission. http://www.ncte.org/standards.

National Educational Technology Standards for Students, Second Edition, © 2007, ISTE® (International Society for Technology in Education), Reprinted with permission. www.iste.org. All rights reserved.

National Science Education Standards Reprinted with permission from the National Science Education Standards, 2008 by the National Academy of Sciences, Courtesy of the National Academies Press, Washington, D.C.

National Standards for History, "National Standards for History, revised edition" (UCLA: 1996). Reprinted with permission. http://nchs.ucla.edu.

Introduction

Destination Collaboration 1: A Complete Research Focused Curriculum Guidebook to Educate 21st Century Learners in Grades 3–5 is designed to assist library media specialists and classroom teachers in creating instructional partnerships. This book includes four chapters with comprehensive instructional units for grades 3, 4, and 5—totaling 30 original lesson plans. Each unit is rooted in classroom content and focuses on: using library resources, incorporating information literacy skills, and using technology to deliver meaningful and memorable instruction to students. Each chapter in this book contains two to three lesson plans for each grade level on a particular media unit: notetaking, public access catalog, informational text, and online resources. These units were chosen as the basis for each chapter, because each topic demands specific skills that are essential for teaching information literacy, copyright, and basic research.

This book is not meant to be read in one sitting or from cover to cover. Instead, we hope that you will use the lessons as needed to cover relevant information literacy topics and content area objectives with your students. The lessons in this book are designed with the assumption that you are *not* fully collaborating with every teacher in your building *all* the time. Each lesson is designed knowing that the possibility exists that you may teach this lesson in isolation, coordination, cooperation, or collaboration. In addition, we also offer the ability to use the lesson topic in an inquiry-based format. These premade lessons and materials can serve as the building blocks for collaborating with other teachers at your school. Our book not only provides complete lessons, technology options, modifications, student project templates, and inquiry-based learning options, but it also supports your efforts in moving from isolation, to coordination, and cooperation and on toward collaboration.

Being Seen as a Leader

The journey toward collaboration requires the use of leadership skills, content knowledge, and information literacy knowledge, along with patience and innovation. Collaboration is most easily implemented when others in the school see you as an instructional leader. Most library media centers are centrally located within a school. We believe the library media center is the "hub" of the school and that library media specialists are in a position where much of the action takes place. We realize that there are many influences that will affect your ability to be a leader in your school: your relationship with administration, your involvement in school improvement meetings, your material selection and evaluation, and the design of your physical space, to name a few. This book is designed to help you be seen as an instructional leader because regardless of what kind of program you find yourself working with today, this book provides the tools and inspiration to move your program toward collaboration.

Information Power (American Association of School Librarians [AASL], 1998) talks about the themes of collaboration, leadership, and technology, but as Keith Curry Lance pointed out, "the three themes [are listed] in the wrong order. Leadership comes first, then collaboration, and then technology. If you want to collaborate, you have to step into those leadership shoes first and establish yourself as a leader that somebody would want to collaborate with" (Achterman, 2007, p. 51).

Collaboration comes when you are seen as an instructional leader. Leadership builds from mutual respect and trust. An instructional leader possesses the ability to design lesson plans, make connections to classroom learning, infuse lessons with technology, include assessment strategies, provide students with modifications and extensions, and have the desire to develop inquiry-based learning units with classroom teachers. This book demonstrates and assists you in putting into practice the aforementioned qualities of an instructional leader.

From Isolation to Collaboration

Effective library media specialists invest a significant amount of time juggling their many duties and jobs. We hope that the materials in this book will help move your relationship with teachers to a higher level; from isolation to coordination, cooperation, or collaboration (ICCC). Each lesson has been designed to enable easy implementation. The introduction in each chapter focuses on the importance of the key topic in that chapter. Relevancy and the importance of the topic are explained. Assessment choices are also discussed.

The circular indicators displayed below will be repeated in each chapter so that you can easily locate how to share the lessons regardless of your location on the ICCC continuum. Information regarding the use of the lessons in isolation can be found at the beginning of each chapter. These tips are located at the beginning of the chapter because isolation tips provide an overview of why the skill covered in the chapter is important, how it can be incorporated in the classroom, and simple ways to improve visibility within the school. Coordination and cooperation tips are located at the beginning of each individual lesson within the unit. These tips are placed close to the lessons because in order to coordinate and cooperate, your efforts must be connected to your instruction and that of the classroom teacher. Suggestions for collaboration can always be found at the end of each grade-level unit. Collaboration tips are placed at the end of the unit because these tips include essential questions that are directly tied to classroom content. Use these essential questions to create inquiry-based learning projects with classroom teachers.

ICCC Continuum

"Not a single state reading assessment used for No Child Left Behind (U.S. Department of Education, 2007) assessments measures our students' ability to read search engine results; locate information online; critically evaluate information on the Internet; or synthesize information online. It is the cruelest irony of No Child Left Behind Act that students who most need to be prepared at school for an online age of information are precisely those who are being prepared the least" (Leu, O'Byrne, Zawilinski, McVerry, and Everett-Cacopardo, 2009, p. 267).

With the implementation of the No Child Left Behind Act in 2002, the importance of moving toward collaboration is clear. Research has shown that improved student learning occurs when learning goals can be unified across many areas of the curriculum. However, in many schools, library media specialists are still working in isolation for a number of reasons. Teaching in isolation is delivering instruction of one subject to one set of students during one time period. Isolation can be a common byproduct of a fixed schedule in a library media center. As a result, library media specialists' fixed schedules allow for very little flexibility for co-teaching opportunities. Classroom teachers may find it difficult to collaborate. There also may not be enough time in the school day to do more than teach classes, troubleshoot technology problems, spend your annual budget, weed your collection, and provide professional development. Taking these factors into account, it is easy to understand how even the most effective library media specialists can find moving toward collaboration complicated. By providing you with proper documentation and complete lesson plans, we hope to alleviate some of the pressure of the demands you face. These lessons will help demonstrate your abilities as a teacher. Recognition as a teacher is an important first step as you move away from isolation. This book lessens the amount of time needed to prepare effective lessons as you move around the ICCC continuum (Austin, 2000) with other teachers.

One way to work toward collaboration is to coordinate a lesson or unit with another teacher. Working in coordination is the process of arranging schedules, activities, or resources with another teacher in order to help your own work run more efficiently. The event, project, or activity is coordinated by one person and communicated to someone else. For example, you may be getting ready to start a geography unit with your 4th grade students that focuses on different cultures around the world. To coordinate a global geography lesson with the classroom teacher, you might ask the classroom teacher when he or she might be teaching global culture. The classroom teacher may ask you to provide him or her with resources that are in your media center. You may also wish to share some materials that you use to teach geography concepts and skills to students. Perhaps the classroom teacher will arrange for you to keep the students for a few extra minutes if you need more time to complete the lessons. If you find yourself in coordination, each lesson in this book provides you with specific examples for how to move from coordination towards cooperation and collaboration.

Cooperation

Cooperation is sometimes mistaken for collaboration; however, it's not the same. The process of cooperation includes setting goals and working with one or more classroom teachers to share responsibility for creating a project, but the parts of the project may be taught separately. One partner in the team may be assigned a major role while others may take on more limited responsibilities. For example, if you were teaching a unit about the planets with your 3rd grade students, you might have a lesson plan that has a large research piece as well as a writing piece. The lesson is mostly planned, but you think that it will be beneficial to cooperate with the classroom teacher, so you meet with the classroom teacher to talk about sharing the work. You offer to teach the research piece, and the classroom teacher takes responsibility for the writing assignment. The research piece may take several sessions in the media center to gather all necessary information to write a comprehensive paragraph for the project. Upon completion of the research, the classroom teacher assists the students by teaching proper grammar and sentence structure, and by giving instruction on how to write a research paper. Cooperation does *not* require shared power. Cooperation can begin a partnership by building mutual respect and trust. Each chapter in this book provides suggestions on how to build on that trust as you move towards collaboration with classroom teachers.

Collaboration

When you work together with other teachers and equally contribute to creating and designing integrated instruction, you are working in collaboration. Sharing the planning, design, and implementation of content and media objectives with other teachers should result in new understandings and experiences for both the teacher and the library media specialist. With a shared vision you will work together through an equal partnership to integrate content and information literacy standards to accomplish objectives. To assist you in reaching collaboration, a number of planning documents and handouts have been included in this book. The companion Web site contains electronic worksheets to assist you in asking the right questions as you meet and plan with your instructional partner to create a collaborative lesson or unit. Not only are you provided with suggestions for approaching classroom teachers, but we've also included essential questions to assist you in creating inquiry-based research projects and templates for creating your own lessons. These documents may be used to initiate conversation with your instructional partner, as well as to build on and improve the lessons provided in this book.

National Standards

Students are more likely to succeed when cross-curricular connections can be made. The lessons in each chapter support not only the new American Association of School Librarians (AASL) *Standards for the 21st-Century Learner* and current National Educational Technology Standards for Students (NETS-S) technology standards, but they also apply national content area standards including science, social studies, history, and language arts. These content areas were chosen because information literacy skills can be taught effectively through these subject areas and because they offer excellent opportunities to collaborate with the classroom teacher (Corey, 2002).

In the process of writing the lessons in this book, the *Standards for the 21st-Century Learner in Action* (AASL, 2009) were explicitly embedded within each of the lessons to show how the content and structure of the lesson supported the AASL strands and benchmarks. Every applicable indicator for skills, dispositions in action, responsibilities, and self-assessment strategies were embedded within each lesson to create clear connections. We have been granted permission from AASL to indicate the standard number at the beginning of each lesson to show what general AASL standards the lesson addresses. However, the embedded numbered strands and descriptions of the skills, dispositions in action, responsibilities, and self-assessment strategies have been removed so as to comply with copyright. Although these indicators and benchmarks have been removed, embedded placeholders remain for your reference. We strongly encourage the use of the *Standards for the 21st-Century Learner in Action* (AASL, 2009) as a guide to locate the indicators and benchmarks for each skill, disposition in action, responsibility, and self-assessment strategy. We suggest writing the indicators directly onto the embedded placeholders in this book. We realize that going back to look at the standards will take a considerable amount of work and effort; however, going through the motion of looking up the indicators and benchmarks will not only assist you in better understanding how to use the lessons in this book, but it will also provide you with the background knowledge and support needed to create your own lesson plans with embedded standards. As you work to embed the skill indicators, be sure to note that the skill indicators will directly correspond with a specific standard (i.e., Standard 1, 2, 3, or 4). However, the dispositions in action indicators, responsibility indicators, and self-assessment strategy indicators, are all fluid. These indicators may be mixed and matched to support any of the four standards. Be sure to note that these indicators do not necessarily follow the general standard for the lesson. Locating these direct connections will assist you as you rework and create lessons that integrate the use of these new standards. Please refer to the *Standards for the 21st-Century Learner in Action* (AASL, 2009) for more information and integrate the full standards directly into each lesson using the template provided.

Using Technology

We understand the need for the ethical use of information and that "information skills will enable students to use technology as an important tool for learning now and in the future" (AASL, 2007, p. 2). As you explore and use the lessons within this book, you will notice that technology is integrated in most of the lessons through various common applications, Web sites, and suggested use of online databases. If technology is not integrated directly into the lesson, technology options are always included and can be used for lesson extensions, activities, or tools for locating more information. These technology options are located at the end of each lesson and are called either "Technology Integration" or an "Enrichment Using Technology." The "Technology Integration" can be used directly within the lesson as it was written. If you decide to use the "Technology Integration" option, the technology standards have also been included. The options provided in the "Enrichment Using Technology" sections could change the focus of the lesson. Depending on your comfort level with technology, build on the lesson by using the suggested podcasts, blogs, or other Web 2.0 tools. As you use this book, you may wish to add other ideas and technology resources to enhance your lessons. Using these technology suggestions may provide you with a springboard for another collaborative opportunity. You may wish to think about how the purpose of the lesson may change by making these alterations.

Materials

Each lesson includes a number of ready-made materials you may use to assist your students in the learning process. These materials will be found either within the book or on our companion Web site. You may access this Web site at **www.destinationcollaboration.com**. You will notice that we include a variety of materials that appeal to kinesthetic, visual, and auditory learners. Each unit includes a blend of electronic materials such as PowerPoint presentations, videos, and electronic worksheets. The PowerPoint presentations in our book are instructional tools and include helpful notes to guide you through instruction, interactive games, and digital photographs. These interactive resources will engage and interest your students in learning information literacy skills and will be found on the companion Web site. In addition, sidebars have been placed within the book to highlight discussion opportunities, time saving tips, communication tools, and classroom connections.

How to Read the Labels for Instructional Materials

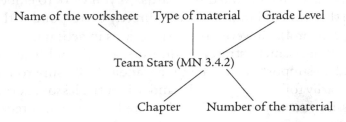

There are several different codes for material types:

MN = Manipulatives are hands-on activities for your students. You may wish to laminate these items and use them from year to year.

WS = Worksheets are for student use and are meant to be printed and photocopied.

EWS = Electronic worksheets are for student use and are meant to be used on a computer or in a computer lab setting. These worksheets can be downloaded from our companion Web site to your computer at any time. We recommend downloading them prior to the lesson for easy access.

RS = Resource sheets are for student use and are meant to provide additional or background information.

ER = Electronic resources are electronic teaching tools and are sometimes interactive.

TRS = Teacher resource sheets are for teachers only and provide background information and answers to student resource sheets and worksheets.

MOD = Modified worksheets or resource sheets are provided to assist those students with special developmental or academic needs. You may wish to modify these sheets even further.

EX = Extension activities are sometimes provided to enhance the lesson with an additional activity or worksheet (print or electronic). You can also use these activities for gifted students or early finishers.

CC = There are three classroom connection documents found at the end of this introduction as a sample for what can be used in coordination and cooperation with other teachers.

O = An "O" at the beginning of any of the aforementioned material codes indicates that the material will be found on our online companion Web site.

Collaborative Documents

The intended use for our book is to provide lesson plans that can be used on an ICCC continuum. In many schools, elementary library media specialists see students on a fixed schedule once a week. As a result, it is very difficult for library media specialists to create inquiry-based learning projects and maintain the cognitive continuity needed for this level of learning by students in just 30 minutes to an hour once a week. Our book includes suggestions for inquiry-based learning projects, which you may wish to use with students. We hope that you will review these lessons and adapt them to meet your needs as well as the needs of your students. This book is designed to support you in your efforts to move toward collaboration with classroom teachers and to improve learning and teaching opportunities within your school.

Inquiry-based learning has been shown to support student achievement. Because of its value, we have included appendices A and B for you to use as you collaborate with classroom teachers to create inquiry-based learning or collaborative lesson plans.

Inquiry-based learning experiences focus on students' own questions about a topic; in this way, student curiosity becomes a driving force for learning. Through such experiences, students locate information, organize it, and share that information with an audience through a variety of forms including writing, multimedia presentations, debates, or Web sites (Moss, 2005).

We hope the examples in appendices A and B will encourage you to work collaboratively with classroom teachers in your building to create integrated learning opportunities. While we know that this book will not be your only lesson planning resource, we hope that it will offer some new ideas and approaches that will enable you to work more effectively with teachers and expand the learning opportunities for your students.

Benefits of Using This Book

"We have to stand by the need for teacher-librarians to be qualified as both teachers and librarians, because if they're not, they're not going to be allowed to do what we want them to do. One thing I'm pretty sure of is that if you're in a public school and you want a teacher to collaborate with you, they'd better perceive you as a teacher or it's just not going to happen" (Lance, 2007).

Library media specialists are a diverse group. Some of us have experience working as classroom teachers, and others may have experience working in public or private libraries prior to beginning work in the preK–12 environment. No matter what our backgrounds, we do share the same goals as our colleagues in the education field—we promote and teach information literacy, ground our instruction in national standards, encourage and integrate the use of technology, encourage a love of reading, and want our students to succeed at whatever career path they choose. This book will help you be recognized by other educators in the building as a teacher, librarian, information specialist, and instructional partner—commonly known as a library media specialist. It will assist changing perceptions about librarians as "just storytellers" or the "sweet lady/gentleman who only knows how to find and recommend books." Library media specialists are men and women from all walks of life who devote themselves to being lifelong learners and educators. We not only answer questions but also teach students and individuals how to find the answers and why the resources used are important. You are a learner, a leader, program administrator, instructional partner, information specialist, and teacher. In providing you with the necessary tools to teach a unit from start to finish, we hope that this book will encourage and enable you to look at your lessons in a new way and give you an opportunity to be recognized as a 21st century library media specialist.

Works Cited

Achterman, Doug. "The Sower: Interview with Keith Curry Lance." *School Library Journal* 53.10 Oct. 2007: 50–53. Print.

American Association of School Librarians. *Information Power: Building Partnerships For Learning.* Chicago: American Library Association, 1998. Print.

American Association of School Librarians. *Standards for the 21st-Century Learner.* Chicago: American Library Association, 2007. American Library Association. Web. 9 Mar. 2008 <http://www.ala.org/ala/mgrps/divs/aasl/guidelinesandstandards/learningstandards/standards.cfm>.

American Association of School Librarians. *Standards for the 21st-Century Learner in Action.* Chicago: American Library Association, 2009. Print.

Austin, James E. *The Collaboration Challenge: How Nonprofits and Businesses Succeed through Strategic Alliances.* San Francisco: Jossey-Bass, 2000. Print.

Corey, Linda. "The Role of the Library Media Specialist in Standards-Based Learning." *Knowledge Quest* (2002): 21–23. *Library Literature and Information Science Full Text.* Web. 12 Nov. 2007.

Leu, Donald J. "New Literacies, Reading Research, and the Challenges of Change: A Deictic Perspective." *The 55th Yearbook of the National Reading Conference.* Video presented at the National Reading Conference, Milwaukee, WI. 30 Nov. 2005.

Leu, Donald J., Rosemarie. Ataya, Julie L. Coiro. *Assessing Assessment Strategies Among the 50 States: Evaluating the Literacies of Our Past or Our Future?* Paper presented at the National Reading Conference, Miami, FL. Dec. 2002.

Leu, Donald J., W. Ian O'Byrne, Lisa Zawilinski, J. Greg McVerry, and Heidi Everett-Cacopardo. "Expanding the New Literacies Conversation." *Educational Researcher* 38.4.1 (2009): 264–269. Web. 30 Sept. 2010.

Moss, Barbara. "Making a Case and a Place For Effective Content Area Literacy Instruction in the Elementary Grades." *The Reading Teacher* 59.1 (2005): 46–55. *Library Literature and Information Science Full Text.* Web. 13 Nov. 2007.

U.S. Department of Education. *No Child Left Behind Act of 2001. United States Department of Education.* Web. 15 Nov. 2007 <http://www.ed.gov/policy/elsec/leg/esea02/index.html>.

Works Consulted

Fine, J. "Hand in Hand: Public and School Library Cooperative Projects." *Journal of Youth Services* 14.3 (2001): 18–22. Print.

Hartzell, Gary N. *Building Influence for the School Librarian: Tenet, Targets and Tactics.* 2nd ed. Worthington: Linworth, 2003. Print.

Loertscher, D.V. "Second Revolution: A Taxonomy for the 1980's." *Wilson Library Bulletin* 56 (1982): 412–21. Print.

Loertscher, D.V. *Taxonomies of the School Library Media Program.* Englewood, CO: Libraries Unlimited, 1988. Print.

Loertscher, D.V. *Taxonomies of the School Library Media Program.* 1988. 2nd ed. San Jose, CA: Hi Willow, 2000. Print.

McKenna, M. C., and R. D. Robinson. "Content Literacy: A Definition and Implications." *Journal of Reading* 34 (1990): 184–86. Print.

Montiel-Overall, Patricia. "Toward a Theory of Collaboration for Teachers and Librarians." *School Library Media Research* 8 (2005). *American Association of School Librarians.* Web. 1 Sept. 2007.

Wiggins, Grant, and Jay McTighe. *Understanding By Design.* Alexandria, VA: Association for Supervision and Curriculum Development, 2005. Print.

FINDING THE MAIN IDEA AND SUPPORTING DETAILS IN NEWSPAPERS

Name: _____

Name of Newspaper: _____

Title of the article you are reading: _____

1. Before you read the entire article, what do you think this article will be about based on the title?

   _____
   _____
   _____
   _____
   _____

2. Read the entire article.

3. What is the *main idea* of this article? Write your answer below:

   _____
   _____
   _____
   _____
   _____

4. What *supporting details* are provided that support the main idea? Write them below:

   _____
   _____
   _____
   _____
   _____

Challenge: Write a question that can be answered by reading this article. Challenge a partner to find the answer. Discuss what information is irrelevant to your question!

From *Destination Collaboration 1: A Complete Research Focused Curriculum Guidebook to Educate 21st Century Learners in Grades 3–5* by Danielle N. DuPuis and Lori M. Carter. Santa Barbara, CA: Libraries Unlimited. Copyright © 2011.

READING INFORMATIONAL TEXT AND LOCATING
THE MAIN IDEA BASED ON YOUR INTERESTS!

Name: _____

1. Locate an informational text that is of interest to you. Informational text is nonfiction.

2. Write the title of the book: _____
_____

3. Look at the cover of the book and the chapters listed in the table of contents. What do you want to learn more about? Write the chapter from the table of contents that you want to explore and learn more about: _____
Page _____

4. Read the chapter that interests you. You may not have time to read the entire chapter. Look at the clock and read for about 10 minutes.

5. What is the main idea for this chapter? Write the main idea here: _____
_____
_____
_____
_____

6. Does the name of the chapter give you a hint about the main idea for that chapter?

   Yes _____ No _____ If no, why not? _____
_____
_____
_____

7. Look back in the table of contents. What chapters are irrelevant to your interests about this topic? List two of the chapters that do not interest you.

   a. _____

   b. _____

   Why do these chapters not interest you? _____
_____
_____
_____

8. Look back at the chapter that you read. List the main idea and a few supporting details that really interest you. When you are at the library media center, ask your library media specialist to help you find more information about this topic. Write the main idea and Supporting details on the back of this paper.

From *Destination Collaboration 1: A Complete Research Focused Curriculum Guidebook to Educate 21st Century Learners in Grades 3–5* by Danielle N. DuPuis and Lori M. Carter. Santa Barbara, CA: Libraries Unlimited. Copyright © 2011.

Write a friendly letter below telling a friend about an interesting nonfiction book that you just read! Be sure to explain why you like this book, and remember to share a few details from the book. Give the letter to a classmate and ask them to underline the main idea of your letter in red, supporting details in blue and irrelevant information in yellow. Discuss whether your friend underlined the correct information using Think-Pair-Share.

Date: _____

Dear _____,

_____

_____

_____

_____

_____

_____

_____

_____

_____

_____

_____

_____

_____

_____

_____

_____

_____,

_____

Chapter 1

Notetaking: Organizing Information

Introduction

Notetaking is a complex skill for young students. This skill is essential to organizing information, which is the reason why it is the subject of the first chapter of this book. By teaching the notetaking units at the beginning of the year, students will be prepared to complete projects throughout the year, thereby maximizing student achievement. To process information, students need to understand the purpose for reading to identify main ideas and supporting details in written, oral, or digital text. The ability to identify key information and take notes from a variety of sources in various formats will assist students as they gain an understanding of content organization.

From Year to Year

Notetaking is a skill that can be expanded on from year to year. As you use the lessons in this book to teach notetaking from 3rd to 4th, and finally to 5th grade, you will see that each unit builds on the knowledge students gained in the previous years' notetaking lessons. The 3rd-grade lessons begin with teaching students how to extract the main idea and supporting details from a text and take notes in their own words. As students move forward into 4th grade, students learn how to create a basic bibliography for book and Web resources. The lessons for 5th grade are designed to teach students notetaking methods as well as get them familiar with copyright laws. Students will also learn the proper Modern Language Association (MLA) citation method when creating a bibliography. By 5th grade, students are also learning how to paraphrase without plagiarizing—a task that is more difficult than it seems. By slowly introducing these critical skills over a period of several years, and allowing students time to process and apply what they have learned while building on prior knowledge, library media specialists can provide students with the necessary tools to be successful organizers of information.

Unintentional Plagiarism

In a study on unintentional plagiarism and proper paraphrasing skills, Angela L. Walker notes "students indicated that identifying plagiarism was simple when a writer failed to provide citation; left the original unchanged, or modified the work by one or two words. When a writer made several minor changes, however, students believed the paraphrasing was accurate suggesting that when writing students may unintentionally plagiarize" (Walker, 2008). By teaching students the basic skills of notetaking and by giving them projects in which they can use their notes to formulate new concepts and ideas, we can assist students in preventing unintentional plagiarism. The earlier students are introduced to the concept, the more likely they will be to use information responsibly and ethically at the middle school, high school, and college level.

Rubrics

Use the rubrics provided in each unit to outline the expectations of the projects. Students who are aware of their expectations ahead of time are more likely to succeed. These rubrics are designed to be used as both assessment and learning tools. As students work toward the project goals, revisit and highlight expectations that may be trouble spots for students as they work toward finishing the project. Some students will need more clarification than others. From year to year, retain exemplary models of student work to share with current year's classes. These works will guide students to working at a higher level as they compare their own work to the exemplary work. While a point value has been assigned to each section of the rubric, you may wish to work in collaboration with the classroom teacher to decide how many points students will need to earn in order to achieve a particular grade. Discuss these options before beginning the lesson so you can inform the students of how many points they will need to receive an "A" or "B" on the project.

Relevancy

In the classroom, students are often asked to answer a question by reading or listening to a passage from a text. The classroom teacher may create the text, ask students to read from a book (fiction or nonfiction), or read information from an Internet site. In order to answer the question, the student must revisit the text, determine the main idea, comprehend what they are reading, and distinguish between relevant and irrelevant information based upon the question. Relevancy is also subject to identifying differences between fact and opinion.

The difficulty of notetaking increases when reading digitally or listening to oral text. Digital text requires the student to read in a nonlinear fashion due to embedded hyperlinks directing the student to new information. Oral text requires the student to take notes while relying on listening skills.

As 21st century learners, our students will be required to take notes—not only for themselves—but collaboratively by using a myriad of Web 2.0 tools. While these Web tools will add a new dimension, the basic skills of notetaking will remain significant to the process.

Working in Isolation

If you find yourself working in isolation, be sure to look through your school district, state or county's curriculum guides to find when and where in the curriculum students may be required to use or learn notetaking skills. If these documents are not available online or in print at your school, call the content area supervisor's office to acquire the most recent version for planning use.

Check your local school system's language arts standards to look for specific content lessons for grades 3, 4, and 5 that teach the skill of distinguishing main ideas and supporting details from irrelevant information. In addition, check the social studies curriculum for specific content lessons for teaching units about your state for 3rd grade, Native Americans for 4th grade, and the American Revolution for 5th grade. Once you have outlined the time frames for teaching these units in the classroom, and have had an opportunity to read the classroom teacher's specific lessons, you will be ready to choose from any of the lessons available in this book to design your teaching plan. Plan to teach your content prior to, along with, or in support of the classroom teachers' content. By doing so, you will elevate yourself as a teacher in the school by showing your understanding of the curriculum being taught in the classroom.

Notetaking is a skill that both the library media specialist and the classroom teacher want students to attain. Library media specialists teach students how to locate information in a wide variety of texts for the purpose of answering an information need by evaluating information critically and competently. Classroom teachers teach students to understand the skill of identifying main ideas and supporting details. They show students how to identify the main idea as their purpose for reading to locate information changes. For many students, this aspect is difficult to understand as the change of focus makes what was once relevant become irrelevant.

The connection between the learning goals for both the classroom teacher and the library media specialist are clear. Classroom teachers teach students to locate the main idea and supporting details based on the reason for reading. A student's reason for reading can be described as their *information need* or *research question*. Young students in grades K–5 are generally provided with a teacher-driven information question that leads the student to locate facts about a topic. These students need the structure and support provided by participating in a guided lesson that introduces how to use library resources. This level of teaching and learning provides the necessary amount of modeling and structure needed for students to be successful as they move toward the higher-order thinking skills necessary for inquiry-based learning.

3RD-GRADE LESSONS

LESSON 1: YOU'RE INVITED!

Coordinate! Your students will be introduced to notetaking by reconstructing a shredded invitation that was mistakenly damaged at the post office. The invitation invites students to participate in a state souvenir idea contest. After determining the main idea and supporting details of the invitation, students list the information they need to gather in order to design an original state souvenir. Students will demonstrate their understanding of proper notetaking procedures by taking notes. This will be the first step for students as they complete the research for their souvenir project. Share this lesson idea with the classroom teacher. Discuss beginning your unit to *coordinate* with the classroom teacher's instruction on how to pick out the main idea from a passage or on learning more about their state.

Cooperate! Challenge students to create their own letter inviting a family member to a party to showcase the unveiling of the state souvenirs created by the class. Instruct students to include some irrelevant information as they write their own invitation. Have students place each sentence for their party invitation on a separate strip of paper and place the strips in an envelope. Students can place their random invitations in envelopes and trade! Once traded, each student should reconstruct the invitation noting the main idea and supporting details, and eliminating the irrelevant information. *Cooperate* with the classroom teacher by sharing this idea for a center activity during language arts.

Lesson Plan

Integrated Goals:

Language Arts

Standard 12. Students use spoken, written, and visual language to accomplish their own purposes (e.g., for learning, enjoyment, persuasion, and the exchange of information).

Library Media

AASL 21st Century Standards

Standard 2: Draw conclusions, make informed decisions, apply knowledge to new situations, and create new knowledge.

Essential Questions:

How can notetaking help you understand and share information?

Desired Understandings:

Students will understand:

How to implement four basic types of notetaking.
How to differentiate between main idea, supporting details, and irrelevant information.
Why notetaking is an important organizational skill.

Integrated Objectives:

- Students will identify main ideas and supporting details of a written text.
- Students will identify and demonstrate proper notetaking techniques.

Time Required:

45 minutes

Provided Materials:

- "Shredded Invitation" (MN 1.3.1) cut out, and placed in an envelope (one for each group of 4–5 students)
- "Contest Invitation" (RS 1.3.1) for the projector
- "Contest Invitation" (TRS 1.3.1) for your reference
- "Take Note!" (OER 1.3.1) PowerPoint
- "3rd-Grade Notebook" (WS 1.3.1)—one per student, copied back to back, folded, and stapled

Materials You Will Need to Obtain:

- Sentence strips with the words "Main Idea," "Supporting Details," and "Irrelevant Information" written on separate pieces
- Projection device
- Pencils
- Business envelopes

Lesson Procedures:

Engagement:

1. Tell students that they have received an invitation in the mail, inviting them to participate in a statewide contest, but that, unfortunately, their invitation was caught in the mail sorter at the post office and was shredded. The post office placed the shredded invitation in an envelope, and now students will have to decide what parts of the invitation are needed. Students must sort the sentences from the invitation into one of three categories: "Main Idea," "Supporting Details," and "Irrelevant Information."

Activity:

2. Display sentence strips of the words: "Main Idea," "Supporting Details," and "Irrelevant Information." Check for student's comprehension of the words.
3. Place students into groups of four or five.

Embedded AASL Skills Indicator: ___.___.___: _____

* Note—While students are completing this benchmark, the actual inquiry-based research process will begin in the next lesson.

4. Distribute the envelopes with the shredded invitation. Tell students they will need to take turns placing the sentences under the appropriate heading.
5. Instruct students to now remove the contents of the envelope and to locate the three headings: "Main Idea," "Supporting Details," and "Irrelevant Information."
6. Tell students to place these headings on their desk, leaving room to place sentences beneath each heading.

Embedded AASL Skills Indicator: ___.___.___: _____

_____

Embedded AASL Dispositions in Action Indicator: ___.___.___: _____

_____

7. Give students time to complete the task.
8. Display the "Contest Invitation" and read aloud to the class.
9. Ask students to volunteer the main idea of the invitation.
10. Circle the main idea on the displayed "Contest Invitation."
11. Ask students which sentences provide supporting details. As students volunteer their answers, underline the correctly identified supporting details.
12. Once all of the supporting details have been underlined, discuss why the information left over is irrelevant to the main idea.

Transition:

13. Ask students to place their pieces back in the envelope and set them aside.
14. Place students into groups of two as you collect the envelopes.

Activity:

Embedded AASL Dispositions in Action Indicator: ___.___.___: _____

_____

Embedded AASL Responsibilities Indicator: ___.___.___: _____

_____

15. Tell students that the person they have been assigned to work with will be their partner in the state souvenir contest. Give students time to brainstorm in order to identify the information and resources needed to properly complete this project. List their ideas along with the resources needed on the board. Suggestions can include state books, Web sites, reference books, and online reference tools to

locate important information about their state. This information can include, but is not limited to facts about landmarks, historic buildings, famous people, and places of interest.

16. Once you have identified the information that is needed, address *how* students will record the information they find. Lead them towards taking notes about their state.

17. Distribute copies of the "3rd-Grade Notebook" (WS 1.3.1) to each student.

18. Display the "Take Note!" (OER 1.3.1) PowerPoint.

19. Explain to students that they will be taking notes about how to take notes. Students should listen and pay close attention as you explain each slide, and they should record notes about notetaking on pages 1 and 2 of their "3rd-Grade Notebook" (WS 1.3.1).

20. Explain why each type of notetaking is an important skill. Discuss with students why this is true.

Closure:

Embedded AASL Self-Assessment Strategies: ___.___.___: _____

_____

21. Ask students to share with the class one of the four types of notes they learned about and have them explain how this kind of notetaking can assist in sharing information.

Evidence of Understanding:

Collect the "3rd-Grade Notebook" (WS 1.3.1) packets. Check to see that students were able to interpret the "Take Note!" (ER 1.3.1) PowerPoint and take notes properly.

Enrichment Using Technology:

Option 1: Students can access an online note-taker at ReadWriteThink (http://www.readwritethink.org/student_mat/student_material.asp?id=55) for practice in taking proper notes.

Extension:

1. Ask students to clip a current newspaper article from home and locate the main idea and supporting details.

Suggested Modifications:

Print a copy of the "Take Note!" (OER 1.3.1) PowerPoint, utilizing the "Handouts—3 slides per page" printing option. This will give students with difficulties a chance to write their notes directly onto the "Take Note!" handout.

SHREDDED INVITATION

MATERIALS YOU WILL NEED

- Different colored printer paper
- Scissors
- Six envelopes

DIRECTIONS FOR USE

Print pages 2–4 for each group of four students in your class. You may want to print each set on different colored paper to keep them in the correct grouping. Cut out each sentence strip and heading and place them all in an envelope. When presenting the invitation to your class, tell them that they received an invitation in the mail inviting them to participate in a statewide contest. Unfortunately, their invitation was destroyed in the mail, and all that's left is fragments. It will be the student's job to sort the main idea and supporting details from the irrelevant information. Ask students to sort the sentence strips under the correct headings.

From *Destination Collaboration 1: A Complete Research Focused Curriculum Guidebook to Educate 21st Century Learners in Grades 3–5* by Danielle N. DuPuis and Lori M. Carter. Santa Barbara, CA: Libraries Unlimited. Copyright © 2011.

The state visitor center is holding a contest. We are looking for a new souvenir to celebrate the upcoming anniversary of our state.

It's hard to believe another year has come and gone.

We are busy preparing for our state's celebration.

We have even ordered a giant cake shaped in the likeness of our state!

Design a new state souvenir that reflects something special and significant about our state.

The souvenir must be original and demonstrate your knowledge about our state.

In addition to the souvenir, you must also design the packaging or tags required to promote your idea.

The packaging/tags must be informative and explain why your souvenir is special and significant.

You may work in groups of two to create your souvenir.

The winner of the contest will be notified on the fifth of the following month.

Be sure and visit our gift shop for our annual sale this Saturday!

Items are discounted up to 50 percent!

Entries must be received no later than the last day of next month.

The winner of the contest will have their suggested souvenir manufactured, and it will be for sale in our gift shop.

Main Idea

Supporting Details

Irrelevant Information

CONTEST INVITATION

Dear 3rd-grade student,

The state visitor's center is holding a contest. We are looking for a new souvenir to celebrate the upcoming anniversary of our state. It's hard to believe another year has come and gone. We are busy preparing for our state's celebration. We have even ordered a giant cake shaped in the likeness of our state!

Contest Details:

- Design a new state souvenir that reflects something special and significant about our state.

- The souvenir must be original and demonstrate your knowledge about our state.

- In addition to the souvenir, you must also design the packaging or tags required to promote your idea.

- The packaging/tags must be informative and explain why your souvenir is special and significant.

- You may work in groups of two to create your souvenir.

The winner of the contest will have their suggested souvenir manufactured, and it will be for sale in our gift shop. Be sure and visit our gift shop this Saturday for this year's annual sale! Items are discounted up to 50 percent! Entries must be received no later than the last day of next month. The winner will be notified on the fifth of the following month.

Sincerely,

The Governor

CONTEST INVITATION

Dear 3rd-grade student,

The state visitor's center is holding a contest. We are looking for a new souvenir to celebrate the upcoming anniversary of our state. It's hard to believe another year has come and gone. We are busy preparing for our state's celebration. We have even ordered a giant cake shaped in the likeness of our state!

Contest Details:

- Design a new state souvenir that reflects something special and significant about our state.

- The souvenir must be original and demonstrate your knowledge about our state.

- In addition to the souvenir, you must also design the packaging or tags required to promote your idea.

- The packaging/tags must be informative and explain why your souvenir is special and significant.

- You may work in groups of two to create your souvenir.

The winner of the contest will have their suggested souvenir manufactured, and it will be for sale in our gift shop. Be sure and visit our gift shop for this Saturday for this year's annual sale! Items are discounted up to 50 percent! Entries must be received no later than the last day of next month. The winner will be notified on the fifth of the following month.

Sincerely,

The Governor

3RD-GRADE NOTEBOOK

Notebook

Name: _____

Grade: 3

Class: _____

Look back at the contest rubric and explain why your souvenir should win this contest:

_____

_____

_____

_____

_____

_____

_____

_____

7

6

My souvenir ideas (think about how the information you found will be reflected in your souvenir)

-
-
-
-
-
-
-
-
-
-
-

Take Note!

Directions: Use the spaces provided to take notes about notetaking.

Types of Notes
Direct quote (DQ)

-
-
-
-

Summary (S)

-
-
-
-

1

2

Paraphrase (P)

• _____

• _____

• _____

• _____

Personal thoughts (PT)

• _____

• _____

• _____

• _____

What resources did you use? List them here.

_____

_____

_____

_____

_____

_____

_____

_____

_____

_____

5

State sport: _____

_____

Direct Quote/ Summary/ Paraphrase/ Personal Thought

Some important facts about our state: for example, historical buildings, famous places, important people, and events.

• _____

• _____

• _____

• _____

• _____

• _____

• _____

• _____

• _____

4

State name: _____

Describe the following.

State flower: _____

_____

Direct Quote/ Summary/ Paraphrase/ Personal Thought

State bird: _____

_____

Direct Quote/ Summary/ Paraphrase/ Personal Thought

State tree: _____

_____

Direct Quote/ Summary/ Paraphrase/ Personal Thought

3

3RD-GRADE LESSONS

LESSON 2: WELCOME TO OUR STATE

Coordinate! Your students will begin taking notes about their own state. They will understand how the main ideas and supporting details change with the purpose for reading. Proper notetaking may be difficult for some students. Point out that students can review the proper ways to take notes by referring back to the notes they took in the previous lesson. Remember to *coordinate* by displaying resources relevant to your students' curriculum in the library media center. This will show the classroom teachers that you are aware of their curriculum. During nonfiction book talks, give students multiple purposes for reading the book.

Cooperate! Your students will be locating information about their own state by reading information from book and online resources. They will understand how the main ideas and supporting details change with the purpose for reading. Ask students to look over a Web site with information about their state. *CultureGrams* (http://www.culturegrams.com/) is a great database for research use, but it is accessible by subscription only. Check with your school to see if you have access to it. Ask students to decide for themselves what information they would be interested in learning more about and design a question based on that interest (purpose for reading). Have students take notes and accurately define the main idea along with supporting details that answers their question by re-reading their notes. Provide the classroom teacher with their work. Use this opportunity to discuss the relevance of teaching this skill *cooperatively*.

Lesson Plan

Integrated Goals:

Language Arts

Standard 8. Students use a variety of technological and information resources (e.g., libraries, databases, computer networks, video) to gather and synthesize information and to create and communicate knowledge.

U.S. History

Topic 2: The History of Students' Own State or Region

3E The student understands the ideas that were significant in the development of the state and that helped to forge its unique identity.

Library Media

AASL 21st Century Standards

Standard 1: Inquire, think critically, and gain knowledge.

Standard 2: Draw conclusions, make informed decisions, apply knowledge to new situations, and create new knowledge.

Essential Questions:

How does your own state's history and natural resources influence the creation of your state souvenir?

Why is it important to use different notetaking methods?

Desired Understandings:

Students will understand:

There are different notetaking methods.

How to apply notetaking methods as they gather information about their own state.

Integrated Objectives:

- Students will identify main ideas and supporting details of a written text in order to create a state souvenir for their own state.
- Students will apply notetaking methods to extract information from factual text.

Time Required:

45 minutes

*Note: In order to meet the U.S. History Standard, students will be creating a souvenir based on the state in which your school is located. You may wish to bring multiple souvenirs and postcards from various locations to demonstrate how a souvenir reflects the resources, history, and unique identity of the state it represents.

Provided Materials:

- "3rd-Grade Notebook" (WS 1.3.1) unfinished packet from the previous lesson
- "Contest Rubric" (RS 1.3.2)

Materials You Will Need to Obtain:

- A large map of the United States displayed in a prominent area of the room
- A book about your own state from the *Discover America State By State* (Sleeping Bear Press; http://www.gale.cengage.com/DiscoverAmerica/index.htm) or another similar series or another state book appropriate for reading aloud
- Nonfiction books about your own state
- Information about your own state. You can use books from your library media center, newspaper and magazine articles, online databases, or encyclopedia articles. The Web site *50 States* is also a good resource (http://www.50states.com)
- Computer access for each group of students
- Projection device
- Pencils
- A souvenir from your own state

Lesson Procedures:

Engagement:

1. Display a map of the United States. Ask students to identify their state on the map. Ask students to give details about their state on the map (bordering states, cities, capital, bodies of water, etc.).

Activity:

2. Select a book about your state from the *Discover America State by State* or another similar series to share with the class. Explain that students should listen for unique characteristic about their own state.
3. Read the book.
4. Redistribute the "3rd-Grade Notebook" (WS 1.3.1) packet and have students sit with their partner. Ask students to redefine the task presented in the previous class. (To create a unique souvenir and package for the state souvenir shop that demonstrates students' knowledge of their own state).
5. Distribute a copy of the "Contest Rubric" (RS 1.3.2) to each pair of students.
6. Display the "Contest Rubric" (RS 1.3.2) and review each of the items with the students so that they are aware of what they need to do in order to successfully complete the project. Students can keep their copies of the rubric with their notebooks to refer back to throughout the project.

Embedded AASL Dispositions in Action Indicator: ___.___.___: _____

_____

7. Distribute the books you selected and provide access to online resources for each pair of students.

Embedded AASL Skills Indicator: ___.___.___: _____

_____

8. Instruct students to jot down notes that will assist them in creating a state souvenir. Read the suggestions in the "3rd-Grade Notebook" (WS 1.3.1) before having students begin their research. Point out that students should circle the type of note they have recorded after they write descriptions of their own state flower, sport, tree, and bird.

Embedded AASL Skills Indicator: ___.___.___: _____

_____

9. Also remind students to place the initial of each type of note they took in the margins as they continue to record their notes. For example, if they take a direct quote from the text, remind students to write the initials *DQ* in the margin of the paper to indicate that they recognize the type of note they recorded.

Embedded AASL Responsibilities Indicator: ___.___.___: _____

_____

10. Point out that on page 5 of the "3rd-Grade Notebook" (WS 1.3.1) students are asked to list any resources they used. Tell students to write on the lines provided

either the name of the Web site, or the title and author of any book they used. Remind students that it is important to record where they find their information to give credit to the author as well as to prove the information they found was a fact and not something they made up on their own.

11. Circulate throughout the room to check for understanding and provide assistance as needed.

Closure:

Embedded AASL Self-Assessment Strategies: ___.___.___: _____

_____

12. Ask students to share some of the notes they took in their "3rd-Grade Notebook" (WS 1.3.1). See if students can identify what type of note they took in their "3rd-Grade Notebook" (WS 1.3.1): direct quote, summary, paraphrase, or personal thought. Ask students to share which notetaking strategies and resources were the most helpful and why. Ask students what they would do differently next time.

Evidence of Understanding:

Collect the "3rd-Grade Notebook" (WS 1.3.1) packets and check to see that students have been correctly taking notes and citing their sources.

Technology Integration:

Technology

NETS–S

3. Research and Information Fluency

Students apply digital tools to gather, evaluate, and use information. Students:

  b. locate, organize, analyze, evaluate, synthesize, and ethically use information from a variety of sources and media.

   Option 1: Students may access an online source to use as a resource for taking notes about their state. Try using the *CultureGrams* database or a pre-approved Internet site such as www.americaslibrary.gov or www.worldalmanacforkids.com.

Extension:

1. Challenge students to come up with a main idea and supporting details from "Images of America" (OEX 1.3.1).

Suggested Modifications:

For challenged readers, you may wish to print out a few articles from online databases or Internet Web sites ahead of time. Highlight passages and key words to focus the student's attention to the important and relevant parts of the text.

CONTEST RUBRIC

Expectations	Not met (1)	Almost there (2)	Great job! (3)	
Students will use accurate facts about our state to create a souvenir.	Students used only background knowledge and did not use facts from available resources.	Students used facts from the resources. Some of the facts they chose reflected misunderstanding or confusion.	Students chose accurate facts from the available resources and demonstrated their understanding of the information they recorded.	
Students' notes should be clear and reflect their knowledge of different notetaking techniques such as paraphrasing, writing down direct quotes, summarizing, and recording personal thoughts.	Students' notes were unclear and did not indicate the proper notetaking techniques.	Students' notes were clear most of the time and showed some demonstration of notetaking techniques.	Students' notes were always clear and well organized and demonstrated knowledge of notetaking techniques.	
Students should demonstrate knowledge about our state and create a souvenir suitable for our state gift shop.	The students did not create a souvenir.	The souvenir the students created demonstrated little knowledge about our state.	The souvenir the students created demonstrated a strong knowledge of our state.	
Students will create a package or tag for their souvenir that explains why their souvenir is significant to our state.	The students did not explain why their souvenir was significant to our state.	The students created a package or tag that briefly explained their souvenir, but not why it was significant to our state.	Students created a package or tag that provided a full explanation of their souvenir and how it was significant to our state.	
The souvenir is original.	The students made no attempt to create an original idea.	The students made an attempt to create an original idea.	The students' souvenir was original and unique.	
The work is neat, complete, and demonstrates proper spelling, punctuation, and grammar usage.	Because of the students' punctuation, spelling, and grammar mistakes, the project was difficult to interpret.	The students made an effort to include proper spelling, punctuation, and grammar. There were only a few mistakes.	The students used proper punctuation, spelling, and grammar throughout the project.	
Total points				

3RD-GRADE LESSONS

LESSON 3: SOUVENIR SHOP

Coordinate! Students will use the information they located about their own state in order to create a souvenir to be sold at the state visitor's center gift shop. Students will create a souvenir and explain why the souvenir they created represents their home state. Share this lesson with the classroom teacher. Consider having students create their souvenir by drawing a picture or bringing in objects to construct the souvenir themselves. Create a bulletin board or showcase of students' work and *coordinate* by inviting the classroom teacher to see the results. Take this opportunity to discuss the possibility of working more cooperatively with the classroom teacher on the instruction of this lesson.

Cooperate! The creation of an authentic state souvenir lends itself to a wide range of project ideas. Consider talking with the classroom teacher several weeks before you teach this lesson. Discuss the project idea and whether the classroom teacher's lessons can incorporate this idea in a *cooperative* way. For example, the classroom teacher may identify certain state landmarks or historical places during social studies instruction. Use factual state information about these places when asking students to design a souvenir.

Lesson Plan

Integrated Goals:

Language Arts

Standard 12. Students use spoken, written, and visual language to accomplish their own purposes (e.g., for learning, enjoyment, persuasion, and the exchange of information).

U.S. History

Topic 2: The History of students' own state or region

3E The student understands the ideas that were significant in the development of the state and that helped to forge its unique identity.

Library Media

AASL 21st Century Standards

    Standard 1: Inquire, think critically, and gain knowledge.
    Standard 2: Draw conclusions, make informed decisions, apply knowledge to new situations, and create new knowledge.
    Standard 3: Share knowledge and participate ethically and productively as members of our democratic society.

Essential Questions:

How does your own states' history and natural resources influence the creation of your state souvenir?

How does your own states' environment affect the products we make and sell?

Desired Understandings:

Students will understand:

How the state's environment affects the state's goods and services.
How to use information in order to create a state souvenir.

Integrated Objectives:

- Students will create an original written work based on their notes.
- Students will design a souvenir to represent their own state.

Time Required:

45 minutes

Provided Materials:

- "3rd-Grade Notebook" (WS 1.3.1) unfinished packet from the previous lesson
- "Contest Rubric" (RS 1.3.2)
- "Sample Souvenir" (RS 1.3.3)—prior to the students' arrival complete this sample as it pertains to your own state
- "State Souvenir" (WS 1.3.2)—one per student pair
- "Souvenir Package Tag" (WS 1.3.3)—one per student pair

Materials You Will Need to Obtain:

- One or two souvenirs from a vacation (e.g., snow globe, postcard, bookmark, pencil, pin, hat, etc.). You may need to provide a souvenir for students who need additional reinforcement. See the "suggested modifications" at the end of this lesson.
- Information about your state. You can use books from your library media center, newspaper and magazine articles, online databases, encyclopedia articles, or the *50 States* Web site (http://www.50states.com).
- Projection device
- Pencils
- Colored pencils or crayons

Lesson Procedures:

Engagement:

1. Show students a souvenir you purchased while on vacation. Ask students to infer information about the place this souvenir represents. Answers will vary depending on the object you bring in to share.

Activity:

2. Distribute the "3rd-Grade Notebook" (WS 1.3.1) packet that students used in the previous lessons.
3. Explain that students will be completing research about their own state in order to create a souvenir that will be sold at their own state visitor's center gift shop. The souvenir can be as simple or as complex as they would like. However, stu-

dents need to support the reasons why they created the souvenir in the way they did on the "Souvenir Package Tag" (WS 1.3.3) package or tag.

4. Remind students to use the "Contest Rubric" (RS 1.3.2) as a guide to help them complete their project.

Embedded AASL Skills Indicator: ___.___.___: _____

_____

5. Give students time to complete their research from the previous week.

Transition:

6. When students are finished their research, have them stop when they reach page 6 in their "3rd-Grade Notebook" (WS 1.3.1).

7. Display the "Sample Souvenir" (WS 1.3.2) and read the package/tag that you created to go along with the souvenir.

Activity:

Embedded AASL Skills Indicator: ___.___.___: _____

_____

Embedded AASL Dispositions in Action Indicator: ___.___.___: _____

_____

8. Ask students to brainstorm with their partner and record some ideas onto page 6 of their "3rd-Grade Notebook" (WS 1.3.1) for a state souvenir. Their souvenir should incorporate and reflect many of the notes they took about their state.

9. Distribute copies of "State Souvenir" (WS 1.3.2) and "Souvenir Package Tag" (WS 1.3.3) to each pair as they complete page 6 in their "3rd-Grade Notebook" (WS 1.3.1).

Embedded AASL Responsibilities Indicator: ___.___.___: _____

_____

10. Give students time to work together to complete their souvenir project.

Closure:

Embedded AASL Skills Indicator: ___.___.___: _____

_____

11. Ask students to share their souvenir ideas with the class.

Embedded AASL Self-Assessment Strategies: ___.___.___: _____

_____

12. As part of their self-evaluation, have students complete page 7 in their "3rd-Grade Notebook" (WS 1.3.1) and explain why their souvenir should win this contest.

Evidence of Understanding:

Use the "Contest Rubric" (RS 1.3.2) to grade the "3rd-Grade Notebook" (WS 1.3.1), "State Souvenir" (WS 1.3.2), and "Souvenir Package Tag" (WS 1.3.3).

Technology Integration:

Technology

NETS–S

1. Creativity and Innovation

Students demonstrate creative thinking, construct knowledge, and develop innovative products and processes using technology. Students:

  b. create original works as a means of personal or group expression.

2. Communication and Collaboration

Students use digital media and environments to communicate and work collaboratively, including at a distance, to support individual learning and contribute to the learning of others. Students:

  a. interact, collaborate, and publish with peers, experts, or others employing a variety of digital environments and media.

    Option 1: Create a class blog "store" at http://edublogs.org to organize, display, and "sell" your souvenirs. Students can scan their souvenir and upload it as a photograph to your blog site. Students can also record a "commercial" about their souvenir and upload it as a podcast to the site.

    Option 2: Have students use the information they recorded on their "Souvenir Package Tag" (WS 1.3.3) to create a slide in PowerPoint to sell their souvenir. Invite a community member who owns a souvenir or variety store to come in to discuss how a store decides what kinds of merchandise it will sell. Have students share some of their slides with the community expert.

Extension:

1. Students may need additional time to complete this lesson. You may wish to continue this project an extra week to allow adequate time for all students to complete the projects. Ask students to locate some souvenirs they have at home to bring to the next class. These souvenirs may give them ideas as to what they could create on their own.

Suggested Modifications:

Provide students in need of assistance with a souvenir that you have brought from home that reflects the student's own state. Ask the student to explain how this souvenir could be improved to better reflect the student's own state.

SAMPLE SOUVENIR

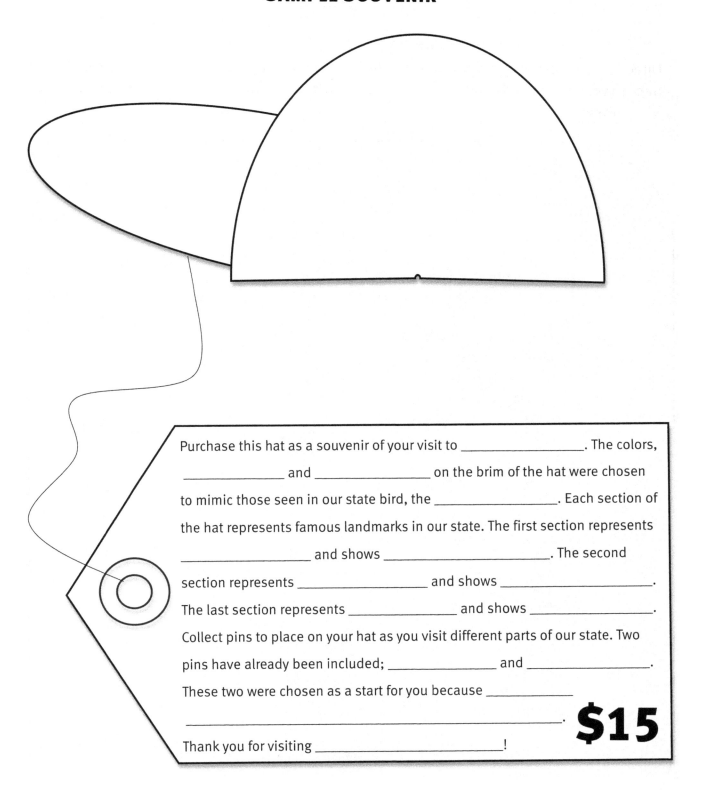

Purchase this hat as a souvenir of your visit to _____. The colors, _____ and _____ on the brim of the hat were chosen to mimic those seen in our state bird, the _____. Each section of the hat represents famous landmarks in our state. The first section represents _____ and shows _____. The second section represents _____ and shows _____. The last section represents _____ and shows _____. Collect pins to place on your hat as you visit different parts of our state. Two pins have already been included; _____ and _____. These two were chosen as a start for you because _____ _____. **$15**

Thank you for visiting _____!

STATE SOUVENIR

Names: _____

Directions: Together with your partner, design a state souvenir in the space below. Refer back to your "Contest Rubric" to make sure you are including everything necessary for this assignment.

SOUVENIR PACKAGE TAG

Names: _____

Directions: Together with your partner, design a state souvenir package or tag using the templates on this page. Refer to your "Contest Rubric" to make sure you include all necessary information.

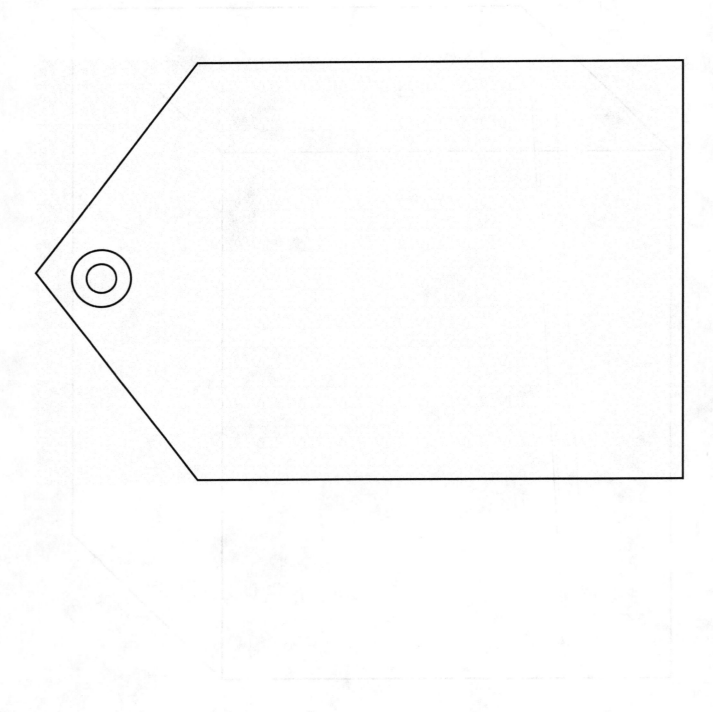

Working in Collaboration

Collaboration

Collaborate! True collaboration requires both the library media specialist and the classroom teacher to share in the design of integrated instruction. Collaboration provides you with an excellent opportunity to design inquiry-based learning activities. Here are some ideas for collaborating with the classroom teachers.

3rd Grade: Your State

Essential Question: How is our state alike and different from other states in our region?

- Have students create a travel brochure for the student's own state advertising the important state features. Compare the student's own state with other states in the region.

Essential Question: How do our natural resources influence the food we eat and celebrate?

- Have students create a restaurant menu based on the natural food products (resources) of the student's own state. Discuss why some foods are used in local festivals.

Essential Question: How is life in our community today different from long ago?

- Have students write a class newspaper with articles about the student's own state. Compare facts about the state long ago with current information. Ask students to research historical places, buildings, or monuments.

For further information, please visit
www.destinationcollaboration.com

4TH-GRADE LESSONS

LESSON 1: TAKE NOTE!

Coordinate! Students will listen to an interview script between a news reporter and Mr. G.O. Odwolf. They will use their listening skills to take notes during the interview to assist Mr. G.O. Odwolf in finding a new location to live. The script is punctuated with humorous moments, which will engage students. Once their notes have been recorded, students will write a letter to the wolf inviting him to live in their neighborhood. *Coordinate* with the classroom teacher by sharing this lesson idea and offering to teach it as an introduction to notetaking or identifying the main idea of a text.

Cooperate! After students complete their letters to Mr. G.O. Odwolf, consider having the students share their letters with the classroom teacher. Discuss with the classroom teacher ways to extend what the students learned by using notetaking and listening skills. Offer to use the Web site, http://storynory.com and download fairy tales and classic stories as an MP3 file to your computer or iPod. *Cooperation* can be achieved if the classroom teacher offers to listen to and assist in selecting the audio stories. Share the stories with students and ask them to summarize the main idea and supporting details of the selected stories.

Lesson Plan

Integrated Goals:

Language Arts

Standard 5. Students employ a wide range of strategies as they write and use different writing process elements appropriately to communicate with different audiences for a variety of purposes.

Library Media

AASL 21st Century Standards

Standard 2: Draw conclusions, make informed decisions, apply knowledge to new situations, and create new knowledge.
Standard 3: Share knowledge and participate ethically and productively as members of our democratic society.

Essential Questions:

How can notetaking help you understand and share information?

Desired Understandings:

Students will understand:

How to concisely extract information from a text.

In order to take notes effectively, they must be able to identify the main idea and supporting details of the information.

How to write a friendly letter.

CLASSROOM CONNECTIONS

If your students are engaged by taking notes based on a script taken from one of their favorite classical stories, think about writing your own! Write a script interviewing Goldilocks, The Little Red Hen, or Cinderella's stepsisters. You may want to include a twist to the story to make taking notes more fun.

Integrated Objectives:

- Students will identify main ideas and supporting details of a written text.
- Students will apply notetaking methods to extract information while listening to an interview.
- Students will apply the information obtained from their notes to create a friendly letter.

Time Required:

45 minutes

Provided Materials:

- "4th-Grade Notebook" (WS 1.4.1)—one per student (the notebook should be copied back to back, folded, and stapled so that it resembles a notebook)
- "Newsflash" (RS 1.4.1)
- " Notetaking Samples" (RS 1.4.2)
- "Interview Script" (TRS 1.4.1)

Materials You Will Need to Obtain:

- Projection device
- Pencils
- Clipboard or steno notepad and pencil

Prior to the Lesson:

Prior to student's arrival, ask the classroom teacher or another adult helper to attend the beginning of the class to share in the engagement by acting out the "Interview Script" (TRS 1.4.1). Use the clipboard or steno pad and pencil as a prop to have your act look more authentic.

Lesson Procedures:

Engagement:

1. Display "Newsflash" (RS 1.4.1) and read aloud to the class.

Activity:

2. Tell students that they are about to witness a live interview with the Big Bad Wolf. Remind students that as they listen to the interview the first time, they should identify the main idea and think about what supporting details may be important in order to help the wolf. Explain to students that they will be taking their notes during the second reading of the script. Give students a bit of background knowledge about the wolf. Tell them that the "Big Bad Wolf" has been around

for a long time. The wolf is a character in many legends, both recent and ancient, including traditional Native American tales.

3. Together with your adult helper, perform the "Interview Script" (TRS 1.4.1) for the class.

4. After performing the script, display "Notetaking Samples" (RS 1.4.2).

5. Actively involve students as you discuss the differences between the sentences and notes on display. Emphasize that notes are concise, and may or may not be incomplete sentences that resemble a list.

6. Distribute the "4th-Grade Notebook" packets (WS 1.4.1).

Embedded AASL Skills Indicator: ___.___.___: _____

_____

7. Display a copy of the "Interview Script" (TRS 1.4.1) and re-read it aloud to the class. Allow students time to jot down the main idea and important supporting details.

Embedded AASL Skills Indicator: ___.___.___: _____

_____

8. Make sure students are correctly taking notes and not writing sentences verbatim. Select students to share their work.

Embedded AASL Dispositions in Action Indicator: ___.___.___: _____

_____

Embedded AASL Responsibilities Indicator: ___.___.___: _____

_____

9. Using their notes, ask students to write a letter to Mr. G. O. Odwolf inviting him to move to their town. This can be done on page 2 in their "4th-Grade Notebook" (WS 1.4.1).

Closure:

10. Ask one or two students to share their letters with the class. Explain to students that they will be using their notetaking skills to learn more about traditional Native American life. They will be using their notes to create an artifact exhibit for a virtual museum.

Evidence of Understanding:

Embedded AASL Self-Assessment Strategies: ___.___.___: _____

_____

Walk around the room and assist students as needed with notetaking and letter writing. Check to see that students can utilize their notes to write a comprehensive letter. Collect and grade the completed pages in the student's "4th-Grade Notebook" (WS 1.4.1).

Technology Integration:

Technology

NETS-S

6. Technology Operations and Concepts

Students demonstrate a sound understanding of technology concepts, systems, and operations. Students:

b. select and use applications effectively and productively.
1. Students can use "Notebook View" in Microsoft Word to take notes using the computer.

Extension:

1. Once students have been engaged with the Big Bad Wolf fictional character in this lesson, encourage them to read more by introducing the story *Once A Wolf: How Wildlife Biologists Fought to Bring Back the Gray Wolf,* by Stephen R. Swinburne (Boston: Houghton Mifflin, 1999). This book explains the myth of the Big Bad Wolf and discusses the connection between the gray wolf and traditional Native Americans. It will provide students with background knowledge for the next lesson.

Suggested Modifications:

For students who will need extra time or will need to see the text close up as well as hear it, provide these students with a copy of the "Interview Script" (TRS 1.4.1).

4TH-GRADE NOTEBOOK

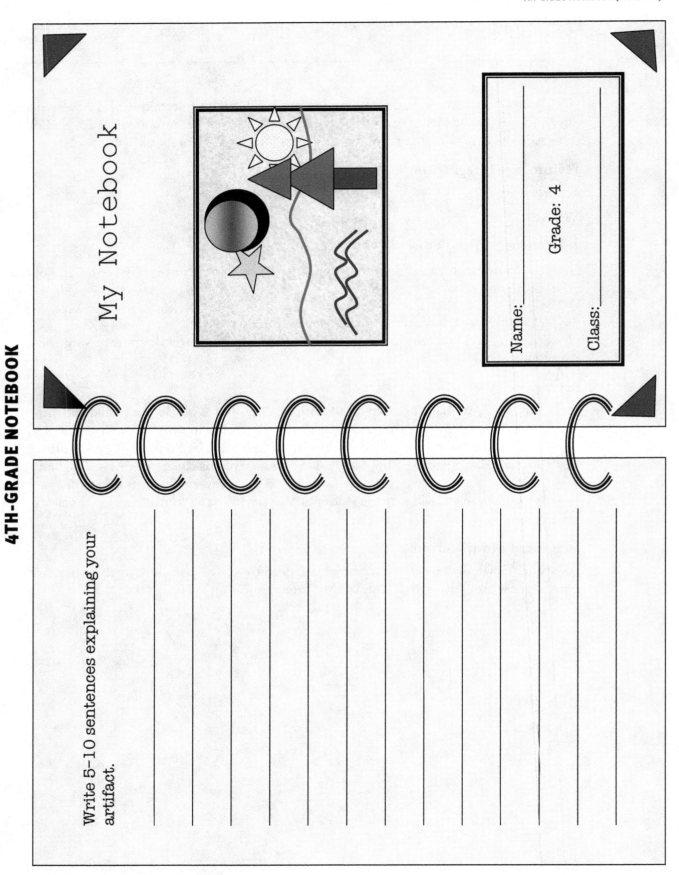

My Notebook

Name: _____

Grade: 4

Class: _____

Write 5–10 sentences explaining your artifact.

Homes:

Artifact:

Web address for digital image of artifact:

Explain how this artifact reflects the environment and culture of your tribe.

6

Big Bad Wolf notes

Main idea:

1

2

Using your notes from the interview, write a letter to Mr. G. O. Odwolf below.

_____
_____
_____
_____
_____
_____
_____
_____
_____
_____
_____

Native American region: _____

Tribe: _____

Environment: _____
_____
• _____
• _____
• _____

Food: _____
• _____
• _____
• _____

Clothing: _____
• _____
• _____
• _____

5

4

Information to collect from the Web site for your bibliography:

- _____
- _____
- _____

Try writing a bibliography entry for a nonfiction book below:

_____

3

Notes about the title page and verso:

Location of the verso: _____

Information to collect from the title page and verso for your bibliography:

- _____
- _____
- _____
- _____
- _____

NEWSFLASH!

This just in . . . Mr. G. O. Odwolf (formerly known as the Big Bad Wolf) wants to move to a new forest!

NOTETAKING SAMPLES

The Forestville library contains 5,235 children's fiction titles. It also has an extensive nonfiction collection that includes over 24,000 titles. The library receives around 250 visitors each day from ages 0–100. The library hopes to work on an expansion project to increase the library's size by 20%. Students can be found at the library every afternoon and on Saturdays and Sundays as they study for school, attend story times, and use the computers.

- Forestville library has
  - 5,235 children's fiction titles
  - 24,000 nonfiction titles
  - 250 visitors per day
- Forestville library wishes to increase by 20 percent
- Students use Forestville library for research and fun

The little brown bat can be found in many areas of the United States and Canada. It uses a special adaptation called echolocation to locate insects to eat. These bats are nocturnal which means they sleep during the day and are awake at night. Bats are perhaps the most unique mammals, since they are the only mammals that can fly. They are from the order, "Chiroptera," meaning hand-wing.

- Little brown bats are found in United States and Canada.
- They use echolocation to find insects.
- They are nocturnal.
- Order "chiroptera" means hand wing.

Resources

Fenton, M. B. "Bat." World Book Online. World Book Online Reference Center. 2007. World Book. 29 Sept. 2007 ‹http://www.worldbookonline.com/wb/Article?id=ar049100›.

INTERVIEW SCRIPT

A WOLF IN SHEEP'S CLOTHING?

Reporter: Good afternoon. I'm here speaking to Mr. G. O. Odwolf, formerly known as the Big Bad Wolf. Mr. Odwolf, I understand that you are looking for a new forest in which to live, is that correct?

Mr. G. O. Odwolf: Yes. That is correct.

Reporter: Mr. Odwolf, you have to admit, not everyone will want a wolf with your reputation living in their town! Can you tell me why you are looking for a new forest?

Mr. G. O. Odwolf: Yes. I will admit that things got a little out of hand in my last forest. In fact, there are lots of stories about me that go way back . . . back to the times of the Cherokee . . . I wasn't always known for being smart back then—you may have read a legend or two about me! *Those* were the days . . . I mean . . . those were *horrible* days. And, lately I've been known for scaring little girls with red hoods and blowing down pigs' homes. But, I have made some pig . . . err . . . I mean *big* changes. I've become a vegetarian!

Reporter: That's wonderful. Now, the reason we're here today is that you hope somewhere in America there are some folks out there that will invite you to live near their town. Is that so?

Mr. G. O. Odwolf: Yes. Well, as you can imagine, in my last forest, I didn't have too many friends. I liked them all very much . . . but for the wrong reasons! Ha, ha . . . ahem . . . I mean . . . I want to live in a new forest, make new friends, and learn how to be a better wolf. I must admit, all that time spent around Native Americans gave me a real appreciation for nature . . . AND doing the right thing . . . and well . . . I just can't eat my fellow animals anymore! Since I've given up meat . . . plump roasted piggies for example . . . I must learn how to cook using only vegetables! In fact, I can make a great corn bread pudding.

Reporter: This will be a big change for you! Do you have a certain region in America that you would like to live?

Mr. G. O. Odwolf: No, not at all! I will move north, south, east, or west. All I ask is that my new home should have some nice, tall trees and a good spot for a huge vegetable garden. And room for a brick house—I've learned that building a house of bricks is probably the best choice! I've tried living in a teepee . . . and well . . . it is a bit drafty!

Reporter: Well, America, you heard it here first! Mr. G. O. Odwolf, formerly known as the Big Bad Wolf, is ready for a new start. Will you invite him to live in your neighborhood or village? Mr. Odwolf do you have any last requests for information or anything else you would like to share with America?

Mr. G. O. Odwolf: Well, I just want to assure everyone that I have indeed changed! Just last night I made a wonderful eggplant piggy . . . I mean *pita* pocket! I hope that in my new forest I will make lots of friends and learn how to cook new vegetarian dishes! Please invite me soon! Send your letters to: Mr. G. O. Odwolf, 121 Blustery Lane, Deep In the Woods, Dark Forest 12345.

Reporter: Thanks for joining us, Mr. G. O. Odwolf! OK, America mail your letters today! Good luck Mr. Odwolf!

4TH-GRADE LESSONS

LESSON 2: DIGGING INTO THE PAST

Coordinate! Students will read an article or access a Web site about Native Americans. They will understand how the main idea and supporting details change with the purpose for reading. To assist students in understanding the text, they will take notes. Ask students to think about what they want to know about Native American culture (purpose for reading). Using the Public Access Catalog (PAC), ask students to locate information that will assist them in locating the answer for their information need. Create a class list and provide the classroom teacher with a bibliography of these resources. You may find that the classroom teacher will ask you to *coordinate* access to these resources for the classroom!

Cooperate! Check the 4th-grade social studies curriculum, curriculum map, or speak to a teacher to find out when students will be learning about Native American culture. Select a variety of books and other resources about Native Americans and display them in your library media center. Be sure to think about audio and video resources. Offer to *cooperate* with the classroom teacher by providing audio and video clips from the Internet or an available database as an engagement activity for their lesson.

Lesson Plan

Integrated Goals:

Social Studies

III People, Places, & Environments

  h. examine the interaction of human beings and their physical environment, the use of land, building of cities, and the ecosystem changes in selected locales and regions.

Library Media

AASL 21st Century Standards

Standard 3: Share knowledge and participate ethically and productively as members of our democratic society.

Essential Questions:

  How did environment affect the lives and culture of Native Americans?
  How can you protect the intellectual property rights of others?

Desired Understandings:

Students will understand:

  How to cite books in print and Web resources.

The meaning of title page and copyright page.

That Native Americans of the past lived in many regions of North America.

That the environment of Native Americans have deeply affected their way of life.

Integrated Objectives:

- Students will identify the kinds of information needed to create a bibliography entry for a book and a Web site.
- Students will identify main ideas and supporting details of a written text.
- Students will apply their notetaking methods to extract information from a factual online text.

Time Required:

45 minutes

Provided Materials:

- "4th-Grade Notebook" (WS 1.4.1) packet that students used in the previous lesson
- "Native American Regions" (ORS 1.4.3)
- "Invite" (RS 1.4.4)
- "Museum Rubric" (RS 1.4.5)—one per student
- "Keeping Track" (OER 1.4.1) PowerPoint

Materials You Will Need to Obtain:

- Computer
- Projection device
- Pencils
- Collection of nonfiction books about Native Americans—one for each student
- Lists of Web sites about Native Americans

Lesson Procedures:

Engagement:

1. Tell students that you have just received an announcement from the National Museum Committee inviting your school's 4th-grade classes to create a virtual display on Native American history and culture.
2. Display or read the announcement "Invite" (RS 1.4.4) to your students.

Activity:

3. Display the "Native American Regions" map (ORS 1.4.3). Ask students to describe the features on the map and determine what the labels on the map depict (Native American Regions of North America).
4. Explain to students that they will be selecting a tribe to research from one of the regions on the map. Ask students to identify their information need in order to successfully complete the task described in the "Invite" (RS 1.4.4)
5. Display the "Museum Rubric" (RS 1.4.5) and explain how students' work will be graded.
6. Ask students how they plan to record the information they locate about their tribe (take notes). Ask students what kinds of sources they might use. Record all appropriate answers on the board.

7. Explain to students that for this task they will only be using books in print or Web sites.
8. Explain to students that as they collect information they must also keep track of the sources they use. Ask students if they know why they must keep track of their sources. Lead students to describing the importance of a creating a bibliography in order to eliminate the possibility of plagiarism.
9. Display the first slide of the PowerPoint "Keeping Track" (OER 1.4.1). Explain to students they will learn the kinds of information necessary to record in order to create a bibliography for a book or a Web site.

Transition:

10. Distribute copies of the "4th-Grade Notebook" (WS 1.4.1) that students worked on in the previous class and tell students to turn to page 3.

Activity:

11. Explain to students that you will tell them when to record information from the "Keeping Track" (OER 1.4.1) PowerPoint into their notebooks. Give students time to jot down notes about the information provided in the title page and copyright page for the bibliography. Provide additional time to jot down information about creating a bibliography entry for a Web site.
12. Circulate throughout the room to check for understanding and provide assistance as needed.
13. Provide each student or pair of students with a nonfiction book about Native American history and culture from your collection.

Embedded AASL Skills Indicator: ___.___.___: _____

_____

14. Ask students to create a bibliography entry in the space provided on page 4 of the "4th-Grade Notebooks" (WS 1.4.1).

Embedded AASL Responsibilities Indicator: ___.___.___: _____

_____

15. Give students time to complete the activity.

Embedded AASL Dispositions in Action Indicator: ___.___.___: _____

_____

16. Ask students to volunteer their bibliography entry with the class. Put the entry on display and discuss. Ask questions such as whether the entry meets the requirements.

Closure:

17. Display the "Native American Regions" (ORS 1.4.3) map. Ask students to record the Native American region that they would like to learn more about into their "4th-Grade Notebooks" (WS 1.4.1) on page 5. Explain that during the next class period they will choose a tribe to research and create their virtual artifact museum. Remind students that as they research they will be expected to create a bibliography for the sources they use. Ask students what information is important to collect for a book in print and a Web site.

Evidence of Understanding:

Embedded AASL Self-Assessment Strategies: ___.___.___: _____

_____

Walk around the room and assist students as needed with finding information on the copyright and title page for their bibliography. Collect and grade the completed portions of the "4th-Grade Notebook" (WS 1.4.1).

Technology Integration:

Technology

NETS–S

5. Digital Citizenship

Students understand human, cultural, and societal issues related to technology and practice legal and ethical behavior. Students:

  a. advocate and practice safe, legal, and responsible use of information and technology.
  1. Show students an online bibliography maker. Some options include: http://www.bibme.org, http://easybib.com, or http://www.noodletools.com (full use of NoodleTools requires a subscription). Have students create their bibliography using this tool.

Extension:

Share with students the book *D is For Drum: A Native American Alphabet,* by Michael and Debbie Shoulders (Chelsea: Sleeping Bear Press, 2006). After reading the story, ask students if they think any of the items in the book came from the region they are researching and discuss why they think so.

Suggested Modifications:

Give students with reading and comprehension difficulties the option of working with a partner. Select resources that meet the learner's reading level. Printing out pages from relevant Web sites and highlighting relevant passages of text for the student may also be helpful. You can use the assisted computer technologies to assist students in reading aloud text from a Web site.

INVITE

Dear Students,

The National Museum Committee members are planning to design a virtual Native American Museum for kids! The Committee is delighted to inform your school that your school's 4th-grade students have been chosen to be among the first to assist us! We hope that you will help us create a display of Native American artifacts for our virtual museum. Please accept this wonderful opportunity to be a part of history! Here are the expectations for your part of the display:

1. Choose a Native American Region and a tribe from that region to research.
2. Take notes about the tribe you have chosen. Carefully look at the geography of the region and decide how the environment may have affected the tribe's culture.
3. Choose an artifact that reflects the culture of the Native American tribe you are researching.
4. Create a virtual display for the artifact. The display must include the name and region of the tribe, the name of the artifact, how it was used, and why this artifact is representative of the culture of this tribe.

Thank you for your help in creating the first virtual Native American museum in our state.

Sincerely,

The State Museum Committee

MUSEUM RUBRIC

Expectations	Not met (1)	Almost there (2)	Great job! (3)
Students will use accurate facts about their tribe and region to determine how the environment affected the tribe's culture.	Students used only background knowledge and did not use facts from available resources.	Students used facts from the resources. Some of the facts they chose reflected misunderstanding or confusion.	Students chose accurate facts from the available resources and demonstrated their understanding of the information they recorded.
Students' notes should be clear and show their desire to understand how the tribe's environment affected their culture.	Students' notes were unclear and did not indicate any understanding of how environment and culture connect.	Students' notes were clear most of the time and showed some demonstration of connecting environment and culture.	Students' notes were always clear and well organized and demonstrated a strong knowledge of how the culture of Native Americans is connected to the environment.
Students should demonstrate their ability to create a bibliography of the resources used in this project.	The students did not create a bibliography.	The bibliography the students created listed most of the resources.	The students demonstrated a strong knowledge of how to create a bibliography for their project. It was complete and citations were listed in alphabetical order.
Students will create a PowerPoint slide to display their artifact.	The students did not create a PowerPoint slide to display their artifact.	The students created a PowerPoint slide to display their artifact. The slide included a picture and a brief explanation; however, the explanation did not fully tie together how the environment affected the culture of the tribe.	Students provided a PowerPoint slide that gave a full explanation of their artifact—what it was, how it was used, and why it was a good representation of the culture of this tribe.
The work is neat and complete, and demonstrates proper spelling, punctuation, and grammar usage.	Because of the students' punctuation, spelling, and grammar mistakes, the project was difficult to interpret.	The students made an effort to include proper spelling, punctuation, and grammar. There were only a few mistakes.	The students used proper punctuation, spelling, and grammar throughout the project.
Total Points			

4TH-GRADE LESSONS

LESSON 3: UNDERSTANDING THE PAST

Coordinate! The final product for this lesson is a Virtual Native American Museum Display for Kids. Students will research the history and culture of a particular Native American tribe and understand how the environment influenced the culture of the tribe they chose. Students will choose an artifact that depicts the ties between environment and culture to display in their virtual museum. You may wish to take each student's PowerPoint slide and combine it into a class show for your virtual museum. Share the students' work with their classroom teacher. *Coordinate* by allowing the classroom teacher to use the show at a time when parents will visit the school.

Cooperate! During the study of Native Americans in the classroom, the classroom teacher may have students creating a piece of artwork inspired by Native American art, such as a sand painting, a dream catcher, a cornhusk doll, a pinch pot, or a diorama. *Cooperate* by offering to take digital photographs of their work. Include their artwork as an additional slide in your Native American Virtual Museum for Kids.

Lesson Plan

Integrated Goals:

Language Arts

Standard 1. Students read a wide range of print and nonprint texts to build and understanding of texts, of themselves, and the cultures of the United States and the world; to acquire new information; to respond to the needs and demands of society and the workplace; and for personal fulfillment. Among these texts are fiction and nonfiction, classic and contemporary works.

U.S. History K–4

Topic 1. Living and Working Together in Families and Communities, Now and Long Ago

> **Standard 1**—Family Life Now and in the Recent Past; Family Life in Various Places Long Ago.

Library Media

AASL 21st Century Standards

1. Inquire, think critically, and gain knowledge.

Essential Questions:

> How did environment affect the lives and culture of Native Americans?
> How can you protect the intellectual property rights of others?

Desired Understandings:

Students will understand:

That Native Americans of the past lived in many regions of North America.
The environment of Native Americans have deeply affected their way of life.
How to display information effectively.

Integrated Objectives:

- Students will create a virtual museum exhibit to represent their Native American region.
- Students will use ethical research methods to research a tribe in their Native American region.
- Students will create a bibliography.

Time Required:

45 minutes

Note: You should give students more than one day to complete this activity—one day for research and one day for creating their virtual museum. See the "Technology Integration" section of this lesson, and select option 1 or option 2 to complete the virtual museum project.

Provided Materials:

- "4th-Grade Notebook" (WS 1.4.1) packet that students used in the previous lesson worksheet
- "Native American Regions" (ORS 1.4.3)
- "Museum Rubric" (RS 1.4.5)
- "Virtual Museum" PowerPoint (OER 1.4.2)
- "Bibliography Notes" (WS 1.4.2)—one per student

Materials You Will Need to Obtain:

- Several artifacts from our current time period (these can include eating utensils, stapler, scissors, paper clips, iPod, cell phone, etc.)
- Information about different Native American regions (you can use books from your library media center, print outs from Web sites, or allow access to Web sites on the Internet). Sort resources by region groups to assist your students as they research a specific Native American tribe.
- Access to http://www.factmonster.com/ce6/society/A0834982.html. Display or print the information about Native Americans for students to use.
- Computers for students
- Projection device
- Pencils

Lesson Procedures:

Engagement:

1. Show students several artifacts from the current time period. Ask students what time period these artifacts are from and how they are used. Explain that thousands of years from now, these items will be looked at as artifacts or something from long ago. Ask students what these artifacts reveal about our culture. Discuss.

Activity:

2. Display the "Native American Regions" (ORS 1.4.3) map. Remind students that at the end of the previous class they chose a Native American region to study.
3. Share with students that today they will identify a Native American tribe from that region to research. Explain that they will choose a digital image of an artifact representative of their tribe's history to place in the Virtual Native American Museum for Kids.
4. Ask students to define "artifact" (an artifact is an object made by humans often discovered much later in time).
5. Distribute the "4th-Grade Notebook" (WS 1.4.1) packets that students used in the previous lesson.
6. Distribute the "Museum Rubric" (RS 1.4.5) to students. Remind students to consult the rubric as they complete their projects.
7. Show students your display of books, Web sites, and other resources about Native American history and culture. Explain how the resources are divided into regional groups. Explain to students where they will most likely find electronic photographs of artifacts for their tribe.

Embedded AASL Skills Indicator: ___.___.___: _____

_____

Give students time to find the resources they will need. Ask them to identify a tribe to research and to record their choice in the "4th-Grade Notebook" (WS 1.4.1) on page 5.

Transition:

8. Provide each student with access to a computer and Internet, as needed.

Activity:

Embedded AASL Skills Indicator: ___.___.___: _____

_____

Embedded AASL Dispositions in Action Indicator: ___.___.___: _____

_____

9. Using the resources provided, ask students to jot down information under each subject heading that will help them understand how the environment shaped their tribe's way of life. Explain that while they are researching, they should think about an artifact that depicts the culture of their tribe to place in the Virtual Native American Museum for Kids.
10. Distribute and instruct students to record the sources they use on the "Bibliography Notes" (WS 1.4.2) sheet.
11. Give students time to complete the activity.
12. Circulate throughout the room to check for understanding and provide assistance as needed.

Closure:

13. Ask students to share which resources gave them the best information for the project and why. Ask student to share how they have used the "Museum Rubric" (RS 1.4.5) to assist them in completing the project so far.

Evidence of Understanding:

Embedded AASL Self-Assessment Strategies: ___.___.___: _____

_____

Have students complete a gallery walk of the virtual museum. Have student pairs grade each other using the "Museum Rubric" (RS 1.4.5). Collect and grade the "4th-Grade Notebooks" (WS 1.4.1).

Technology Integration:

Technology

NETS–S

1. Creativity and Innovation

Students demonstrate creative thinking, construct knowledge, and develop innovative products and processes using technology. Students:

  a. apply existing knowledge to generate new ideas, products, or processes.
  b. create original works as a means of personal or group expression.

Day 2 Option 1:

Allow students to finish up their research. Show students the "Virtual Museum" (OER 1.4.2) PowerPoint slide. Instruct students on how to create their own PowerPoint slide, insert a photograph, and write their description of the artifact. Review the rubric. Give students time to create their slides. Put all of the slides together to create a class museum.

Day 2 Option 2:

Allow students to finish up their research. Instead of using the "Virtual Museum" (OER 1.4.2) PowerPoint, use the virtual museum on the Thinkport Web site http://museum.thinkport. org/. Although you have to join Thinkport to have full access to the online museum, it is free and it contains many other innovative technology options to use with your class.

Extension:

1. Ask students to think about some everyday items they use and choose one. Have students think about what that item would look like 1,000 years from now and write about it. Will it be in existence, or will it have changed?

Suggested Modifications:

Guide students with reading difficulties to resources that are easy for the student to read and interpret.

> **CLASSROOM CONNECTIONS**
>
> Invite the classroom teacher to view the student's gallery walk. A gallery walk is when students display their work and have an opportunity to walk around and view each other's projects. Students and teachers alike can provide positive feedback for student work.

BIBLIOGRAPHY NOTES

Name:

Web site

"Title of Website", Date you accessed the Web site,
<URL of the Web site>.

Books

Last Name, First Name. Name of Book. Publisher's City
Name: Name of Publisher, Year book was published.

From *Destination Collaboration 1: A Complete Research Focused Curriculum Guidebook to Educate 21st Century Learners in Grades 3–5* by
Danielle N. DuPuis and Lori M. Carter. Santa Barbara, CA: Libraries Unlimited. Copyright © 2011.

Working in Collaboration

Collaborate! True collaboration requires both the library media specialist and the classroom teacher to share in the design of integrated instruction. Collaboration provides you with an excellent opportunity to design inquiry-based learning activities. Here are some ideas for collaborating with the classroom teachers.

4th Grade: Native Americans

Essential Question: How did the environment shape the culture of Native Americans in North America?

- Create a Native American Virtual Museum that includes a wide variety of artifacts (e.g., music, food, clothing, games and sports, homes, jewelry, art, and legends). Celebrate your students' work by displaying their PowerPoint shows in a gallery walk.

Essential Question: How do Native Americans live today?

- Research Native American tribes that are currently in existence in our country. How do the tribes live today? Have students create a brochure, podcast, or newspaper that shares this information. Include places of interest where students can learn more about the heritage of Native Americans.

For further information, please visit
www.destinationcollaboration.com

5TH-GRADE LESSONS

LESSON 1: GET A CLUE ABOUT COPYRIGHT©

Coordinate! Students will be introduced to copyright and plagiarism terms through concrete examples and hands-on activities. Students will learn about copyright, including how it originated, why it is important, and how it affects them. After this introduction, students will have the opportunity to use what they learned to create some copyright tips, and to properly cite sources of information by creating a bibliography. Citing resources used in class is a skill your classroom teachers will want you to reinforce for students. Share copyright information with the classroom teachers to assist them in remaining up-to-date on current policies and laws regarding the proper use of information. *Coordinate* when to teach the lesson with the classroom teachers or offer to teach this lesson alongside a project they have assigned.

Cooperate! Students will use their listening and reasoning skills to decide how to ethically use information. Have students interpret what they learned by creating a class fair use policy. *Cooperate* with the classroom teacher by offering to create a poster on copyright information to display in the classroom for student use.

Lesson Plan

Integrated Goals:

Language Arts

Standard 8. Students use a variety of technological and information resources (e.g., libraries, databases, computer networks, video) to gather and synthesize information and to create and communicate knowledge.

Library Media

AASL 21st Century Standards

Standard 1: Inquire, think critically, and gain knowledge.

Essential Questions:

How can individuals respect the principles of intellectual freedom?

Desired Understandings:

Students will understand:

Specific terms and their meanings as they relate to copyright.
The basics of copyright laws and procedures.

> **CLASSROOM CONNECTIONS**
>
> Check with a classroom teacher to have this lesson coincide with a unit about the American Revolution. Students can use what they learned about copyright and apply it to the completion of a class project.

How to create a bibliographic citation for books and Web sites.
How to be responsible when using information.

Integrated Objectives:

- Students will identify and define copyright terms.
- Students will recall information about copyright and plagiarism by taking notes.
- Student will recognize appropriate information to include in a bibliography.

Time Required:

45 minutes

Provided Materials:

- "Clue into Copyright" (MN 1.5.1)—These can be printed on card stock and laminated so that they will last longer.
- "Copyright Introduction" (OER 1.5.1) PowerPoint
- "Copyright Clips" (WS 1.5.1)—one per student
- "Copyright Bibliography" (OER 1.5.2) PowerPoint

Materials You Will Need to Obtain:

- Computer
- Projection device
- Pencils

Lesson Procedures:

Engagement:

1. Give every student a "Clue into Copyright" (MN 1.5.1) card. Follow the directions includeed in the "Clue Into Copyright" (MN 1.5.1) document to play the game.

Activity:

2. Collect the "Clue Into Copyright" (MN 1.5.1) cards from the students and ask for them to recall a term and definition used in the game.
3. Display the first slide from the "Copyright Introduction" (OER 1.5.1) Power-Point.

Embedded AASL Skills Indicator: ___.___.___: _____

_____

4. Distribute copies of "Copyright Clips" (WS 1.5.1) to each student and instruct them to take notes about each term as you review the "Copyright Introduction" (OER 1.5.1) PowerPoint.

Embedded AASL Responsibilities Indicator: ___.___.___: _____

_____

5. After you display the first term on the "Copyright Introduction" (OER 1.5.1) PowerPoint, review with students the definition of copyright. Model how to take notes. Also, demonstrate by thinking aloud how you would personally reflect upon this slide. Remind students not only to take notes about each slide but also to record any personal thoughts about how the terms relate to them and how they use information.

6. Review the "Copyright Introduction" (OER 1.5.1) PowerPoint, and use the "notes" section to assist in giving examples for each term and how it relates to student achievement.

7. Allow time between each slide for students to take proper notes.

8. After sharing the last slide from the "Copyright Introduction" (OER 1.5.1) PowerPoint, you may wish to share the first book ever copyrighted with students, *The Philadelphia Spelling Book,* by John Barry, from the Library of Congress Web site (http://www.loc.gov/rr/rarebook/digitalcoll/digitalcoll-american.html).

Transition:

9. Instruct students to Think-Pair-Share for the last two questions on the "Copyright Clips" (WS 1.5.1).

Activity:

10. After students are finished completing their "Copyright Clips" (WS 1.5.1), ask that they share the number one way that they can prevent plagiarism and avoid breaking copyright (by creating a bibliography or resource list).

11. Display the first page of "Copyright Bibliography" (OER 1.5.2) PowerPoint.

12. Explain that a bibliography can include a variety of citations. Ask students to name some of the works that need to be cited if they are used to complete a project. Examples may include but are not limited to photographs, pictures, diagrams, maps, sound recordings, and documents, as well as books, newspaper articles, and Web sites.

13. Move to the next slide of the "Copyright Bibliography" (OER 1.5.2) PowerPoint and ask students to identify what type of resource is being cited. Once the correct answer has been identified, ask students how they came up with their answer. Use the notes section of the "Copyright Bibliography" (OER 1.5.2) PowerPoint to assist you in teaching about bibliographies. Be sure and discuss the important pieces of information that should be included in a bibliographic citation.

14. Continue through the slides to demonstrate the two types of citations most commonly used by 5th-grade students.

Closure:

Embedded AASL Self-Assessment Strategies: ___.___.___: _____

_____

15. Ask for students to share their reflections they recorded about copyright or bibliographies and what they thought as they recorded this information. Ask students how this new knowledge will change how they use information in the future.

Evidence of Understanding:

Check for participation throughout the lesson. Collect "Copyright Clips" (WS 1.5.1) and assess for completion of the worksheet, and the students understanding of copyright terms and future application.

Enrichment Using Technology:

Option 1: Students can access Library of Congress's Web site on "Taking the Mystery Out of Copyright" (http://www.loc.gov/teachers/copyrightmystery/) to learn more information about copyright.

Option 2: For more assistance on how to create a bibliography, direct students to this Web site: http://www.hobbyhorsebooks.com/bibliography5.html.

Extension:

1. Read the book, *Chickens May Not Cross the Road and Other Crazy (But True) Laws,* by Kathi Linz (Boston: Houghton Mifflin, 2002).
2. Challenge students to write their own song, play, or short story, and apply to have their idea copyrighted at http://www.loc.gov/teachers/copyrightmystery/#/steps/.

Suggested Modifications:

For students with reading and processing difficulties, print the "Copyright Introduction" (OER 1.5.1) PowerPoint utilizing the "Hand Outs 3 slides per page" option. Students can use these print-outs and record their notes directly onto the hand-outs.

DISCUSSION OPPORTUNITY

Your students will find *Chickens May Not Cross the Road and Other Crazy (But True) Laws* absolutely hilarious! Ask students to make connections and discuss how this book ties in with copyright.

CLUE INTO COPYRIGHT

MATERIALS FOR GAME PLAY

2 sets of copyright cards: Print each set (pages 4–5 and pages 6–7) in a different color to help the student easily determine their team (you may wish to laminate these cards so they will last longer).

4 rolls of masking tape

4 small balls or beanbags

HOW TO PLAY THE GAME

Distribute both sets of the "Clue Into Copyright" cards to the students. Students should each have one card. However, depending on the class size, some students could be assigned two cards. Make sure that if a student does have two cards, they have two of the same color card. As students play the game, each team will have two students with the same correct answer and will have an opportunity to earn up to two points for each question.

Instruct the students to form a line with other students who have their same color card. The students in each line should be facing the students in the opposite line. The lines should have approximately 8–10 feet of space separating them from one another. Place the balls or beanbags inside the rolls of masking tape (so they don't roll around on the floor) in between the two rows (see diagram below). Explain to the students that you will be reading a series of questions. Any student who thinks she has the correct answer should grab a ball/beanbag from the center of the room and quickly get back in line. Explain that teams receive one point for each correct answer, but that they lose one point for each incorrect answer. If they don't answer a question, they don't lose any points. Start with the first question on page three. Certain words in each question are in bold italics—you may wish to place emphasis on these words to clue students in to the answer.

Play the game until you have asked all of the questions and all students have had a turn.

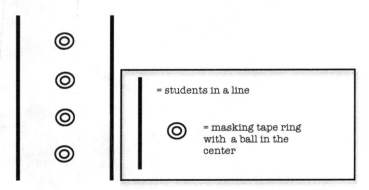

GAME QUESTIONS

1. When copyright expires, the work is available to be used by the **public** for personal, educational, or commercial purposes.

   Answer: public domain

2. Represented by the **letter C surrounded by a circle**, this word means the **right** given to an artist, author, or creator of a work to promote, sell, and distribute their work.

   Answer: copyright

3. A condition that allows you to **use** copyrighted work for limited educational purposes without paying royalties to the copyright owner.

   Answer: fair use

4. Using, **copying**, or **stealing** someone else's work, words, or idea and claiming it as your own.

   Answer: plagiarism

5. The United States Copyright Office is located in this **building**. This building houses **millions of books**, documents, sound recordings, and maps.

   Answer: Library of Congress

6. The symbol of the **letter P** surrounded by a circle indicates that these **sound recordings** are copyrighted.

   Answer: phonorecords

7. This will protect someone's **invention** and give the owner of the invention the right to reproduce and sell their invention for a limited amount of time.

   Answer: patent

8. **A list of resources** used to demonstrate where information or ideas were found.

   Answer: bibliography

9. This shows where you found a quote or piece of information in the body of your text or in a bibliography.

   Answer: citation

10. **Images** that are visibly seen and can be produced with assorted mediums and formats.

    Answer: picture

11. An expression of art and emotion through **sounds** with different rhythms, harmonies, melodies, beats, or words.

    Answer: music

12. A **motion picture** typically used as a form of entertainment.

    Answer: movies

13. A **printed** or electronic work of **fiction or nonfiction text**. Printed works contain pages and are protected with a cover; electronic works can be read online or by using a special reader.

    Answer: books

14. A set of pages connected together containing information posted by an individual, institution, or company to deliver information on the **Internet**.

    Answer: Web sites

15. The **creator** and copyright owner of an original work.

    Answer: author

Copyright	**Fair Use**
Public Domain	**Plagiarism**
Author	**Pictures**
Music	**Movies**

Books

Websites

Citations

Bibliography

Patent

Library of Congress

Phonorecords

Intentionally blank

From *Destination Collaboration 1: A Complete Research Focused Curriculum Guidebook to Educate 21st Century Learners in Grades 3–5* by Danielle N. DuPuis and Lori M. Carter. Santa Barbara, CA: Libraries Unlimited. Copyright © 2011.

Copyright	**Fair Use**
Public Domain	**Plagiarism**
Author	**Pictures**
Music	**Movies**

Books	**Websites**
Citations	**Bibliography**
Patent	**Library of Congress**
Phonorecords	Intentionally blank

COPYRIGHT CLIPS

Name: _____

Directions: As we discuss the "Copyright Introduction" PowerPoint, take notes about the various copyright terms, and reflect on each by adding your own personal thoughts about how these apply to you.

COPYRIGHT

© _____

© _____

Personal reflection:

_____

_____

_____

PLAGIARISM

© _____

© _____

Personal reflection:

_____

_____

_____

FAIR USE

© _____

© _____

Personal reflection:

_____

_____

_____

PUBLIC DOMAIN

© _____

© _____

Personal reflection:

_____

_____

_____

BIBLIOGRAPHY

© _____

© _____

Personal reflection:

_____

_____

_____

CITATION

© _____

© _____

Personal reflection:

_____

_____

_____

Use the spaces below to create some of your own tips.

What should you do when using images, documents, books, and Web sites for a project?

_____

_____

_____

_____

_____

_____

_____

What are some tips or guidelines you could post in the media center to remind others of how to use information responsibly?

_____

_____

_____

_____

_____

_____

_____

5TH-GRADE LESSONS

LESSON 2: PLAGIARISM OR NOT?

Coordinate! When students learn proper notetaking skills and how to record bibliographic citations, they will be better prepared to prevent committing plagiarism in future projects. Students will use what they learned to take notes about the inventions of Benjamin Franklin and add their own thoughts by reflecting on how his inventions have affected the way they currently do things in their own life. Share this lesson idea with the classroom teacher. Discuss beginning your unit to *coordinate* with the classroom teacher's instruction on the American Revolution.

Cooperate! Unintentional plagiarism is commonplace in elementary school. Challenge students to create an instructional commercial, blog, or poster to advertise the proper use of information for students in younger grades. Instruct students to include some appropriate examples as well as inappropriate examples to show other students the difference between plagiarism and the proper use of information. Students can share their information on your school Web site, on the announcements, or display posters in the hall. *Cooperate* with the classroom teacher by sharing the possibility of creating display posters or blog entries for a center activity during language arts.

Lesson Plan

Integrated Goals:

Language Arts

Standard 8. Students use a variety of technological and information resources (e.g., libraries, databases, computer networks, video) to gather and synthesize information and to create and communicate knowledge.

Social Studies

VIII Science, Technology, & Society

a. identify and describe examples in which science and technology have changed the lives of people, such as in homemaking, childcare, work, transportation, and communication.

Library Media

AASL 21st Century Standards

Standard 1: Inquire, think critically, and gain knowledge.
Standard 3: Share knowledge and participate ethically and productively as members of our democratic society.

Essential Questions:

How have inventions changed our daily lives?
How does organizing information help us to understand?
How can you protect the intellectual property rights of others?

Desired Understandings:

Students will understand:

How inventions from the past can still have an impact on our lives today.
How to utilize a graphic organizer to organize information.
How to create a bibliographic citation for books and Web sites.

Integrated Objectives:

- Students will review plagiarism.
- Students will use proper notetaking methods and citations to avoid unintentional plagiarism.
- Students will locate information about the inventions of Benjamin Franklin and create a web to organize their information.
- Students will write a comprehensive paragraph that describes inventions of Benjamin Franklin and explain how they affect our lives today.

Time Required:

45 minutes

Provided Materials:

- "Web of Ideas" (WS 1.5.2)—one packet per student—you may not wish to print these pages back-to-back to allow students to easily flip between pages.

Materials You Will Need to Obtain:

- An image of Benjamin Franklin.
- *Now & Ben: The Modern Inventions of Benjamin Franklin,* by Gene Barretta (New York: Henry Holt, 2006).
- Information about Benjamin Franklin and his inventions. You can use books from your library media center, or Web sites.
- Projection device
- Pencils

Lesson Procedures:

Engagement:

1. Display an image of Benjamin Franklin. Ask students to identify the man in the picture. Talk about evidence that supports their answer. Explain that today students will learn more about the life of Benjamin Franklin and his impact on the American Revolution as well as his impact on the way we live life today.

Activity:

2. Read the book *Now & Ben: The Modern Inventions of Benjamin Franklin* by Gene Barretta.

3. After reading the book, tell students that Benjamin Franklin made lots of inventions. Ask students how they think he would feel if someone stole one of his ideas and claimed it as their own?

4. Review plagiarism with the students. Ask students to define the word (stealing someone else's work and claiming it as your own). Ask students to recall some ways that they can avoid plagiarism (using your own words when taking notes, creating a bibliography to cite your sources, etc).

5. Tell students that one way to take notes is to record just the facts or main ideas along with one or two supporting details in your own words. Tell students that today they try taking notes in a new format, by using a web to organize their ideas.

Transition:

6. Display a copy of "Web of Ideas" (WS 1.5.2).

Embedded AASL Skills Indicator: ___.___.___: _____

_____

7. Tell students that they will learn more about Benjamin Franklin and his inventions by using the materials you have selected (books or Web sites). Students will place their notes into a web. A web is a graphic organizer and can help students organize and reorganize their thoughts in a clear, visual way.

Activity:

8. The "Web of Ideas" (WS 1.5.2) already has an invention included (the lightning rod) to start students on their way to creating their own web.

9. Demonstrate the proper way to construct a web by adding information about the lightning rod that was found using one of the sources selected. Together with the class, discuss how this invention has had impact on the way we live today.

Embedded AASL Skills Indicator: ___.___.___: _____

_____

10. Once you have used your resource, show students how to correctly cite that resource on the third page of "Web of Ideas" (WS 1.5.2). Explain that not only do students have to take notes in their own words but they also need to record where they found information to avoid plagiarism.

11. Distribute copies of "Web of Ideas" (WS 1.5.2) along with the resources about Benjamin Franklin and his inventions. These resources could be books or articles, or you can provide students with computers and access to Web sites that you have preselected.

Embedded AASL Dispositions in Action Indicator: ___.___.___: _____

_____

Embedded AASL Responsibilities Indicator: ___.___.___: _____

_____

12. Give students time to complete their web and cite their sources on the bibliography page.
13. Display the second page of the "Web of Ideas" (WS 1.5.2) packet for students to see. Model for the students how to take the notes from the web and create a comprehensive paragraph.
14. Allow students time to write a paragraph or two about two of Benjamin Franklin's inventions and how these inventions have affected the way we live our lives today.

Closure:

Embedded AASL Self-Assessment Strategies: ___.___.___: _____

_____

15. Ask students to trade papers with the person sitting next to them and quietly take a moment to read what that student has written. Students will use the checklist included on the last page of the packet to assess the work of their classmates.
16. Have students give back the papers they assessed to their classmate. Give students time to read and reflect on the comments made by their peer assessors.

Evidence of Understanding:

Use the checklist on the last page of the "Web of Ideas" (WS 1.5.2) packet to assist in assigning a grade for this assignment.

Technology Integration:

Technology

NETS–S

3. Research and Information Fluency

Students apply digital tools to gather, evaluate, and use information. Students:

b. locate, organize, analyze, evaluate, synthesize, and ethically use information from a variety of sources and media.

Option 1: Use the online webbing tool on Read Write Think (http://www.readwrite think.org/classroom-resources/student-interactives/readwritethink-webbing-tool-30038. html) instead of using the provided worksheet.

Enrichment Using Technology:

Option 1: Go to http://en.childrenslibrary.org/ and click on "Read Books." In the language scroll bar, scroll down to the "English" and then search for "Ben Franklin." Choose the *Stories of Great Men* book (rare books collection, c1903). Search through the book and find the section about Benjamin Franklin. Read the story to the class. Discuss the sayings of Benjamin Franklin from *Poor Richard's Almanac*, which is discussed in the story. Discuss how we still use these sayings and what they mean. Discuss the childhood of Benjamin Franklin and the obstacles he had to overcome to become an important historical figure.

Extension:

1. Tell students that Benjamin Franklin invented the items he did because he wanted to come up with a better way of doing things. Ask students to think about things they do every day that could be done more efficiently. Challenge students to design, draw, and explain an invention that would make something they do easier for them to accomplish.

Suggested Modifications:

For students with writing difficulties, use the modified "Web of Ideas" (MOD 1.5.1). This version asks for students to select only one of Benjamin Franklin's inventions to write about, is written in a larger font, and instructs students to cut out their bibliography to organize in alphabetical order (if necessary).

WEB OF IDEAS

Name: _____

Directions: Complete the web below by including three additional invention bubbles. From these bubbles, continue your web to include information about these inventions and why they were important.

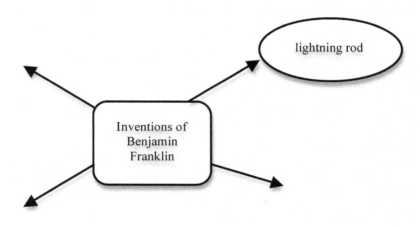

Once you have recorded all of your ideas about the various inventions of Benjamin Franklin, select two to write about on the lines below. Make sure you include a good opening and closing sentence, write the information you found in your own words, and include a personal reflection for how these inventions affect our lives today.

_____

_____

_____

_____

_____

_____

_____

_____

_____

_____

_____

_____

_____

_____

_____

_____

_____

_____

_____

_____

_____

_____

_____

_____

_____

_____

BIBLIOGRAPHY SAMPLE

HOW TO CITE A BOOK

Authors last name, Author's first name. Title (underlined). City where the book was published: Publishing company, Year the book was published. Page numbers used.

HOW TO CITE A WEB SITE

Title of the Web site (underlined). Date the Web site was last updated. Organization responsible for the Web site. Date that you accessed the Web site < URL of the Web site >.

Cite the sources you used for your "Inventions of Benjamin Franklin" web in the spaces below. Be sure your sources are in alphabetical order!

_____

_____

_____

_____

_____

_____

_____

_____

_____

_____

_____

_____

_____

_____

_____

_____

_____

_____

_____

_____

_____

PEER FEEDBACK CHECKLIST

Question	Yes	Partly	No
Does your classmate's web include at least three additional inventions?			
Does your classmate's web include information about each invention and why it was important?			
Did your classmate write a paragraph about two of the inventions from their web?			
Did your classmate include a personal reflection as to how these inventions have impacted our lives today?			
Did your classmate record where they found their information?			
Did your classmate use more than one source?			
Did your classmate use more than one type of source (i.e., Web site, book, magazine, newspaper article)?			
Did your classmate cite their source using the proper format (i.e., in alphabetical order, second line indented, information in the correct order)?			

Include some constructive feedback to your classmate (i.e., name something they did well, that could be improved, they missed).

_____

_____

_____

_____

_____

_____

_____

_____

_____

Peer Reviewer: _____

_____

WEB OF IDEAS

Name: _____

Directions: Complete the web below by including one additional invention bubble. From this bubble, continue your web to include information about this invention and why it was important.

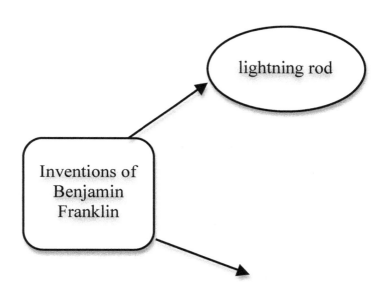

Once you have recorded your facts and ideas about one of the inventions of Benjamin Franklin, write about it on the lines below. Make sure you include a good opening and closing sentence, write the information you found in your own words, and include a personal reflection for how this invention affects your life today.

_____

_____

_____

_____

_____

_____

_____

_____

_____

_____

_____

_____

_____

_____

_____

_____

_____

_____

_____

_____

_____

_____

_____

_____

_____

_____

_____

_____

BIBLIOGRAPHY SAMPLES

HOW TO CITE A BOOK

Authors last name, Author's first name. Title (underlined). City where the book was published: Publishing company, Year the book was published. Page numbers used.

HOW TO CITE A WEB SITE

Title of the Web Site (underlined). Date the Web Site was last updated. Organization responsible for the Web Site. Date that you accessed the Web Site ‹ URL of the Web Site ›.

Cite the sources you used for your "Inventions of Benjamin Franklin" web in the spaces below. If your sources are not in alphabetical order, you can cut out each one and glue it on the back of the previous page in the correct order.

Use the template below to cite a **book**.

_____, _____. _____.
Author's last name   Author's last name   Title

_____: _____, _____. _____.
City where the book   Publishing company   Year the book   Page numbers
was published   was published   used

Use the template below to cite a **website**.

_____, _____. _____.
Title of the Web site   Date the Web site   Organization responsible for the
was last updated   Web site

_____ ‹ _____ ›.
Date you looked at the Web site   The URL of the Web site

PEER FEEDBACK CHECKLIST

Question	Yes	Partly	No
Does your classmate's web include one additional invention?			
Does your classmate's web include information about that invention and why it was important?			
Did your classmate write a paragraph about the invention from their web?			
Did your classmate include a personal reflection as to how this invention has impacted our lives today?			
Did your classmate record where they found their information?			
Did your classmate use more than one source?			
Did your classmate use more than one type of source (i.e., Web site, book, magazine, newspaper article.)?			
Did your classmate cite their source using the proper format (i.e., in alphabetical order, second line indented, information in the correct order)?			

Include some constructive feedback to your classmate (i.e., name something they did well, that could be improved, they missed).

_____

_____

_____

_____

_____

_____

_____

_____

Peer Reviewer: _____

_____-_____

5TH-GRADE LESSONS

LESSON 3: ARCHIVING INFORMATION

Coordinate! Students will locate information and take notes about Benjamin Franklin and his various accomplishments. Students will use their notes and follow current copyright procedures to create an archive of information about Benjamin Franklin for their classroom. Depending on their learning style, students can use a web or more linear technique to record their notes. *Coordinate* with the classroom teacher to have this lesson occur during the time they are teaching the American Revolution.

Cooperate! Citing resources and abiding by proper copyright laws and regulations is an important 21st century skill for both students and teachers. Ask students to work on an archive based on another school curriculum-based project. Be sure students double check to make sure they are properly documenting and citing their sources. *Cooperate* with the classroom teacher by creating a classroom archive of information for them to keep from year to year based on the teacher's interests. Include a bibliography in the classroom archive.

Lesson Plan

Integrated Goals:

Language Arts

Standard 8. Students use a variety of technological and information resources (e.g., libraries, databases, computer networks, video) to gather and synthesize information and to create and communicate knowledge.

U.S. History

5–12 Historical Thinking Standards

Standard 3: Historical Analysis and Interpretation

  C.   Analyze cause-and-effect relationships and multiple causation, including the importance of the individual, the influence of ideas.

Library Media

AASL 21st Century Standards

  Standard 1: Inquire, think critically, and gain knowledge.
  Standard 2: Draw conclusions, make informed decisions, apply knowledge to new situations, and create new knowledge.
  Standard 3: Share knowledge and participate ethically and productively as members of our democratic society.

Essential Questions:

How have Benjamin Franklin's accomplishments contributed to him being a founding father of the United States?

Why is it essential to have a national archive?

Desired Understandings:

Students will understand:

That our founding fathers played a significant role during the American Revolution by providing our nation with new ideas and beliefs.

The meaning and purpose for an archive.

How to create a bibliographic citation for books and Web sites.

Integrated Objectives:

- Students will apply notetaking methods to extract information from various sources.
- Students will cite sources appropriately.
- Students will create an "archive" of Benjamin Franklin's accomplishments.

Time Required:

45 minutes

Provided Materials:

- "Declaration of Independence" (RS 1.5.1)
- "Archiving Benjamin Franklin" (WS 1.5.3)—one packet for each student
- "Archiving Information" (MN 1.5.2)—copy and separate so that you have one card for each student. Depending on your class size, you will need to make between two and four copies of this sheet.

Materials You Will Need to Obtain

- Information about Benjamin Franklin, the Declaration of Independence, and the United States Constitution. Check to make sure these materials will assist students in explaining/supporting the following statement, "Benjamin Franklin is considered to be one of the founding fathers of the United States of America." You can use books from your library media center or Web sites.
- Access to the following Web sites http://www.archives.gov/exhibits/charters/constitution_founding_fathers_pennsylvania.html#Franklin (this will give students access to primary sources); http://bensguide.gpo.gov/benfranklin/; http://www.ushistory.org/franklin/info/index.htm.
- Computers for student use
- Projection device
- Pencils

Lesson Procedures:

Engagement:

1. Display the "Declaration of Independence" (RS 1.5.1). Ask students to share why the Declaration of Independence was so important. Explain that the Declaration of Independence is a primary source and is on display at the National Archives.

Activity:

2. Explain to students that an archive is "a place where people can go to gather first-hand facts, data, and evidence from letters, reports, notes, memos, photographs, and other primary sources" (http://www.archives.gov/about/info/whats-an-ar chives.html). Check that students understand the definition of primary source.

3. Take a moment and have students share their ideas for why it is important to archive information.

4. Tell students that they will be using the notetaking techniques they learned as well as following proper copyright procedures to create a classroom archive of Benjamin Franklin's accomplishments.

5. Distribute a copy of "Archiving Benjamin Franklin" (WS 1.5.3) to each student.

6. Tell students that they will be taking notes in order to determine why Benjamin Franklin is considered to be one of our founding fathers.

Embedded AASL Skills Indicator: ___.___.___: _____

_____

7. Give students access to the materials you obtained about Benjamin Franklin for this assignment. Explain that they may take notes on either the first or second page of their "Archiving Benjamin Franklin" (WS 1.5.3) packet, depending on the method they prefer to use when taking notes.

8. Give students time to complete their notes.

Transition:

9. Distribute an "Archiving Information" (MN 1.5.2) card to each student.

10. Tell students to find their group by locating other students who have the same card.

Activity:

11. Tell students that they are to use their "Archiving Information" (MN 1.5.2) cards to assist them in completing the final portion of their assignment. As a group, students will create an archive of information about their Benjamin Franklin topic area they have been assigned. Note that this is the same as what is written on their "Archiving Information" (MN 1.5.2) card.

Embedded AASL Responsibilities Indicator: ___.___.___: _____

_____

12. Explain the directions of the assignment on page 3 of the "Archiving Benjamin Franklin" (WS 1.5.3) packet. Emphasize that even though the information they are using falls into the fair use category, they still need to properly cite their re-sources. (This information was covered on the "Copyright Introduction" [OER 1.5.1] PowerPoint delivered in lesson 1 of this unit.).

13. Before students begin, ask that they work with their group to select a variety of items for their archive so that not everyone in the group is locating the same information. This will add diversity and variety to the archive.

14. Give students access to the Web sites selected as well as the books you have gathered for this lesson.

Embedded AASL Skills Indicator: ___.___.___: _____

_____

Embedded AASL Skills Indicator: ___.___.___: _____

_____

15. Allow students time to complete the assignment.

Embedded AASL Dispositions in Action Indicator: ___.___.___: _____

_____

Closure:

Embedded AASL Self-Assessment Strategies: ___.___.___: _____

_____

16. Ask students to complete the reflection log located on the bottom half of the last page of the "Archiving Benjamin Franklin" (WS 1.5.3) packet.

17. Once completed, have students share their reflections with the other members of their group.

Evidence of Understanding:

After gathering the "Archiving Information" (MN 1.5.2) packets, compile them and share with the classroom teacher. The teacher can use this student-created archive as a reference when discussing the founding fathers of our country.

Check the reflections for understanding, the citations for completeness, and the appropriateness of the archived items.

Technology Integration:

Technology

NETS–S

3. Research and Information Fluency

Students apply digital tools to gather, evaluate, and use information. Students:

   b. locate, organize, analyze, evaluate, synthesize, and ethically use information from a variety of sources and media.

   1. Once students have researched their Benjamin Franklin assignment, use the "Classroom Archives" (OER 1.5.3) PowerPoint for students to compile their information and add photos and links to Web sites and documents.

Enrichment Using Technology:

1. If students have extra time, they can sign their own name to the Declaration of Independence by following the directions at: http://www.archives.gov/exhibits/char ters/declaration_sign.html.

Extension:

1. Read the book *John, Paul, George & Ben,* by Lane Smith (New York: Hyperion, 2006). Students can make connections from the characters in the book to the founding fathers of the American Revolution.

Suggested Modifications:

For students in need of both visual and auditory assistance, have them view the "We the People: Behind the Scenes with Benjamin Franklin" video from the Cyberbee Web site (http://www.cyberbee.com/constitution/). There is also an option for students to download a transcript of the movie. This will assist them as they take notes for the first part of this lesson.

DECLARATION OF INDEPENDENCE

IN CONGRESS, JULY 4, 1776.

The unanimous Declaration of the thirteen united States of America.

[handwritten text of the Declaration of Independence, followed by signatures of the signers]

"Declaration of Independence." *The National Archives.* 2007. 25 Sept. 2007 ‹http://www.archives.gov/national-archives-experience/charters/declaration.html›.

ARCHIVING BENJAMIN FRANKLIN

Name: _____

Directions: Use the lines below or the web on the next page to take notes to support and explain the following statement,

"Benjamin Franklin is considered to be one of the founding fathers of the United States of America."

-
-
-
-
-
-
-
-
-

Cite your source below _____

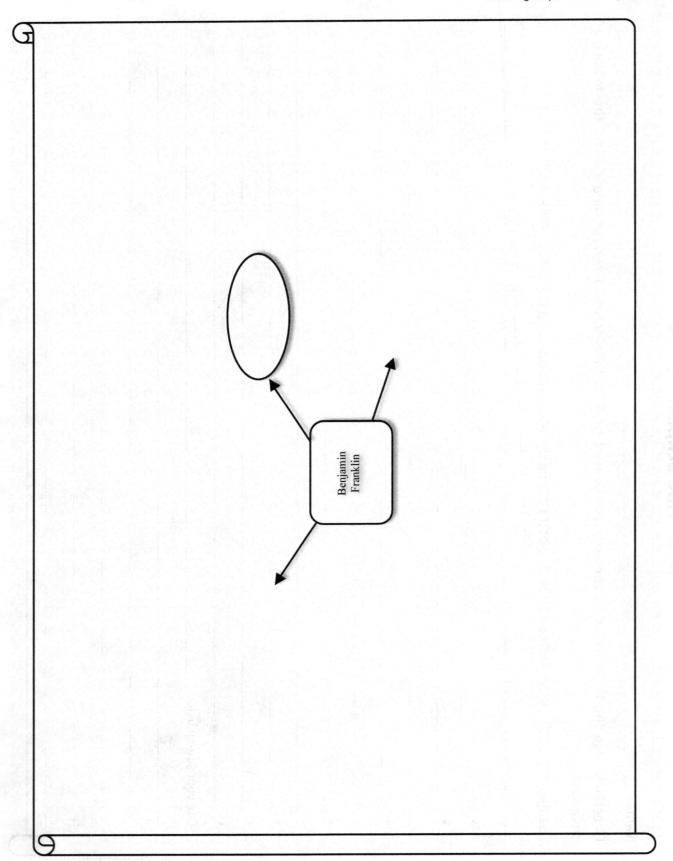

With the other members of your team, create an archive (collection) of information about Benjamin Franklin as it pertains to the significant part of his life you have been assigned. First, locate information about the part of Benjamin Franklin's life that you have been assigned. Try to have a variety of items in your archive. Use the checklist below to assist you as you gather information. Use the space to the right of the checklist box to take notes to explain why the artifact you chose should be placed in the archive. Also, be sure to cite your sources and include page numbers for where you found your information on the next page.

I found my information from a book / website (circle one).
My information was in the form of a...

☐ Photograph
☐ Picture
☐ Drawing
☐ Primary Document
☐ Table

I found my information from a book / website (circle one).
My information was in the form of a...

☐ Photograph
☐ Picture
☐ Drawing
☐ Primary Document
☐ Table

I found my information from a book / website (circle one).
My information was in the form of a...

☐ Photograph
☐ Picture
☐ Drawing
☐ Primary Document
☐ Table

Use this page to cite any resources you gathered for your archive.

_____

_____

_____

_____

_____

_____

_____

_____

_____

Reflection Log:
What was the best resource you used today? Why was it the best?

_____

_____

What accomplishments would you think are necessary to be named a founding father of our country?

_____

_____

Share these thoughts with your group.

ARCHIVING INFORMATION

United States Constitution	Declaration of Independence
Treaty of Paris	Scientist/ Inventor
Poor Richard's Almanac	Printer
Postmaster	Family Life

Working in Collaboration

Collaborate! True collaboration requires both the library media specialist and the classroom teacher to share in the design of integrated instruction. Here are some ideas that for collaborating with the classroom teachers.

5th Grade: American Revolution

Essential Question: How has the Declaration of Independence shaped our country?

• Have students create a podcast. Students can role-play and pretend to live during 1776 and act out what life was like at that time for Americans. A student role playing as a present-day radio commentator can ask questions regarding freedoms and how the Declaration of Independence has helped to shape our freedom and country. Students can work in pairs to conduct research together and then each take on a role for the podcast.

Essential Question: How have the contributions of Benjamin Franklin influenced the way we do things today?

• Have students explain the importance of post offices, libraries, and sanitation departments: all of which are around today because of Benjamin Franklin. Students could create a newspaper explaining what life might be like without these institutions.

For further information, please visit
www.destinationcollaboration.com

Bibliography

Works Cited

America at Home. Photograph. 2001. CNN International. 2007. Cable News Network. 29 Sept. 2007. Web. <http://i.cnn.net/cnn/SPECIALS/2001/trade.center/images/america. at.home.jpg>.

Benjamin Franklin. Archiving Early America. 2007. Web. 29 Sept. 2007. <http://www.early america.com/portraits/franklin.html>.

Carter, Lori. *Capitol.* Photograph. 2006. Lori Carter, Baltimore.

"Declaration of Independence." *The National Archives.* 2007. 25 Sept. 2007. Web. <http:// www.archives.gov/national-archives-experience/charters/declaration.html>.

Fenton, M. B. "Bat." *World Book Online. World Book Online Reference Center.* 2007. World Book. 29 Sept. 2007. Web. <http://www.worldbookonline.com/wb/Article?id=ar049100>.

Nordamerikanische Kulturareale en. Map. *Wikimedia Commons.* 7 Apr. 2007. Web. 29 Dec. 2008. <http://commons.wikimedia.org/wiki/File:Nordamerikanische_Kulturareale_en.png>.

"United States." *CultureGrams Kids Edition.* 2007. Web. 6 Sept. 2007 <http://online.culture grams.com/>.

"United States." Map. *The World Factbook.* 8 Oct. 2008. Web. 29 Dec. 2008 <https://www.cia. gov/library/publications/the-world-factbook/reference_maps/united_states.html>.

Walker, Angela L. "Preventing Unintentional Plagiarism: A Method for Strengthening Para-phrasing Skills." *Journal of Instructional Psychology* 35.4 (2008): 387–95. *EBSCO.* Web. 27 Feb. 2009.

What's an Archives? The National Archives. Web. 14 Mar. 2009. <http://www.archives.gov/ about/info/whats-an-archives.html>.

Suggested Book Resources

Barretta, Gene. *Now & Ben: The Modern Inventions of Benjamin Franklin.* New York: Henry Holt, 2006. Print.

Linz, Kathi. *Chickens May Not Cross the Road and Other Crazy (But True) Laws.* Boston: Hough-ton Mifflin, 2002. Print.

Shoulders, Michael, and Debbie Shoulders. *D is for Drum: A Native American Alphabet.* Chel-sea: Sleeping Bear Press, 2006. Print.

Smith, Lane. *John, Paul, George & Ben.* New York: Hyperion, 2006. Print.

Swinburne, Stephen R. *Once a Wolf: How Wildlife Biologists Fought to Bring Back the Gray Wolf.* Boston: Houghton Mifflin, 1999. Print.

Suggested Web Resources

"American Digitized Materials." *Rare Book & Special Collections Reading Room.* 4 Mar. 2009. Web. The Library of Congress. 14 Mar. 2009. <http://www.loc.gov/rr/rarebook/digital coll/digitalcoll-american.html>.

"America's Library." *America's Story.* The Library of Congress. Web. 29 Dec. 2008. <http:// www.americaslibrary.gov/bin/.cgi>.

Aroldi, Susan. "Fifth Grade Bibliographical Format." *Instructional Media Center.* Oradell Pub-lic School. Web. 14 Mar. 2009. <http://www.hobbyhorsebooks.com/.html>.

"Benjamin Franklin." *Ben's Guide to U.S. Government for Kids.* U.S. Government Printing Of-fice, 17 Feb. 2009. Web. 18 Oct. 2009. <http://bensguide.gpo.gov/benfranklin/>.

Ben's Guide to U.S. Government for Kids. 18 Dec. 2008. U.S. Government Printing Office. Web. 29 Dec. 2008. <http://bensguide.gpo.gov/3-5/index.html>.

BibMe. 2009. GreenRiver. Web. 14 Mar. 2009. <http://www.bibme.org/>.

"Create Your Own Museum." *Thinkport.* 2007. MPT & Johns Hopkins Center for Technology in Education. Web. 15 Mar. 2009. <http://museum.thinkport.org/>.

CultureGrams. 2009. Web. 14 Nov. 2009. <http://www.culturegrams.com/>.

"Declaration of Independence." *The National Archives.* 2007. Web. 25 Sept. 2007. <http://www.archives.gov/national-archives-experience/charters/declaration.html>.

EasyBib. 2009. ImagineEasy. Web. 14 Mar. 2009. <http://easybib.com >.

Edublogs. 2008. Web. 29 Dec. 2008. <http://edublogs.org/>.

"Educators and Students." *The National Archives.* U.S. National Archives and Records Administration. Web. 29 Dec. 2008. <http://www.archives.gov/education/>.

"The Electric Ben Franklin." *USHistory.* Independence Hall Association, 2009. Web. 18 Oct. 2009. <http://www.ushistory.org/franklin/info/ index.htm>.

Future State. U.S. Department of State. Web. 29 Dec. 2008. <http://future.state.gov/educators/online/us/>.

International Children's Digital Library. Web. 29 Dec. 2008. <http://en.childrenslibrary.org/>.

Kindig, Thomas. "Signers of the Declaration of Independence." *US History.* 2007. Web. 25 Sept. 2007. <http://www.ushistory.org/declaration/signers/index.htm>.

"Meet Dr. Franklin." *Adventures of Cyberbee.* Ed. Linda C. Joseph. 11 Dec. 2008. Web. 14 Mar. 2009. <http://www.cyberbee.com/constitution/>.

The National Archives. America's Founding Fathers. Web. 14 Mar. 2009. <http://www.archives.gov/exhibits/charters/constitution_founding_fathers_pennsylvania.html#Franklin>.

NoodleTools, Inc. 2009. Web. 14 Mar. 2009. <http://www.noodletools.com/.php>.

"ReadWriteThink Notetaker." *ReadWriteThink.* 14 Mar. 2009. Web. 14 Mar. 2009. <http://www.readwritethink.org/student_mat/student_material.asp?id=55>.

"ReadWriteThink Webbing Tool." *ReadWriteThink.* 2004. Web. 14 Mar. 2009. <http://interactives.mped.org/view_interactive.aspx?id=127&title >.

"Natives, North American." *Fact Monster.* 2008. Pearson Education. Web. 29 Dec. 2008. <http://www.factmonster.com/ce6/society/A0834982.html>.

"States and Capitals." *50 States.* 2008. Marchex. Web. 30 Dec. 2008. <http://www.50states.com/>.

Storynory. Blog Relations Ltd. Web. 15 Mar. 2009. <http://storynory.com>.

"Taking the Mystery Out of Copyright." *The Library of Congress.* Web. 14 Mar. 2009. <http://www.loc.gov/teachers/copyrightmystery/>.

Time For Kids. 2008. Time Inc. Web. 29 Dec. 2008. <http://www.timeforkids.com/TFK/>.

World Almanac for Kids. 2008. World Almanac. Web. 29 Dec. 2008. <http://www.worldalmanacforkids.com>.

"The Writings of Benjamin Franklin." *The History Carper.* 22 Dec. 2008. Web. 22 Dec. 2008. <http://www.historycarper.com/resources/twobf2/contents.htm>.

Chapter 2

Public Access Catalog: Locating Information

Introduction

The Public Access Catalog (PAC) is a necessary tool for students to locate resources in the library media center. The students' ability to locate resources depends upon their background knowledge of subjects and their ability to make inferences. These two components are necessary in the identification and implementation of conducting a keyword search. To be effective users of information, students must be able to expand or narrow their search depending upon their informational needs. The three-lesson unit for 3rd grade and the two-lesson units for 4th and 5th grade will assist students in accomplishing this goal. The units should be taught in the beginning of the year for optimal library use.

From Year to Year

The PAC is a tool that can be used by both basic and proficient library users. The lessons in this book build on each other. The primary goal of all the lessons is to help students become proficient library users. The 3rd-grade lessons begin with the basics of performing a basic keyword, title, and author search. In the 4th-grade lessons, students learn how to broaden and narrow search terms to locate desired information. The lessons for 5th grade are designed to teach students how to extract keywords from a research question in order to conduct a successful search and to locate relevant information sources in the PAC. Through the gradual introduction of these search methods, you can ensure your students will have time to process and practice each technique so that they are better prepared for whatever projects the school year may bring.

Lifelong Library Use

Learning to use the PAC in an elementary school library media center may be the first opportunity students have to explore and locate relevant information. Providing students with a successful searching experience in the PAC will give them the confidence that is needed to locate information for a school project or personal inquiry. Students will be more likely to "persist in information searching despite challenges" (American Association of School Librarians, 2009) if they have already experienced success with searching in the PAC. The connection between the library media center and local public library should be made clear. Explain how the catalog search and the general order of the materials in a school library media center mirrors those of a public library. Once students have made the connection that the two entities are similar, they will be more likely to explore and locate information in the public library, thereby encouraging them to be lifelong library users.

Self-Assessment Strategies

Self-assessment is an important part of the learning process. It is important for learners to step back to see what learning has occurred, how it can be improved, and what can be changed in the future. It is through consistent self-reflection and self-assessment that students can gain a deeper understanding for the learning process as well as for the information gained. We included self-assessment strategies within this chapter because learning how to search with keywords successfully requires students to make inferences and reflect on their own processes. Only then will they be able to modify their search process and find the information they desire. Being able to make inferences is a higher order thinking skill that will take practice before students are able to make connections without a prompt or guidance from their teacher or library media specialist.

Relevancy

As students progress from elementary to middle school, high school, and on to higher education, one thing will remain consistent each year—students will be expected to complete various research projects from simple reports to large collaborative group projects involving digital presentation tools. To be successful at locating appropriate, accurate, and reliable information, students need to understand how to access books and online materials. As students move forward in their educational careers, the search process becomes more complicated; however, the basic steps involved in locating information remains the same.

Working in Isolation

Basic knowledge of the PAC and the concept of keywords are foundation blocks for information literacy. Traditionally, informational literacy has been a library skill. Today, understanding how to find or organize information by assigning keywords or tags is a 21st century skill that will affect your students' ability to become information literate in a digital environment. As such, your students must learn how to think about an information question to determine the topic and brainstorm synonyms and/or related concepts in order to assign keywords. Teach students how to use the PAC early in the year.

Frequently, students will be assigned projects that will require them to find information in the school or the public library. Their ability to use the PAC to find relevant information will be very useful to students, as they become successful 21st century learners. While teaching students how to use the PAC can be taught in isolation, the skill should no longer be taught in isolation from other content areas. Use the provided lessons as a template to create your own lessons in which you can tie in science, social studies, math, or language arts objectives. Incorporation of these objectives will help you begin a conversation with other teachers as you move toward full collaboration.

Take notice when students come to you with an informational need: whether it is an assigned classroom project or their own personal interest. The library media collection should reflect the needs of the school's students and staff. Having books in the collection that reflect the wants and needs of the community will result in a higher circulation rate as students search for these resources, thereby encouraging continual library media center use.

Classroom teachers may assign favorite projects each year. Take note of these projects and file notes according to the date assigned. By reviewing these notes the following year, you will be in a better position to discuss the project with the classroom teacher prior to the project's assignment. Also, develop the collection to better serve the school's curriculum by purchasing titles aligned to the curriculum. In this way, your library media center will begin to serve its purpose at the center of the school's curriculum.

3RD-GRADE LESSONS

LESSON 1: PAC SCRAMBLE

Coordinate! This PAC Scramble lesson will teach students how to search the library media center's collection by conducting subject, title, and author searches in the PAC. After selecting a subject, title, or author of interest to search, students will then have an opportunity to locate and check out one of the books they found in the PAC. *Coordinate* with the classroom teacher by offering to create a bibliography of titles available in your media center for an upcoming classroom project.

Cooperate! After this lesson, students will be eager to use the PAC to locate books of interest. *Cooperate* with the classroom teacher by offering to bookmark your school's PAC on their classroom computer. Students can use the PAC during a center activity to create a list of titles they might like to check out the next time they come to the library media center. Students can also use the bookmarked PAC in their classroom to create a list of possible resources for an upcoming classroom project.

Lesson Plan

Integrated Goals:

Language Arts

Standard 8. Students use a variety of technological and information resources (e.g., libraries, databases, computer networks, video) to gather and synthesize information and to create and communicate knowledge.

Library Media

AASL 21st Century Standards

Standard 1: Inquire, think critically, and gain knowledge
Standard 4: Pursue personal and aesthetic growth

Essential Questions:

How can the PAC help you locate information?

Desired Understandings:

Students will understand:

How to search the PAC depending on their informational need.
How to conduct a subject, title, and author search in the PAC.

Integrated Objectives:

- Students will become familiar with the purpose of the PAC.
- Students will search the PAC using subject, title, and author.

Time Required:

45 minutes

Provided Materials:

- "PAC Scramble" (WS 2.3.1)—one per student
- "PAC Search" (WS 2.3.2)—one third of a sheet per student

Materials You Will Need to Obtain:

- Computer with Internet access to the school's PAC
- Projection device
- Pencils
- Before meeting with the class, decide whether you will be using computers with the entire class, part of the class, or not at all. Book the stationary or mobile lab accordingly.

Lesson Procedures:

Engagement:

*Be sure that your media center owns the titles/authors/subjects used for the engagement activity. Change the items accordingly with what you have available to you.

1. Come into the room with pages of notebook paper and tell students that you are excited to get started, but don't know where to begin. Explain that teachers have been approaching you left and right for books they can use in their classrooms. A kindergarten teacher wants books written by and about Eric Carle, a 4th-grade teacher wants books about animals of the rainforest, and a 2nd-grade teacher wants a book called *Diary of a Worm*. Ask students what's the fastest way to locate these books. Students should be able to suggest that you should look up the titles, authors, and subjects in the PAC.

Activity

2. Display the school's PAC for students to see. Tell students that the acronym used to shorten the name of the "Public Access Catalog" is PAC. Explain to students that there are three main ways to search the PAC. Ask students to share their ideas for these search methods.
3. Ask students if they have ever had the problem where they couldn't remember the title of the book they were looking for, but they remembered the author. Or maybe they remembered the title, but couldn't remember the author. Or perhaps they just wanted to read a book about a particular subject. Give students time to share their answers.
4. Use the title *The Very Hungry Caterpillar* by Eric Carle as an example. Type the title into the PAC, and do a search. Show students that by doing a title search, you are able to find the title you are looking for quickly.
5. Next, begin a new search, and type the author's name, "Eric Carle," into the PAC. Explain that you just wanted to see what else the media center owned that was written by Eric Carle. Ask students what they can see that is different about the new search results (e.g., the list is longer, there are multiple titles, etc.).

6. Explain to students that perhaps after reading *The Very Hungry Caterpillar*, they wished to learn more about butterflies. Explain how this would require a subject search in the PAC because you are not concerned with who wrote the book, or even the title. You just wish to locate more information about butterflies. Type the word "butterflies" into the PAC. Ask students what they notice about this new list. Be sure and point out the number of results, ways to navigate through pages of results, the difference in call numbers for fiction vs. nonfiction, the format of the item, and then demonstrate how students are able to see if the titles are available or not.

7. Ask for students to volunteer a title that can be searched for together as a class.

8. Search for the title in the PAC and ask students to identify the author, subject, and call number. Ask students to note whether the title is available or not. With the students, determine where to find this book in the media center.

Transition:

9. Option 1: Distribute copies of "PAC Scramble" (WS 2.3.1)

10. Option 2: If you are using computers with the class, use this time as an opportunity for students to log on to the library media center's PAC and distribute copies of "PAC Search" (WS 2.3.2)

Activity:

11. Option 1: Explain the worksheet "PAC Scramble" (WS 2.3.1) to students and allow time to complete.

Embedded AASL Skills Indicator: ___.___.___: _____

_____

Embedded AASL Skills Indicator: ___.___.___: _____

_____

12. Option 2: Explain to students that they must use the PAC to conduct a title, author, or subject search of their choosing. Highlight the fact that they must record the author, subject, call number, and the availability of the book they chose.

Embedded AASL Dispositions in Action Indicator: ___.___.___: _____

_____

Embedded AASL Dispositions in Action Indicator: ___.___.___: _____

_____

13. Circulate around the room to assist students with searching the PAC. Students will need encouragement and redirection as they complete this activity.

Closure:

14. Option 1: Have students swap the "PAC Scramble" (WS 2.3.1) worksheets. Discuss the correct answers as a group to check for understanding.

Embedded AASL Responsibilities Indicator:

___.___.___: _____

15. Option 2: Allow students time to either conduct a new search or locate the book they found in the PAC if it sounds like something they wish to check out.

Evidence of Understanding:

Embedded AASL Self-Assessment Strategies: ___.___.___: _____

_____

Option 1: Collect and grade "PAC Scramble" (WS 2.3.1).

Option 2: Collect the "PAC Search" (WS 2.3.2). Check to make sure the students were successful in completing a search in the PAC.

Enrichment Using Technology:

Access your local library's Web site and PAC to give students practice in using a different catalog. Have students compare and contrast the similarities and differences between the library media center's PAC and the PAC at the local library.

Extension:

1. Have a librarian from the local public library come in and discuss and demonstrate the library's PAC with students.

Suggested Modifications:

Use the modified "PAC Scramble" (MOD 2.3.1) for students that may have difficulty in completing the assignment.

PAC SCRAMBLE

Name: _____

Directions: Read each statement and question carefully. Place a check next to the correct answer for questions 1–6. Write the correct answer for questions 7 and 8.

1. Molly knows that she wants to read more books written by Beverly Cleary. What search does Molly need to do in the PAC?

   ☐ Title   ☐ Author   ☐ Subject

2. Steven loves books about snakes. He's already read *The Complete Guide to Snakes of North America,* but wants to try a different book. What kind of search would you recommend Steven try?

   ☐ Title   ☐ Author   ☐ Subject

3. Kara's mom is having a birthday. Kara really wants to do something special for her mom's birthday. She was thinking of making her a card or special craft. What type of search should Kara look for in the PAC?

   ☐ Title   ☐ Author   ☐ Subject

4. Billy loves the Henry and Mudge book series by Cynthia Rylant. What type of search should Billy do if he is looking for other books written by Cynthia Rylant?

   ☐ Title   ☐ Author   ☐ Subject

5. Carol loves *If You Give a Mouse a Cookie* by Laura Numeroff. What type of search should she do when looking for this book's location on the shelf?

   ☐ Title   ☐ Author   ☐ Subject

6. Think about a favorite book you have checked out. If you tried to locate this book again, what type of search would you do?

   ☐ Title   ☐ Author   ☐ Subject

7. Samantha dreams about being a famous ballerina when she grows up. If she were to do a subject search in the PAC, what subject would she search for? _____
_____

8. Bobby wants to know how cars work. Would he want books that are fiction or non-fiction? _____

PAC SEARCH

Name: _____

Directions: Choose a title from the board to search for in the Public Access Catalog (PAC). Record the information you find in the spaces provided below.

Title: _____

Author: _____ Call number: _____

Subject: _____

This book is ☐ Available ☐ Not Available

Name: _____

Directions: Choose a title from the board to search for in the Public Access Catalog (PAC). Record the information you find in the spaces provided below.

Title: _____

Author: _____ Call number: _____

Subject: _____

This book is ☐ Available ☐ Not Available

Name: _____

Directions: Choose a title from the board to search for in the Public Access Catalog (PAC). Record the information you find in the spaces provided below.

Title: _____

Author: _____ Call number: _____

Subject: _____

This book is ☐ Available ☐ Not Available

PAC SCRAMBLE

Name: _____

Directions: Read each statement and question carefully. Place a check next to the correct answer for questions 1–6. Write the correct answer for questions 7 and 8.

1. Molly knows that she wants to read more books **written by Beverly Cleary.** What search does Molly need to do in the PAC?

   □ **Title**   □ **Author**   □ **Subject**

2. Steven loves books about **snakes.** He's already read *The Complete Guide to Snakes of North America,* but wants to try a different book. What kind of search would you recommend Steven try?

   □ **Title**   □ **Author**   □ **Subject**

3. Kara's mom is having a birthday. Kara really wants to do something special for her mom's birthday. She was thinking of making her a card, or special **craft.** What type of search should Kara look for in the PAC?

   □ **Title**   □ **Author**   □ **Subject**

4. Billy loves the Henry and Mudge book series by Cynthia Rylant. What type of search should Billy do if he is looking for other books **written by Cynthia Rylant?**

   □ **Title**   □ **Author**   □ **Subject**

5. Carol loves *If You Give a Mouse a Cookie* by Laura Numeroff. What type of search should she do when looking for this book's location on the shelf?

   □ **Title**   □ **Author**   □ **Subject**

6. Think about a favorite book you have checked out. If you tried to locate this book again, what type of search would you do?

   Write the name of the book here:_____

   □ **Title**   □ **Author**   □ **Subject**

7. Samantha dreams about being a famous **ballerina** when she grows up. If she were to do a subject search in the PAC, what subject would she search for? _____

   _____

   What is the root word for ballerina? This word will help you!

8. Bobby wants to know how **cars** work. Would he want books that are fiction or nonfiction? _____

   Are cars real or not real? This will help you decide!

3RD-GRADE LESSONS

LESSON 2: LOCKED IN THE LIBRARY

Coordinate! In this Locked in the Library lesson, students will use keyword searches in the PAC to locate clues. One clue leads to the next, requiring students to determine and enter different keywords in the PAC. A surprise awaits students when they locate the last clue. *Coordinate* with the classroom teacher by offering to show or demonstrate features of the PAC.

Cooperate! After having actively participated in this lesson, students will understand how to conduct a keyword search in the PAC. Students will also be familiar with Marty the Media Mouse. *Cooperate* with the classroom teacher by offering to share Marty the Media Mouse as a motivational engagement activity for their class. Marty could visit the classroom and bring along books that support an upcoming lesson topic. Marty and the classroom teacher could have a conversation with the students about how to locate more book resources if the selection of books does not meet their informational needs.

Lesson Plan

Integrated Goals:

Language Arts

Standard 8. Students use a variety of technological and information resources (e.g., libraries, databases, computer networks, video) to gather and synthesize information and to create and communicate knowledge.

Library Media

AASL 21st Century Standards

> **Standard 1:** Inquire, think critically, and gain knowledge.
> **Standard 4:** Pursue personal and aesthetic growth.

Essential Questions:

> How can the PAC help you locate information?

Desired Understandings:

Students will understand:

> How to search the PAC depending on their informational needs.
> How to conduct a keyword search in the PAC.

Integrated Objectives:

- Students will use keywords to locate information in the PAC.

Time Required:

45 minutes

Provided Materials:

- "Marty Letter" (RS 2.3.1)
- "Mouse Clues" (OER 2.3.1)—printed using the six slides per page option

Materials You Will Need to Obtain:

- Computer with Internet access to the school's PAC
- Projection device
- Pencils
- Envelope—Write the word "Urgent" on the front.
- A picture of a mouse, or preferably a small stuffed mouse or mouse puppet—The mouse finger puppets made by Folkmanis are perfect for this lesson (item #2652— mini mouse, field; available from http://www.folkmanis.com/).

Prior to the Lesson

Prior to student arrival, place the clues in the appropriate parts of the media center for the students to find during the scavenger hunt activity.

Lesson Procedures:

Engagement:

1. Tell students that you have received a letter on your desk marked "Urgent." Ask your student's advice on whether you should open the letter now, or begin the class. (Students should encourage you to open the letter). Open the "Marty Letter" (RS 2.3.1) and act surprised. Read it aloud to the class.

Activity:

2. After reading the letter from Marty, ask students what they think should be done (encourage them to be sympathetic toward Marty and want to help him).
3. Ask students how they should go about finding Marty in the media center. Did his letter contain any clues to help locate his whereabouts?
4. Remind students about the Tyrannosaurus Rex clue. What should they do with this information? If students are having difficulty coming up with an answer, remind them what they did in the last media class.
5. Discuss the options for conducting a search in the PAC. Have students volunteer ways to search title, author, and subject. Tell students that there is one more way they can search the PAC that hasn't been discussed. They can do a keyword search.
6. Explain to students that a keyword is a word in the question or task at hand that will guide them to the answer they seek.
7. Read the letter again and have the students listen for a keyword they can use to begin their search in the PAC (Tyrannosaurus Rex).
8. Display your PAC for students to view. Type in "Tyrannosaurus Rex" into the PAC's search box as a keyword search. Display the results. In the results, there might be a picture book or a fiction book about a Tyrannosaurus Rex. Ask students why this would ***not*** be the section that Marty visited (because Marty gave a fact about a Tyrannosaurus Rex and facts are found in nonfiction books).
9. Once you have determined where the section is in the media center, send a pair of students to look for a clue that Marty left there. Once the students find the clue, have them bring it to the front of the class to read aloud.

Embedded AASL Skills Indicator: ___.___.___: _____

_____

Embedded AASL Skills Indicator: ___.___.___: _____

_____

Embedded AASL Dispositions in Action Indicator: ___.___.___: _____

_____

10. Repeat steps 7–9 again until all the clues are found. Be sure and discuss which options in the PAC are not the best options based on the clue that has been given. Allow students to type the keyword and conduct the search in the PAC. Offer encouragement and help when the student's first attempts are not successful.

Embedded AASL Responsibilities Indicator: ___.___.___: _____

_____

11. Ask the class to assist the student conducting the search in PAC by providing them with suggestions for appropriate search terms to use.

Closure:

12. Ask students to explain their reasoning as they suggest search terms during the lesson. Ask students to name all four ways they can complete a successful search in the PAC.

Embedded AASL Self-Assessment Strategies: ___.___.___: _____

_____

13. Once Marty has been found, congratulate the students on a job well done and allow them to pet Marty before they leave.

Evidence of Understanding:

Make sure everyone gets a turn at either doing a keyword search in the PAC or locating a clue on the shelf. Check for understanding and encourage students throughout the lesson.

Enrichment Using Technology:

1. Introduce students to the Internet Public Library (http://www.ipl.org/div/kid space). Show students how to do a subject keyword search in order to find Web

sites related to their interests. Discuss the differences between this online data-base and the PAC.

Extension:

1. Read the book *Mouse Views: What the Class Pet Saw* by Bruce McMillan (New York: Holiday House, 1993). Use the ideas in this book to create close-up pictures of books in the library media center. Students can identify the different areas where the pictures were taken by looking at the call numbers.

Suggested Modifications:

If you feel that you won't have enough time to locate all of the clues, you may choose to ab-breviate the lesson by selecting only a handful of clues to hide in your library media center.

MARTY LETTER

Dear Media Specialist,

Please help me! I'm lost in the library! I bet you didn't know that mice can read, but we can (and write too!). I've learned a lot from living in the library.

I love telling my friends all about the neat things that I learn. Unfortunately, I think I went a little too far this time. You see—I like to drop clues in every section I visit so my friends can find me and learn a little something along the way. Only this time I took too long and got lost myself! I hope you can help me. As you know, we mice don't like coming out during the day and now I'm too scared to move because I am in broad daylight! I'm stuck on a shelf I've never been in before. My friends won't come to find me because they only play at night. Please hurry. I am little scared and I missed eating breakfast this morning, so I'm really hungry. I think I left a clue somewhere in the section where I was learning all about the Tyrannosaurus Rex. Did you know that some of the teeth from a T-Rex were the same size as bananas? Bananas!? That just made me even *more* hungry. I hope you'll find me soon!

Sincerely,

Marty the Media Mouse

3RD-GRADE LESSONS

LESSON 3: MOUSE TRACKS

Coordinate! This Mouse Tracks lesson will encourage students to conduct searches in the PAC to pursue their own interests. *Coordinate* this lesson with the classroom teacher by offering to show or demonstrate other features in the PAC that will assist students in locating a book of interest. Knowing about these features, such as sorting results or looking for information in a database link, will assist the teacher and student as they pursue future investigations and informational needs.

Cooperate! Using keywords in the PAC, students locate a thank-you gift left by Marty the Media Mouse. *Cooperate* with the classroom teacher by offering to add a lesson at the end of this unit to assist students in finding resources for a planned classroom project. Students will enjoy using their new knowledge in a practical way. Assist the students as necessary as they find resources to investigate for completion of the project.

Lesson Plan

Integrated Goals:

Language Arts

Standard 8. Students use a variety of technological and information resources (e.g., libraries, databases, computer networks, video) to gather and synthesize information and to create and communicate knowledge.

Library Media

AASL 21st Century Standards

   Standard 1: Inquire, think critically, and gain knowledge.
   Standard 4: Pursue personal and aesthetic growth.

Essential Questions:

   How can the PAC help you locate information?

Desired Understandings:

Students will understand:

   How to search the PAC depending on their informational needs.
   How to conduct a keyword search in the PAC.
   How to use the PAC to locate books of personal interest.

Integrated Objectives:

- Students will apply information they learned about keywords to locate titles and call numbers of interest about a given subject.
- Students will successfully complete a keyword scavenger hunt.

Time Required:

45 minutes

Provided Materials:

- "Mouse Tracks" (WS 2.3.3)—one packet for each student or pair of students
- "Marty's Thank-You Note" (RS 2.3.2)
- "Marty Bookmarks" (RS 2.3.3)—Copy onto cardstock or colored paper and cut into individual bookmarks so that each student can have one.
- "Mouse Tracks Answer Sheet" (TRS 2.3.1)—for your reference

CLASSROOM CONNECTIONS

Consider sharing lesson ideas in a monthly/quarterly communication newsletter. This will help classroom teachers make the connection between curriculum and information literacy skills.

Materials You Will Need to Obtain:

- Computer with Internet access to the school's PAC
- Projection device
- Pencils
- 1 computer per group of students with access to the school's PAC

Prior to the Lesson

Prior to student's arrival, place a stack of "Marty Bookmarks" (RS 2.3.3) in the nonfiction section about pet cats. Students will locate these bookmarks at the end of the class.

Lesson Procedures:

Engagement:

1. Read "Marty's Thank-You Note" (RS 2.3.2) aloud to the class.

Activity:

2. Display an image of the "Mouse Tracks" (WS 2.3.3) worksheet packet.
3. Answer the first clue together as a class.
4. Divide students into pairs and decide whether each student will record information individually or as a group.
5. Distribute copies of the "Mouse Tracks" (WS 2.3.3) worksheet packet to each student or pair of students. If students are working in pairs, they should take turns recording a book that is of interest to them.
6. Tell students to take turns recording answers and looking up information in the PAC.

Embedded AASL Skills Indicator: ___.___.___: _____

_____

7. Explain that students will use their background knowledge to answer each of the 11 questions.

Embedded AASL Skills Indicator: ___.___.___: _____

_____

Embedded AASL Skills Indicator: ___.___.___: _____

_____

8. As they answer each question, students should then use that word to conduct a keyword search in the PAC.

Embedded AASL Dispositions in Action Indicator: ___.___.___: _____

_____

9. Students should record the title and call number of a book they find of interest in the blank spaces provided in their "Mouse Tracks" (WS 2.3.3) worksheet packet.
10. Once students locate all of the answers, you can verbally give them directions on how to locate the secret message.
11. Instruct students to take the first letter from each keyword answer and place them in order to fill the blanks at the bottom of the last page in their packet. This will give them a special secret message from Marty the Mouse.
12. Ask for a volunteer to read the message aloud (pet cats have a surprise).
13. Ask students what needs to happen next? What does Marty want us to do (use the PAC to locate books about pet cats on the shelf)?
14. Together as a class, look up the location for pet cats in the library media center.
15. Select a student to go to the shelf and find the surprise Marty the Mouse has left for the class.

Closure:

Embedded AASL Responsibilities Indicator: ___.___.___: _____

_____

16. Allow students time to locate and check out one of the titles they found of interest to them as they completed the "Mouse Tracks" (WS 2.3.3) worksheet.

Embedded AASL Self-Assessment Strategies: ___.___.___: _____

_____

17. Have students evaluate whether or not the title they found was of interest to them and explain why it was or wasn't. Ask students to share their ideas for how they could better locate a book of personal interest in the PAC. A possible response could be; "Next time, I might read the description for the book to see if it is really something I am interested in reading about."
18. At the end of the class, distribute a Marty Bookmark from "Marty Bookmarks" (RS 2.3.3) to each student.
19. Collect the "Mouse Tracks" (WS 2.3.3) worksheet packets.

Evidence of Understanding:

Collect the "Mouse Tracks" (WS 2.3.3) worksheet packets and check for completion and understanding.

Enrichment Using Technology:

1. Introduce students to an online database such as SIRS Discoverer (http://www.discoverer.sirs.com). Allow students to try different kinds of searches including the subject tree and keywords options.

2. Another option is to provide access to the "Kids Click" Web site (http://www.kidsclick.org). Choose "advanced search" and allow students to explore Kids Click by doing subject, title, or keyword searches. Discuss the URL search option. Compare this online database to the PAC.

> **DISCUSSION OPPORTUNITY**
>
> After completing the lesson and reading the book *Seven Blind Mice* by Ed Young, challenge students to think about and share other problem solving possibilities.

Extension:

1. Read the book *Seven Blind Mice* by Ed Young (New York: Philomel Books, 1992).

Suggested Modifications:

For students in need of additional assistance, you may wish to pair them with the above gradelevel students in the class. They may benefit from working in a group as opposed to independently.

MOUSE TRACKS

Name:_____

Directions: Read each of the statements carefully. Fill in the blanks with the best possible word choice. Next, use the word to complete a keyword search in the PAC. Write down the title and call number of one of the titles found in your search that interests you.

1. Captain Hook was one of these. ____ ____ ____ ____ ____ ____

   Title: _____

   Call number: _____

2. Dr. Seuss created a character named Horton the

   ____ ____ ____ ____ ____ ____ ____ ____

   Title: _____

   Call number: _____

3. The short name for a steam-powered locomotive is a ____ ____ ____ ____ ____

   Title: _____

   Call number: _____

4. Red, blue, and yellow are all primary ____ ____ ____ ____ ____ ____

   Title: _____

   Call number: _____

5. The ____ ____ ____ ____ ____ ____ ____ ____ contains 26 letters. It begins with the letter A and ends with the letter Z.

   Title: _____

   Call number: _____

6. A terrapin is another name for a ____ ____ ____ ____ ____ ____ that lives in fresh water. They are reptiles and have a hard shell on their back.

   Title: _____

   Call number: _____

7. A minus sign is the symbol for this type of math.

   ____ ____ ____ ____ ____ ____ ____ ____ ____ ____ ____

   Title: _____

   Call number: _____

8. This subject involves famous people, places, and events of the past.

   ____ ____ ____ ____ ____ ____ ____

   Title: _____

   Call number: _____

9. Commonly mistaken for a crocodile, this reptile's snout is much wider.

   ____ ____ ____ ____ ____ ____ ____ ____

   Title: _____

   Call number: _____

10. One of the original 13 colonies, the state of

    ____ ____ ____ ____ ____ ____ ____ ____ has Richmond as its capital.

    Title: _____

    Call number: _____

11. This majestic bird is the national bird of the United States of America. Its name is the

    Bald ____ ____ ____ ____ ____.

    Title: _____

    Call number: _____

    Secret message

    ____ ____ ____   ____ ____ ____ ____   ____ ____ ____ ____ a surprise!

MARTY'S THANK-YOU NOTE

Dear Class,

Thank you so much for all your help. I'm so glad that you found me when you did. I was trying to think of a way I could show my appreciation for all you have done for me and here is what I came up with. Remember how I told you I liked leaving clues for my friends and making fun games? Well, I decided that I would make a game for you! I've left you with a clue sheet that you can use to explore the Public Access Catalog (PAC). For each question you answer, you will be given a clue to help you uncover a secret message! I hope you enjoy my game and that we see each other again soon!

Thanks again,

Marty

MARTY BOOKMARKS

_____'s bookmark Marty doesn't take up much space – use him in a book to mark your place!	_____'s bookmark Marty doesn't take up much space – use him in a book to mark your place!	_____'s bookmark Marty doesn't take up much space – use him in a book to mark your place!	_____'s bookmark Marty doesn't take up much space – use him in a book to mark your place!

_____'s bookmark Marty doesn't take up much space – use him in a book to mark your place!	_____'s bookmark Marty doesn't take up much space – use him in a book to mark your place!	_____'s bookmark Marty doesn't take up much space – use him in a book to mark your place!	_____'s bookmark Marty doesn't take up much space – use him in a book to mark your place!

MOUSE TRACKS ANSWER SHEET

1. pirate
2. elephant
3. train
4. colors
5. alphabet
6. turtle
7. subtraction
8. history
9. alligator
10. Virginia
11. eagle

Pet cats have a surprise!

Working in Collaboration

Collaboration

Collaborate! True collaboration requires both the library media specialist and the classroom teacher to share in the design of integrated instruction. Collaboration provides you with an excellent opportunity to design inquiry-based learning activities. Here are some ideas for collaborating with the classroom teachers.

3rd Grade: Reading for Pleasure

Essential Question: How can the books we read for pleasure inspire us to read more or help us understand our reading preferences?

- Have students share a book with the class, and give reasons why they found it enjoyable or not enjoyable. Discuss how this book gave them ideas for new book subjects and genres to try. If they did not find it enjoyable, have them discuss how this knowledge helps them shape their future reading choices.
- Have students create a blog to share and discuss stories they have read with their classmates.

For further information, please visit
www.destinationcollaboration.com

4TH-GRADE LESSONS

LESSON 1: BRANCHING OUT

Coordinate! In this Branching Out lesson, students will have an opportunity to learn how to broaden and narrow a search using familiar topics. *Coordinate* with the classroom teacher by sharing the "Subject Tree Graphic Organizer" (WS 2.4.1) for students to record their ideas for an upcoming classroom project. Explain how using the organizer will assist students as they broaden or narrow their topic ideas.

Cooperate! After students complete this lesson, *cooperate* with the classroom teacher by offering to extend this learning experience. Offer to assist the classroom teacher by helping students narrow or broaden their topic for an upcoming class project. Consider adding another lesson to this unit to allow students time to locate resources based on their search terms.

Lesson Plan

Integrated Goals:

Language Arts

Standard 8. Students use a variety of technological and information resources (e.g., libraries, databases, computer networks, video) to gather and synthesize information and to create and communicate knowledge.

Library Media

AASL 21st Century Standards

> **Standard 2:** Draw conclusions, make informed decisions, apply knowledge to new situations, and create new knowledge.
> **Standard 4:** Pursue personal and aesthetic growth.

Essential Questions:

> How can broadening or narrowing a search help to organize information in a useful way?

Desired Understandings:

Students will understand:

> The meaning of the words "broad" and "narrow."
> How to broaden and narrow a subject term.
> How broadening and narrowing a subject term in the PAC offers different results.

Integrated Objectives:

- Students will understand the concept of subject trees and produce their own subject trees.

- Students will distinguish the difference between broadening and narrowing a search term.

Time Required:

45 minutes

Provided Materials:

- "Subject Trees" (OER 2.4.1) PowerPoint
- "Best Book Buds" (OER 2.4.2) PowerPoint
- "Subject Tree Graphic Organizer" (WS 2.4.1)—one per student
- "Word Boxes" (MN 2.4.1)—one set per group

Materials You Will Need to Obtain:

- Computer
- Projection device
- Pencils
- Access to the school's PAC
- Envelopes
- Before meeting with the class, decide whether to use computers with the entire class or part of the class. Book the stationary or mobile lab accordingly.

Prior to the Lesson

Prior to student arrival, copy "Word Boxes" (MN 2.4.1) so that you have one set per group and the words are cut out and placed in envelopes.

Lesson Procedures:

Engagement:

Embedded AASL Responsibilities Indicator: ___.___.___: _____

_____

1. Divide students into six groups. Distribute an envelope with the set of "Word Boxes" (MN 2.4.1) to each group. Tell students that they should look carefully at each word contained in the envelopes and should organize the words in a way that makes sense to them. Remind students to share their ideas and be respectful to one another as they organize their thoughts.

Activity

2. Ask students to share the various ways they chose to organize the word boxes. Be sure to congratulate students on their creative thinking.
3. Explain that for the purposes of this activity, there is a special way to organize the words. Students will learn how to broaden and narrow a subject search. This will help them find information in the PAC.
4. Spend time discussing the terms "broad" and "narrow." Check for student understanding of the terms prior to moving forward with this lesson.

> **CLASSROOM CONNECTIONS**
>
> Gather information about what students are learning in their classrooms as you prepare to teach this lesson. Feel free to substitute the subject tree words with ones that better suit the needs of your students.

5. If there are students in the class that organized the words in the way that reflects narrow to broad or broad to narrow subject search, ask these students to explain their thinking to the class.

6. Display the "Word Boxes" (MN 2.4.1) and demonstrate how to broaden and narrow search terms using these words. Take time to answer questions and address any confusion before moving forward.

7. Collect the "Word Boxes" (MN 2.4.1) and envelopes.

8. Next, display the "Subject Trees" (OER 2.4.1) PowerPoint to the class.

9. As you go from one slide to the next, ask students to predict which words could be on the next level as you narrow the search terms. Explain that in the visual, the trunk of the tree represents the broadest search term. As the limbs and leaves appear, the terms become narrower.

10. Once you arrive at the end of the "Subject Trees" (OER 2.4.1) PowerPoint, click backward through the PowerPoint to demonstrate going from a narrow term to a broad term.

11. After going back through the entire "Subject Trees" (OER 2.4.1) PowerPoint, display the school's PAC. Use the term "animals" to do a broad subject search. Point out how many results are received. Next, conduct a search for "cats" and show students how to narrow a search, meaning less results were given because other animals were not included. Lastly, conduct a search for "Abyssinian" and show students the results again. *Note—if there are not any books in the collection about Abyssinian cats, select a different type of cat to search. Try searching for Abyssinian and cat together in the same search to further narrow results.

Transition:

12. Distribute copies of "Subject Tree Graphic Organizer" (WS 2.4.1).

13. Point out that there are visual clues on the "Subject Tree Graphic Organizer" (WS 2.4.1). Note that the broad topic is in a large, bold font. As the topics become smaller, the font sizes get smaller. This will help students associate the terms with the words they should place in the blanks.

Activity:

14. Explain that students are to think of a broad subject, write it on the trunk of their tree, and then narrow that subject as they move into the branches and leaves of the tree. Display the "Subject Trees" (OER 2.4.1) PowerPoint for students again to assist them in remembering how to create a subject tree of their own.

15. Brainstorm some ideas/broad subjects that they could use. For example, ask students what sorts of things they study in school, or what activities they do after school (e.g., math, science, sports, etc.). Explain how to take the subjects and narrow them. Students should choose a topic of interest to them, and one that they know enough about to make a subject tree about it.

Embedded AASL Skills Indicator: ___.___.___: _____

_____

16. Allow students time to complete the "Subject Tree Graphic Organizer" (WS 2.4.1).

Embedded AASL Skills Indicator: ___.___.___: _____

_____

17. Select a volunteer to come up to the front of the room and type the broad subject term they selected into the PAC. Display the results. Next, ask the student to select a narrow term from their "Subject Tree Graphic Organizer" (WS 2.4.1) to type into the PAC. Discuss the results with the class.

Embedded AASL Dispositions in Action Indicator: ___.___.___: _____

_____

Embedded AASL Self-Assessment Strategies: ___.___.___: _____

_____

18. Allow students time to do the same at their own computers if computer use has been arranged for this opportunity. Students should record their results on the back of the "Subject Tree Graphic Organizer" (WS 2.4.1) and indicate how many results they received for their broad and narrow searches.

Closure:
19. Ask for students to share their results and explain why the numbers are different for a broad or narrow search. Check for understanding.
20. Display the "Best Book Buds" (OER 2.4.2) PowerPoint to the class. Explain that when they return, they will be using broad and narrow search terms to create a list of recommended books for the students on the "Best Book Buds" (OER 2.4.2) PowerPoint.
21. Collect the "Subject Tree Graphic Organizer" (WS 2.4.1).

Evidence of Understanding:
Check for student participation throughout the lesson.
   Grade the "Subject Tree Graphic Organizer" (WS 2.4.1).

Enrichment Using Technology:
1. Allow students to use an online database such as SIRS Discoverer (http://www.discoverer.sirs.com). Allow students to try different kinds of searches including the subject tree and keywords options.

Extension:

1. Use the "Visual Subject" (OEX 2.4.1) PowerPoint to extend student thinking. Print the selection "Handouts—3 slides per page." Distribute this handout to students and instruct them to look at each of the three pictures and then identify subject search terms for each picture. They should record their answers from broad to narrow on the lines provided to the right of each picture.

Suggested Modifications:

Use the modified "Subject Tree Graphic Organizer" (MOD 2.4.1) for students who need to have the words available to them to create their own subject tree.

SUBJECT TREE GRAPHIC ORGANIZER

Name: _____

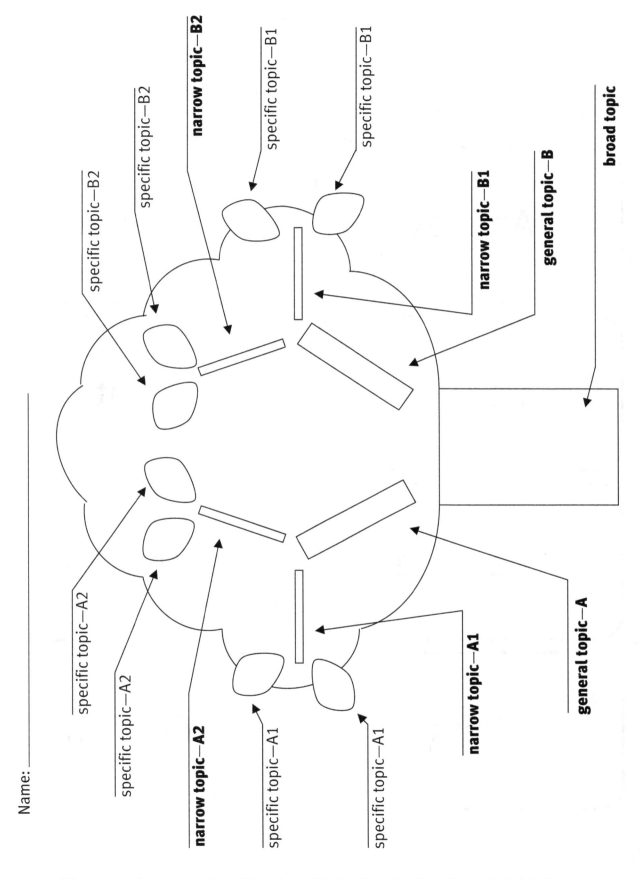

specific topic—B2

specific topic—B2

narrow topic—B2

specific topic—B1

specific topic—B1

narrow topic—B1

general topic—B

broad topic

specific topic—A2

specific topic—A2

narrow topic—A2

specific topic—A1

specific topic—A1

narrow topic—A1

general topic—A

WORD BOXES

Directions for use:

Make six copies of this page onto colored copier paper. Cut out each word box and laminate if desired. Place each set of words into an envelope to use in groups with your classes.

Animal	Dog
Poodle	Cat
Siamese	Labrador
Pets	Persian

SUBJECT TREE GRAPHIC ORGANIZER

Name: _____

4th grade word bank

New England Patriots

San Francisco 49ers

New York Yankees

baseball

Baltimore Orioles

entertainment

football

sports

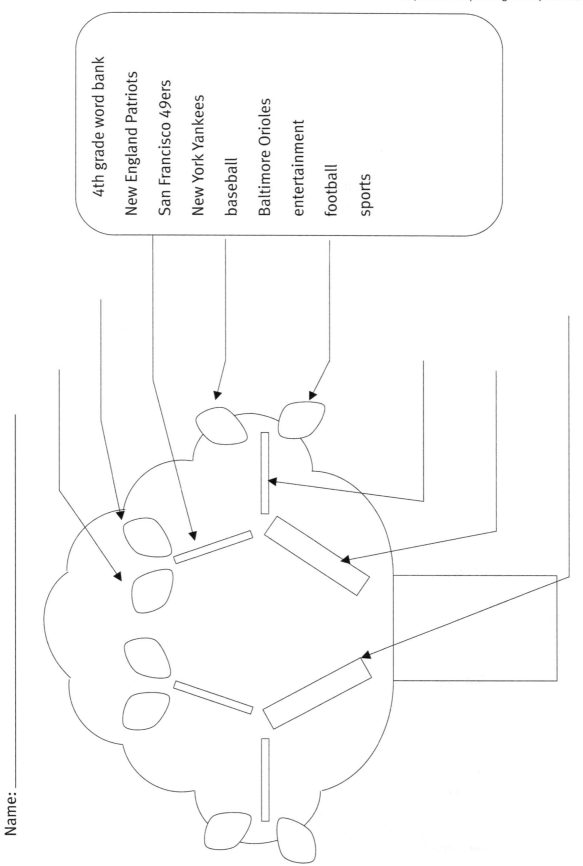

4TH-GRADE LESSONS

LESSON 2: BEST BOOK BUDS

Coordinate! Create a template using the "Best Book Buds" (OER 2.4.2) PowerPoint as a guide. Coordinate with the classroom teacher by sharing the template. The classroom teacher can use the template with their students to get to know them better. Students could also share information about their family and culture in addition to their likes and dislikes. Consider adding the student's photographs and then printing and posting the completed student profiles to a bulletin board.

Cooperate! Create a template of a slide from the "Best Book Buds" (OER 2.4.2) PowerPoint. *Cooperate* by sharing the template with the classroom teacher. Students can create their own "Best Book Bud" profile in the classroom by recording their likes and dislikes directly on the template. Include a space for students to add their own picture identification. Suggest that students exchange profiles and bring them to the library media center during their next visit. They can practice finding a book for one of their classmates.

Lesson Plan

Integrated Goals:

Language Arts

Standard 8. Students use a variety of technological and information resources (e.g., libraries, databases, computer networks, video) to gather and synthesize information and to create and communicate knowledge.

Standard 12. Students use spoken, written, and visual language to accomplish their own purposes (e.g., for learning, enjoyment, persuasion, and the exchange of information)

Technology

NETS-S

3. Research and Information Fluency

Students apply digital tools to gather, evaluate, and use information. Students:

a. plan strategies to guide inquiry.

Library Media

AASL 21st Century Standards

   Standard 1: Inquire, think critically, and gain knowledge.
   Standard 2: Draw conclusions, make informed decisions, apply knowledge to new situations, and create new knowledge.
   Standard 4: Pursue personal and aesthetic growth.

Essential Questions:

How can broadening or narrowing a search help to locate information?

Desired Understandings:

Students will understand:

The meaning of the words "broad" and "narrow."

How to broaden and narrow a subject term.

How broadening and narrowing a subject term in the PAC offers different results.

DISCUSSION OPPORTUNITY

Use this lesson as an opportunity to discuss online safety with students. Be sure and point out the fact that the "Best Book Buds" is just a PowerPoint. Students featured in the profiles are safe in that they do not use names, place names, or people to describe who they are or where they are located.

Integrated Objectives:

- Students will brainstorm topics of interest for other students at the school.
- Students will use the PAC to find a book of interest for a friend.
- Students will create a shelf marker to promote books to other students at the school.

Time Required:

45 minutes

Provided Materials:

- "Best Book Buds" (OER 2.4.2) PowerPoint—This should be loaded on to student computers prior to the start of the class.
- "Best Search Terms" (WS 2.4.2)—one page per student
- "Leaf Shelf Marker" (WS 2.4.3)—one shelf marker per student (These will need to be printed on legal size paper.)

Materials You Will Need to Obtain:

- Computer
- Projection device
- Pencils
- Access to your school's PAC
- Tagboard (if you wish for students to back their shelf markers to make them more sturdy)
- Before meeting with the class, decide whether to use computers with the entire class or part of the class. Book the stationary or mobile lab accordingly.

Lesson Procedures:

Engagement:

1. Display the "Best Book Buds" (OER 2.4.2) PowerPoint to the class. Explain that the "Best Book Buds" (OER 2.4.2) PowerPoint resembles an online social networking site. Ask students to share any experiences they have had with social networking sites (e.g., Disney's Club Penguin, Webkinz, etc.).
2. Demonstrate how the "Best Book Buds" (OER 2.4.2) PowerPoint can be easily navigated by first clicking on "Slide Show" and then selecting a "profile" to view. Show students how to toggle between the main page and student profiles by clicking on the "back to main page" button located at the bottom of the profile screens.

Activity:

Embedded AASL Skills Indicator: ___.___.___: _____

_____

3. Explain to students that they will select a "Best Book Buds" (OER 2.4.2) Power-Point profile. Students will use the information given on the profile to compile a list of appropriate search terms. Students will use the search terms in the PAC to locate a book to recommend to their "best book bud." Remind students that they may need to broaden or narrow their search terms in order to find the perfect book.

4. Choose a best book bud profile and model to the class how you would think it through. (There are two "extra" profiles located at the end of the "Best Book Buds" [OER 2.4.2] PowerPoint profile that are not linked from the first page. You may wish to use one of these as a sample.) Demonstrate how to record the information onto the "Best Search Terms" (WS 2.4.2) worksheet.

5. Distribute copies of "Best Search Terms" (WS 2.4.2) to the students.

6. If you do not wish for students to navigate through the "Best Book Buds" (OER 2.4.2) PowerPoint, you may choose to print out the profiles ahead of time for student use.

Embedded AASL Skills Indicator: ___.___.___: _____

_____

7. Explain to students that they are to choose a profile and then they will record the likes and dislikes of their best book bud onto their "Best Search Terms" (WS 2.4.2) sheet. While the best book bud profiles are fictitious, the interests of the best book buds are based on the interests of real students. After figuring out what their best book bud likes, students will then need to create a list of broad and narrow search terms that will assist them in locating a book that other students with interests similar to that of their best book bud might enjoy.

Transition:

8. When students have completed the "Best Search Terms" (WS 2.4.2) worksheet give them a "Leaf Shelf Marker" (WS 2.4.3).

Activity:

Embedded AASL Skills Indicator: ___.___.___: _____

_____

Embedded AASL Dispositions in Action Indicator: ___.___.___: _____

_____

9. Explain to students that they must use their search terms to locate a perfect book for their best book bud. Once they have located this perfect book in the PAC, they will need to complete the "Leaf Shelf Marker" (WS 2.4.3).

10. Students should be sure to include all of the necessary information listed on the shelf marker, and should do so neatly so that others can easily read the shelf marker.

11. Once students have completed the "Leaf Shelf Marker" (WS 2.4.3), they can color in the leaf to make it more visible.

12. Explain that their shelf marker will be used in two ways—it can be inserted on the shelf next to the book they are recommending, with the leaf portion of the shelf marker extending beyond the shelf so that it will get the attention of students browsing the shelves. It can also be used as a shelf marker that students can use when they come to the library media center. When students read the recommendation on the shelf marker, they may chose to look in the PAC for similar books, or they may go right to the shelf to find the title the students themselves recommended. This handy tool will mark their place on the shelf as they browse and select titles.

Closure:

Embedded AASL Responsibilities Indicator: ___.___.___: _____

_____

Embedded AASL Self-Assessment Strategies: ___.___.___: _____

_____

13. Ask students to share with a neighbor the book they recommended and to explain why they chose that particular book based on the interests of their best book bud. The students neighbor should offer suggestions for additional terms to use when searching.

14. Collect the "Best Search Terms" (WS 2.4.2) and "Leaf Shelf Markers" (WS 2.4.3). If desired, back the "Leaf Shelf Markers" (WS 2.4.3) with tag board and laminate them so they last longer.

Evidence of Understanding:

Check for student participation throughout the lesson.

Grade the "Best Search Terms" (WS 2.4.2) and "Leaf Shelf Markers" (WS 2.4.3) by checking to see that the books students chose reflect the interests of their best book bud.

Enrichment Using Technology:

1. Have students visit the International Children's Digital Library (http://www.icdl books.org) to find a book for their best

> **CLASSROOM CONNECTIONS**
>
> Meet with classroom teachers to discuss and plan class best book bud profiles. Students from each grade level can begin recommending books to one another. This is a great way for you to get to know your students and for your students to learn more about each other.

book bud. Ask students how they approached finding a book on this site. What kinds of keywords did they use? Did they search by age, language, or other ways? Did they think this site was easy to use for their purpose?

Extension:

1. Challenge students to find a Web site that their best book bud would enjoy. If available, go to SIRS Discoverer Online and search using the WebFind option.

Suggested Modifications:

Print out a slide from the "Best Book Buds" (OER 2.4.2) PowerPoint presentation for student use. Have students circle the words that describe what their best book bud enjoys. Have students use these words to conduct a search in the PAC. If needed, pull together a smaller shelf of books and allow students time to find the perfect book from the provided shelf.

BEST SEARCH TERMS

Name: _____

Name of best book bud: _____

Likes: _____

Dislikes: _____

SEARCH TERMS I WILL USE

BROAD	*NARROW*
_____	_____
_____	_____
_____	_____
_____	_____
_____	_____
_____	_____
_____	_____
_____	_____
_____	_____

LEAF SHELF MARKER

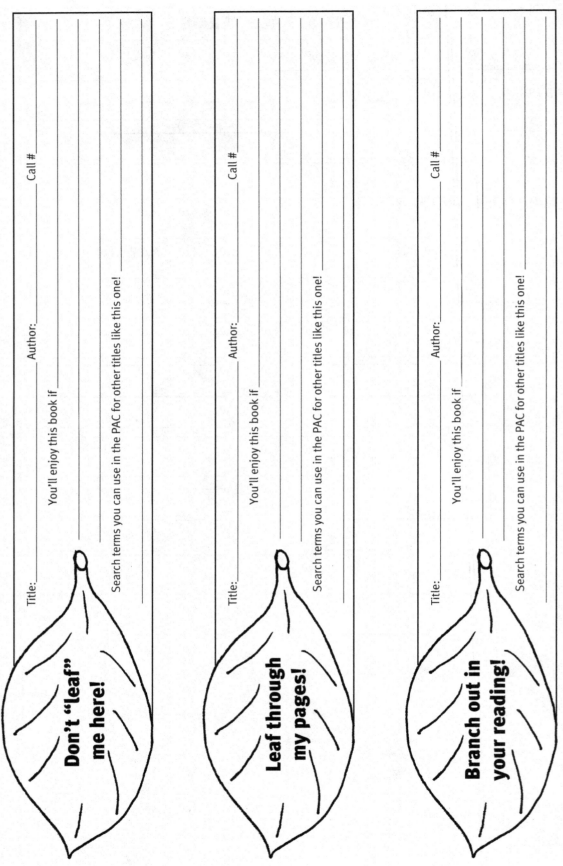

Title: _____

Author: _____

Call # _____

You'll enjoy this book if _____

Search terms you can use in the PAC for other titles like this one! _____

Don't "leaf" me here!

Title: _____

Author: _____

Call # _____

You'll enjoy this book if _____

Search terms you can use in the PAC for other titles like this one! _____

Leaf through my pages!

Title: _____

Author: _____

Call # _____

You'll enjoy this book if _____

Search terms you can use in the PAC for other titles like this one! _____

Branch out in your reading!

Working in Collaboration

Collaboration

Collaborate! True collaboration requires both the library media specialist and the classroom teacher to share in the design of integrated instruction. Collaboration provides you with an excellent opportunity to design inquiry-based learning activities. Here are some ideas for collaborating with the classroom teachers.

4th Grade: Reading for Pleasure

Essential Question: How can sharing information with others help us gain new knowledge and understanding?

- Create a classroom wiki and have students collaborate on ideas and insights about books they have read. Students can share links to author Web sites, blogs, and so forth.

For further information, please visit
www.destinationcollaboration.com

5TH-GRADE LESSONS

LESSON 1: UNLOCKING INFORMATION

Coordinate! If the teachers at your school are creating inquiry-based projects in the classroom, you may wish to share the students completed "5th-Grade Content Questions" (WS 2.5.1). This will facilitate a discussion with the classroom teacher about how well the students can identify keywords in order to locate information. *Coordinate* with the classroom teacher for the next inquiry-based project by helping students identify keywords for their upcoming project.

Cooperate! Share the extension ideas at the end of this lesson with the classroom teacher. Change the challenge by asking students to come up with a question based on an upcoming classroom topic. *Cooperate* by offering to assist the class in designing an appropriate research question based on what the students want to know about the topic.

Lesson Plan

Integrated Goals:

Language Arts

Standard 12. Students use spoken, written, and visual language to accomplish their own purposes (e.g., for learning, enjoyment, persuasion, and the exchange of information).

Library Media

AASL 21st Century Standards

Standard 1: Inquire, think critically, and gain knowledge.
Standard 2: Draw conclusions, make informed decisions, apply knowledge to new situations, and create new knowledge.

Essential Questions:

How does the identification of keywords in a research question assist in locating information?

Desired Understandings:

Students will understand:

What it means to be an information consumer.
How to identify keywords.
How to make inferences about topics in order to identify keywords.

Integrated Objectives:

- Students will determine the appropriate keywords to use when locating specific information.
- Students will apply this skill to answer a specific informational need.

Time Required:

45 minutes

Provided Materials:

- "Unlocking Keywords" (MN 2.5.1)—Printed on cardstock, laminated, and cut out
- "5th-Grade Content Questions" (WS 2.5.1)—Prior to student arrival, copy and cut questions for students.
- "Information Consumers" (OER 2.5.1) QuickTime movie

Materials You Will Need to Obtain:

- Computer
- Projection device
- Pencils
- Access to your school's PAC

Prior to the Lesson:

Prior to student arrival, print "Unlocking Keywords" so that you have one key for each student.

Lesson Procedures:

Engagement:

1. As students enter the room, randomly distribute a key from "Unlocking Keywords" (MN 2.5.1) to each student. Ask that students then group themselves in a way they feel is appropriate and makes sense to them. Once students are in groups, ask a student to speak for the group and explain why they think their keys go together.

2. After students have shared their organization strategies, place the lock questions on the board or in a pocket chart. Read each question aloud, and ask that students come up by group to place their keys under the appropriate lock. Explain to students that the locks represent questions that any learner might have and the keys represent keywords that can be used in the PAC in order to find the answer. Be sure and tell students that a "keyword" helps guide someone to an answer and is not the answer itself.

Activity:

3. Explain to students that as they progress through their 5th-grade year, they will be expected to learn about many different topics in subject areas such as science and social studies. As students learn about these subjects and topics, they will be expected to create projects, displays, and reports to demonstrate what they learned. In order to do this, students will need to collect information from a variety of sources such as books, encyclopedia articles, databases, and Web sites. Tell students that they will be "consumers" of this information.

4. Ask students where they have heard the word "consumer" before. Have students define the word, or look it up in a dictionary and explain it to the class. Explain to students that they have an informational need and their need will be answered by placing appropriate keywords into the PAC. Tell students that for the purpose of this lesson, they should think of themselves as consumers of information or "information consumers."

5. Show students the "Information Consumers" (OER 2.5.1) QuickTime movie.

6. After the QuickTime movie, ask students what Ned's "information need" was and have them explain how he was able to solve his problem.

7. Display the following question for students to see: "How is climate change affecting our environment?" Ask students to assist you in determining the keywords needed to locate resources to answer this question. Some example of good keywords for this search are: "global warming," "environment," "climate," and "earth." Place these words on the board for students to see.

Transition:

8. Distribute the "5th-Grade Content Questions" (WS 2.5.1) to each pair of students.

Activity:

Embedded AASL Skills Indicator: ___.___.___: _____

_____

Embedded AASL Dispositions in Action Indicator: ___.___.___: _____

_____

9. Remind students that like Ned, they are information consumers. Explain to students that they will be identifying keywords from the list of provided questions to put in their "shopping cart." Add that each pair of students has different questions. As each pair of students looks at their questions, they should share their ideas with one another before writing them down.

Embedded AASL Skills Indicator: ___.___.___: _____

_____

Embedded AASL Responsibilities Indicator: ___.___.___: _____

_____

10. Allow students time to complete the activity.

Closure:

Embedded AASL Self-Assessment Strategies: ___.___.___: _____

_____

11. Ask students to swap their questions with other students in the class to see if there are any other keywords to add. Ask students to share some of their questions and keywords with the class. Discuss their choices and ask students what changes they might make if they were to locate keywords in this activity again, and why.

12. As each pair of students shares their results, collect their "5th-Grade Content Questions" (WS 2.5.1).

Evidence of Understanding:

Check for student participation throughout the lesson.

Check the "5th-Grade Content Questions" (WS 2.5.1) for student understanding. Suggest appropriate keywords as needed.

Enrichment Using Technology:

1. Have students visit the public library's PAC. Encourage students to think of an information question they have regarding something of interest to them. Have students write down keywords for this question and enter them into the public library's PAC. Are they satisfied with the results? If not, ask them to try different keywords and explain why the change resulted in more or fewer results. Have students record the titles, authors, and call numbers of their results so that they can easily find these items when they visit the library with their family.

Extension:

1. Challenge students to come up with a question based on personal interest to give to a partner. Have the partner see if they can locate the keywords of the question.

Suggested Modifications:

Check with the classroom teacher ahead of time to find out which students have reading and comprehension difficulties. Be sure to pair these students with the stronger readers in the class.

UNLOCKING KEYWORDS

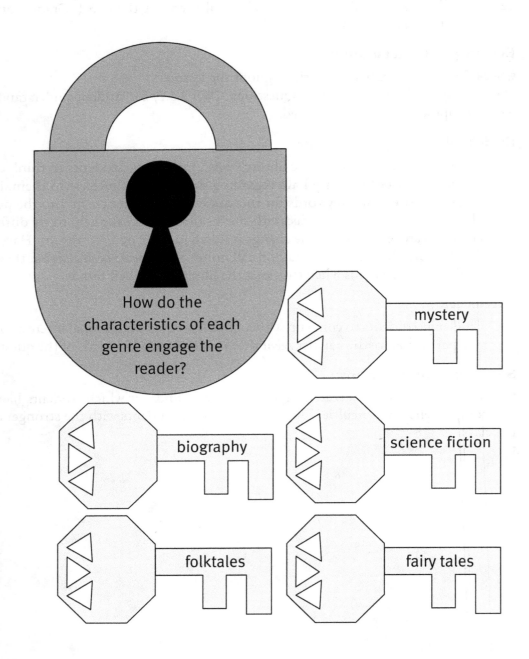

How do the characteristics of each genre engage the reader?

mystery

biography

science fiction

folktales

fairy tales

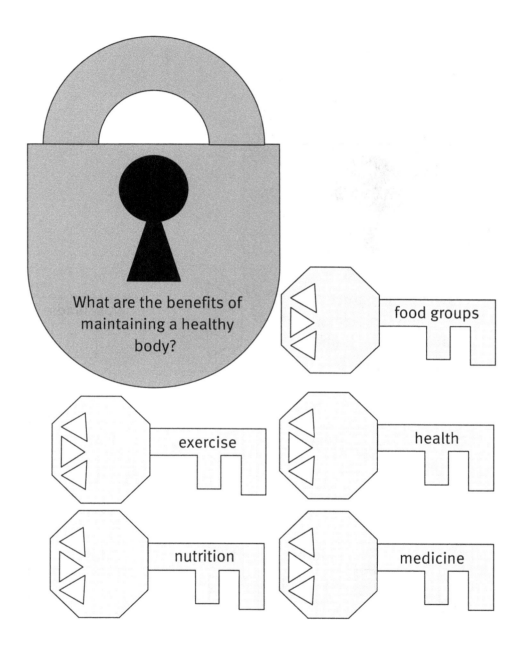

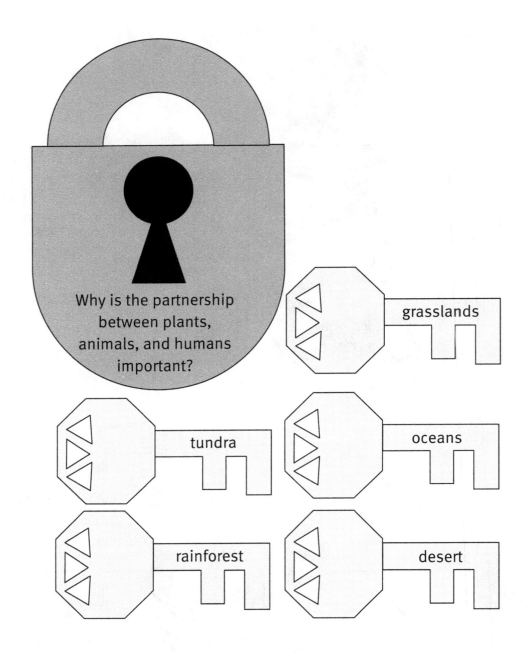

Why is the partnership between plants, animals, and humans important?

grasslands

tundra

oceans

rainforest

desert

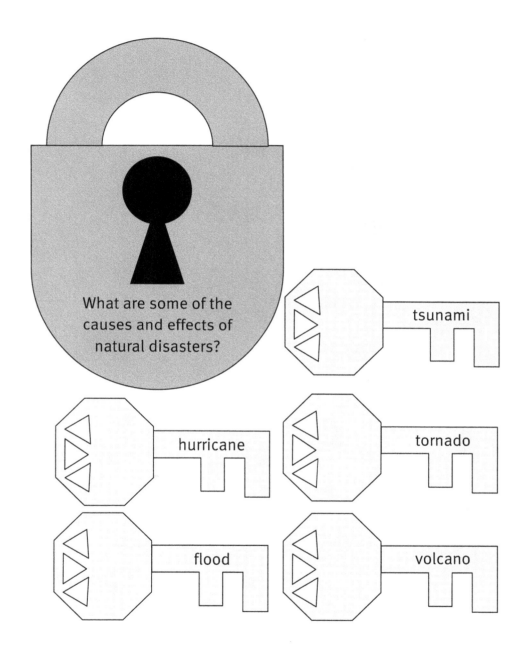

What are some of the causes and effects of natural disasters?

tsunami

hurricane

tornado

flood

volcano

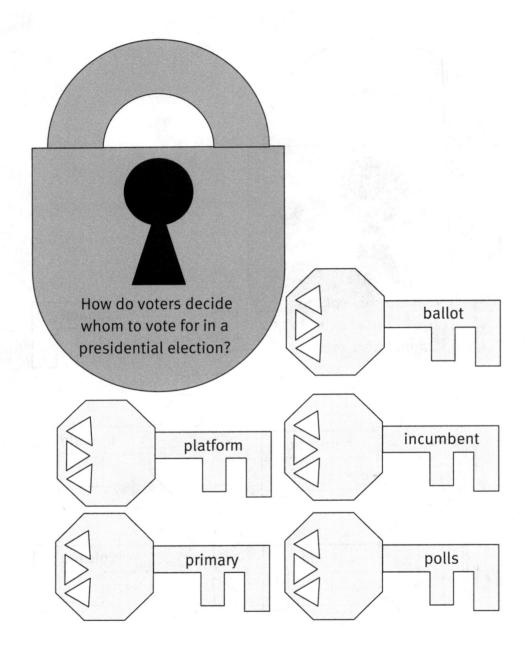

How do voters decide whom to vote for in a presidential election?

ballot

platform

incumbent

primary

polls

5TH-GRADE CONTENT QUESTIONS

1. How does the Earth experience day and night?

    _____   _____
    _____   _____

2. Why do scientists study comets, asteroids, and meteors?

    _____   _____
    _____   _____

3. Why are the patterns of rotation and revolution of the Earth and Moon important?

    _____   _____
    _____   _____

4. How do the changes in the seasons in the northern and southern hemi-spheres affect us?

    _____   _____
    _____   _____

5. How did slavery help to shape life in colonial America?

    _____   _____
    _____   _____

6. How can recycling help the environment?

    _____   _____
    _____   _____

7. How does pollution affect the quality of groundwater and surface water?

    _____   _____
    _____   _____

8. How did Benjamin Franklin, James Madison, and other leaders of their time contribute to the progress in colonial America?

    _____   _____
    _____   _____

9. Why was the Mayflower Compact and the House of Burgesses important in early America?

_____   _____

_____   _____

10. Why did early settlers and Native Americans experience difficulties with one another?

_____   _____

_____   _____

---

11. How are force, energy, and motion related?

_____   _____

_____   _____

12. How can sunlight and water be used for alternative energy?

_____   _____

_____   _____

---

13. How was shipping and trading important to the economic development of the colonies?

_____   _____

_____   _____

14. How do single and multicell organisms compare?

_____   _____

_____   _____

---

15. How did technology change the way goods and services were produced in colonial America?

_____   _____

_____   _____

16. How did the wars with the Native Americans affect the settlement of the colonists?

_____   _____

_____   _____

17. How do animals and plants adapt to their biome?

_____   _____

_____   _____

18. How were the American colonies able to defeat the British in the Revolutionary War?

_____   _____

_____   _____

----

19. How are endangered species protected in our country?

_____   _____

_____   _____

20. Why was the Declaration of Independence created?

_____   _____

_____   _____

----

21. Why is our flag an important symbol to our country?

_____   _____

_____   _____

22. Why was Paul Revere important to the American Revolution?

_____   _____

_____   _____

----

23. How do the three branches of United States Government work together?

_____   _____

_____   _____

24. How did events in United States history lead to the writing of the U.S. Constitution?

_____   _____

_____   _____

25. Why is the Bill of Rights important?

_____   _____

_____   _____

26. Why was Martin Luther King Jr. important to the civil rights movement?

_____   _____

_____   _____

----

27. How is a day in the life of an American colonist in Williamsburg different from a day in your life?

_____   _____

_____   _____

28. How can physical, political, and economy maps help you learn more about a place?

_____   _____

_____   _____

----

29. How were the three colonial regions similar and different from one another?

_____   _____

_____   _____

30. How were indentured servants and slaves different?

_____   _____

_____   _____

----

31. How do our state resources impact the types of goods and services our state provides?

_____   _____

_____   _____

32. Millers, silversmiths, and shoemakers were all craftsmen who lived in colonial America. Why were their trades so important?

_____   _____

_____   _____

5TH-GRADE LESSONS

LESSON 2: FINDING THE KEY

Coordinate! Show the classroom teacher the binder "5th-Grade Information Consumers: Resource Lists" your students created in library media class. Have the classroom teacher identify the research questions that will be covered in upcoming classroom lessons. *Coordinate* by offering to pull the resources the students recorded for the classroom teacher to use with the upcoming lessons.

Cooperate! Share the "5th-Grade Information Consumers: Resource Lists" your students created in library media class with the classroom teacher. *Cooperate* by offering to assist students in creating a classroom project-driven resource list. Add their findings to the binder. Share that you are interested in assisting the students with upcoming projects and are available to assist the classroom teacher as well.

Lesson Plan

Integrated Goals:

Standard 8. Students use a variety of technological and information resources (e.g., libraries, databases, computer networks, video) to gather and synthesize information and to create and communicate knowledge.

Standard 12. Students use spoken, written, and visual language to accomplish their own purposes (e.g., for learning, enjoyment, persuasion, and the exchange of information).

Library Media

AASL 21st Century Standards

  Standard 1: Inquire, think critically, and gain knowledge.

Essential Questions:

  How does the identification of keywords in a research question assist in locating information?

Desired Understandings:

Students will understand:

  How to modify a keyword search to locate information.
  How to select appropriate resources to meet an informational need.

Integrated Objectives:

• Students will use the PAC to create an informal bibliography or list of books to support their 5th-grade curriculum.

- Students will evaluate sources to determine which one is the most appropriate for their informational need.

Time Required:

45 minutes

Provided Materials:

- "Information Consumers" (OER 2.5.1) Quick-Time movie
- "Shopping Cart" (WS 2.5.2)—one per student, three hole-punched
- "Resource Shopping List" (RS 2.5.1)—tuck these copies inside the binder for future student use

Materials You Will Need to Obtain:

- Computer
- Projection device
- Pencils
- Computers for each pair of students with access to your school's PAC
- ½" three-ring binder—Label with the title "5th-Grade Information Consumers: Resource Lists." Make sure this is available to show to students at the time the lesson is delivered.

Lesson Procedures

Engagement:

1. Show students the "Information Consumers" (OER 2.5.1) QuickTime movie again.
2. After students watch the "Information Consumers" (OER 2.5.1) QuickTime movie, remind them that during their last class, they located keywords to assist them in answering their assigned questions.

Activity:

3. Explain to students that just like Ned, they must use the keywords they came up with to conduct a search in the PAC.
4. Tell students that throughout the year, they may be expected to complete various projects and research topics in both social studies and science. By creating resource lists about these topics, students can help each other, and save time in the future. The resource lists created in the class today will be stored in a binder and kept in the media center's reference collection for easy student access. Students can add resources to the binder and use it when they return to the media center. *Note: Students will be

CLASSROOM CONNECTIONS

Show classroom teachers the binder your students will make. Emphasize that it is a work in progress and will improve as students add to it. With this knowledge, perhaps teachers will want to add a Web site or book title to the lists students begin.

CLASSROOM CONNECTIONS

Meet with the classroom teachers to discuss upcoming projects throughout the year. Together, come up with some additional questions that can be added to the "5th-Grade Content Questions" Worksheet.

better equipped to add online resources to the resource lists after completing the lessons in chapter 4, "Online Resources."

5. Using the sample prompt, "Explain how climate change is affecting our environment," and keywords from the previous class, model how to conduct a search in the PAC. Be sure to point out how to select an appropriate and reliable resource. For example, students should use nonfiction text and check the publication date for currency as well looking at the subject and note to determine if the title will meet their informational needs.

6. Redistribute the "5th-Grade Content Questions" (WS 2.5.1) to students.

7. Explain to students that each student in the pair is responsible for locating resources for one of the two questions.

8. Distribute copies of the "Shopping Cart" (WS 2.5.2) worksheet. Each student should indicate on the sheet the content area of the provided question (science or social studies).

9. Display and explain the "Shopping Cart" (WS 2.5.2) worksheet to students. Be sure and point out the information that must be included: title, author, and call number. Students should neatly write their question and keywords at the top of their "Shopping Cart" (WS 2.5.2) sheet.

Transition:

Embedded AASL Skills Indicator: ___.___.___: _____

_____

10. Assign each pair of students to a PAC computer.

Activity:

Embedded AASL Skills Indicator: ___.___.___: _____

_____

11. Allow students time to complete the assignment. Students should include all necessary information listed on their "Shopping Cart" (WS 2.5.2) worksheet.

Embedded AASL Dispositions in Action Indicator: ___.___.___: _____

_____

Embedded AASL Self-Assessment Strategies: ___.___.___: _____

_____

12. Give students time to use their keywords to complete a search in the PAC. After a few minutes, ask students to share whether they were successful. Explain to

students that they may need to revise their search if they did not receive their desired results. Ask students to share their thinking if they had to revise their search.

Embedded AASL Responsibilities Indicator: ___.___.___: _____

_____

13. Point out to students that they should be evaluating the sources that they are recommending. They should be prepared to support their reasons for adding a title to the list.

Closure:

Embedded AASL Self-Assessment Strategies: ___.___.___: _____

_____

14. Select volunteers to share their work with the class and to explain the thinking processes they used while searching for resources in the PAC. Be sure to ask students to share their thinking if they had to modify their search.
15. Collect the "Shopping Cart" (WS 2.5.2) worksheets.

Evidence of Understanding:

Check for student participation throughout the lesson.

Check the "Shopping Cart" (WS 2.5.2) worksheets for accuracy, and place the exemplary sheets into the "5th-Grade Information Consumers: Resource Lists" binder. Find time to conference with the students who did not complete the activity satisfactorily. Work with these students to complete the activity accurately so their resource sheet may be included in the "5th-Grade Information Consumers: Resource Lists" binder.

Enrichment Using Technology:

1. Show students how to use the online tool NoodleTools (http://www.noodletools. com/) if the subscription has been purchased for the school or district. Using the "MLA Starter" in NoodleTools will walk students through the steps of creating a successful bibliography of their sources. It's a great way to keep multiple source lists and links together. Students can even add their own ideas or notes by using the "notecard" option. The students can create a bibliography of their sources to print out for future reference.

Extension:

1. Have students check the public library's PAC for books on a particular topic, and have students send a letter to the librarian explaining what books they will need and when throughout the year.
2. Have students come up with some Web sites and database links that might be helpful to include on their "Shopping Cart" (WS 2.5.2) worksheet.

Suggested Modifications:

Check with the classroom teacher ahead of time to find out which students have reading and comprehension difficulties. Be sure to pair these students with the stronger readers in the class.

SHOPPING CART

Indicate which subject area your essential question covers (circle one):

science   social studies

Question:

_____

_____

Keywords used to locate resources.

_____   _____

_____   _____

Resource #1

Title: _____

Author: _____ Call # _____

Resource #2

Title: _____

Author: _____ Call # _____

Resource #3

Title: _____

Author: _____ Call # _____

Internet resource

Page title: _____

URL: _____

Date visited: _____

This list was created by _____

Did you find a good resource not listed on the front portion of this page? Add in your own here!

Additional resource #1

Title: _____

Author: _____ Call # _____

Additional resource #2

Title: _____

Author: _____ Call # _____

Additional resource #3

Title: _____

Author: _____ Call # _____

Additional resource #4

Title: _____

Author: _____ Call # _____

Additional resource #5

Title: _____

Author: _____ Call # _____

Additional Internet resource #1

Page title: _____

URL: _____

Date visited: _____

Additional Internet resource #2

Page title: _____

URL: _____

Date visited: _____

RESOURCE SHOPPING LIST

MY RESOURCE SHOPPING LIST

Books that I'd like to look
for that might be helpful for my research.

1. Title: _____
   Author: _____ Call# _____

2. Title: _____
   Author: _____ Call# _____

3. Title: _____
   Author: _____ Call# _____

4. Title: _____
   Author: _____ Call# _____

Other search terms or keywords I can use in the Public Access Catalog.

_____
_____
_____
_____

Websites that might be helpful to me.

Web site Name: _____
URL: _____

Web site Name: _____
URL: _____

Web site Name: _____
URL: _____

MY RESOURCE SHOPPING LIST

Books that I'd like to look
for that might be helpful for my research.

1. Title: _____
   Author: _____ Call# _____

2. Title: _____
   Author: _____ Call# _____

3. Title: _____
   Author: _____ Call# _____

4. Title: _____
   Author: _____ Call# _____

Other search terms or keywords I can use in the Public Access Catalog.

_____
_____
_____
_____

Websites that might be helpful to me.

Web site Name: _____
URL: _____

Web site Name: _____
URL: _____

Web site Name: _____
URL: _____

From *Destination Collaboration 1: A Complete Research Focused Curriculum Guidebook to Educate 21st Century Learners in Grades 3–5* by Danielle N. DuPuis and Lori M. Carter. Santa Barbara, CA: Libraries Unlimited. Copyright © 2011.

Working in Collaboration

Collaboration

Collaborate! True collaboration requires both the library media specialist and the classroom teacher to share in the design of integrated instruction. Collaboration provides you with an excellent opportunity to design inquiry-based learning activities. Here are some ideas for collaborating with the classroom teachers.

5th Grade: Astronomy

Essential Question: Why do scientists study comets, asteroids, and meteors?

- After conducting their research, students could create a news show. Students can role-play and pretend to be interviewers and scientists. Film the presentation. Use copyright-free images to include in the movie to illustrate important points.

5th Grade: Colonial America

Essential Question: How was a day in the life of an American colonist in Williamsburg different from a day in your life?

- After locating information and researching their question, students can create a diorama illustrating their life today compared to that of an American colonist.

For further information, please visit
www.destinationcollaboration.com

Bibliography

Work Cited

American Association of School Librarians. *Standards for the 21st-Century Learner in Action.* Chicago: American Library Association, 2009. Print.

Suggested Book Resources

McMillan, Bruce. *Mouse Views: What the Class Pet Saw.* New York: Holiday House, 1993. Print.

Young, Ed. *Seven Blind Mice.* New York: Philomel, 1992. Print.

Suggested Web Resources

Abilock, Damon, and Debbie Abilock, eds. *NoodleTools.* 2009. Web. 11 Nov. 2009. <http://www.noodletools.com/>.

Folkmanis Puppets. Folkmanis. 2009. Web. 11 Nov. 2009. <http://www.folkmanis.com>.

International Children's Digital Library. University of Maryland, 2009. Web. 11 Nov. 2009. <http://en.childrenslibrary.org/.shtml>.

SIRS Discoverer. ProQuest, 2009. Web. 11 Nov. 2009. <http://www.discoverer.sirs.com>.

Chapter 3

Informational Text: Locating Information

Introduction

Historically, students' interaction with informational texts has been mainly through the use of textbooks. Today, students have the advantage of selecting a wide variety of informational texts for their own pleasure and information needs. As 21st century library media specialists, we cannot afford to stop there—there is much more to consider. Using informational texts and online resources are a part of the foundational skills required for acquiring information literacy skills. Michael B. Eisenberg states, "There are three essential contexts for successful learning and teaching: the information process, technology in context, and real needs—either work, educational, or personal" (2008, 40). This chapter on informational text provides elementary students with an initial opportunity to learn and practice the skills of inquiry-based learning and information literacy. As a 21st century learner, students will learn how to prepare their own research questions, locate and choose reliable resources to answer their research questions, and progress towards sharing their information effectively with an audience beyond their own classroom and school.

Inquiry-based learning supports a child's naturally inquisitive nature. Our educational system has often been organized in a manner that makes inquiry-based teaching difficult. Fixed library class schedules make collaboration challenging, and according to Katherine Miller, "The research and the professional literature overwhelmingly suggest that most teachers do not understand the role of the teacher-librarian, particularly the teaching and instructional partner role" (2005, 9). Ideas throughout this chapter will assist you in being recognized as a teacher as well as a librarian. Collaborative suggestions are available along with essential questions to assist your students in participating in inquiry-based learning.

From Year to Year

The effective use of informational text, whether digital or print, to satisfy an information need requires information literacy skills that students must master in order to become lifelong learners. The lessons in this book build on the understandings from the previous year. The 3rd-grade lessons begin with a review of how to use the table of contents, index, glossary, and text feature skills. Students also learn how to create a researchable question in order to begin an inquiry-based project. Students complete their project by creating a newsletter as a real-world product. In the 4th-grade lessons, students are provided with less background knowledge in using informational texts and text feature skills. However, resources are provided in order to do a quick review if needed. Students will use informational texts to research butterflies and butterfly gardens, and they will write their own research question and locate information in order to answer the question. Using their research, students will create their own butterfly garden. The butterfly garden can be created on paper or in the schoolyard—the choice is up to you. The lessons for 5th grade are designed to take students through the inquiry process. During these lessons students will research the impact of climate change on our environment and how humans can help. They will answer the research question, "How have the effects of climate change impacted our environment, and how can we make a difference?" Students will then create a real-world agenda and share their information in a meeting format. The gradual progress of learning how to use informational texts will ready students for more independent projects.

Information Literacy in the Library

Many new literacies have been introduced in the 21st century—among these new literacies, information literacy is in the forefront. As the school's library media specialist, you are the key educator equipped to teach your students information literacy skills. Informational texts are the cornerstone to building these skills. Informational texts include nonfiction books and magazines, Web sites, and databases. Students must be able to use informational texts in all formats—print and electronic. Utilizing electronic or digital text requires students to have additional literacy knowledge. Digital text is unique because unlike print text, it can include hyperlinks, which are not linear. Digital texts will be expanded upon in the next chapter, "Online Resources."

Students have a natural interest in learning about the real world. Take advantage of this innate curiosity by making sure your library media center has resources on a wide variety of nonfiction topics. Check your state or district's curriculum documents for specific topics addressed by grade level in mathematics, science, health, and social studies. This will help you decide what resources to purchase. Keep track of the different topics that pique students' interests. Update your collection by staying current with student interests, new technologies, changes in political maps and countries, scientific news, and mathematical concepts.

Teach your students how to read informational texts. Model for them your thinking as you approach a nonfiction book. Show them the table of contents and index. Model for students how an informational text does not have to be read from beginning to end in a linear fashion. Show them that they can begin anywhere in the text and encourage them to begin with a topic that interests them. Choose to read aloud from an informational text during instruction time in the library media center.

Self-Assessment Strategies

The American Association of School Librarians (AASL) describes self-assessment strategies as three-directional. "(1) Looking backwards at work that has been done to see how successful it was, (2) Looking at the present to determine the next steps, and (3) Looking at the future to decide what has been learned that will make the learning process more effective in the future" (2009, 57). In addition, AASL states: "Self-assessment is enhanced by applying it in a social context because learning itself is social. Learners can assess their own performance and progress more effectively by: gathering feedback from others, looking at how their individual skills contribute to group learning, thinking about the responsibilities and dispositions that are most appropriate for the learning situation and others around them, and considering the applications of their learning to the real world" (2009, 58).

Throughout this chapter, students are given opportunities to self assess their learning using a variety of strategies. These strategies include the use of reflection logs as a tool to assist students in monitoring their own learning, opportunities to reflect with peers, and encouragement to think about future investigations.

Relevancy

There has been much written about the importance of read-alouds in classroom instruction. Studies show that most teachers select fictional books to read aloud. However, reading informational books aloud "inspires curiosity in children, and for some struggling readers, informational books may hold the key to learning to read" (Kletzien and Dreher, 2004, 45). Informational books (such as nonfiction books, magazines and newspapers) can expand a child's vocabulary and increase their comprehension skills.

In *Informational Text in K-3 Classrooms: Helping Children Read and Write* (2009), Kletzien and Dreher tell us that informational text is best read interactively. Allow students to interact with the text by asking questions. Read the table of contents and then give students the opportunity to decide which chapter will be explored first. These kinds of experiences will help students develop interests and encourage them to ask questions and develop ideas. Questioning will lead them to developing research skills and evaluating information to answer their questions. They will feel excited to share their knowledge in written, oral, or electronic formats. Practicing how to present information in written, oral, and electronic formats will prepare students for the demands of many types of jobs of the 21st century.

Working in Isolation

Isolation

This unit will take your students beyond learning text feature skills. Students learn how to develop and answer a simple research question, and they create a real-life product to share their learning. Share these products with the classroom teacher. This will be a great way to begin a discussion that may lead toward coordination, cooperation, and collaboration.

In order to support the classroom teacher, keep your school library media center stocked with a wide variety of informational texts. Students enjoy reading informational magazines and newspapers. Some Sunday editions of newspapers carry a kid's section. Consider laminating these sections to save year to year. In addition, databases like SIRS Discoverer carry a wide variety of informational texts in magazine or newspaper formats.

3RD-GRADE LESSONS

LESSON 1: PLANT AN IDEA

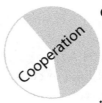

Coordinate! Students will use informational texts to research a variety of topics about plants. During this lesson, students will review how to use the table of contents, index, glossary, and text feature skills by viewing the "Informational Text" (OER 3.3.1) PowerPoint. Coordinate with the classroom teacher by letting them know students are reviewing text features to be better prepared to locate information as they research a variety of topics about plants. Share the provided Web sites and show the classroom teacher the kinds of resources available in the library media center relating to this topic. The classroom teacher may wish to use these resources for an upcoming science-focused project.

Cooperate! Students will be introduced to text features and how to use them in order to extract facts from informational text. Students will use a plant topic list to assist in creating a research question about plants. Share with the classroom teacher the media center's collection of plant resources that students will use to begin their research. Offer to bring this collection to the classroom or place the collection on a library cart for easy access.

Lesson Plan

Integrated Goals:

Language Arts

Standard 3. Students apply a wide range of strategies to comprehend, interpret, evaluate, and appreciate texts. They draw on their prior experience, their interactions with other readers and writers, their knowledge of word meaning and of other texts, their word identification strategies, and their understanding of textual features (e.g., sound-letter correspondence, sentence structure, context, graphics).

Life Science

Content Standard C: Grades K–4

As a result of activities in grades K–4, students should develop an understanding of

- The characteristics of organisms
- Life cycles of organisms
- Organisms and environments

Library Media

AASL 21st Century Standards

> **Standard 1:** Inquire, think critically, and gain knowledge.
> **Standard 2:** Draw conclusions, make informed decisions, apply knowledge to new situations, and create new knowledge.

Essential Questions:

How does creating an open-ended question help to guide research?

How do text features, table of contents, index, and keywords assist in locating information?

Desired Understandings:

Students will understand:

How to use text features when locating information.

How to write a research question.

How to locate, evaluate, and use information to answer a research question.

Integrated Objectives:

- Students will learn how to read and interpret informational text in order to complete a research project.
- Students will select a life science topic about plants and develop a research question.

Time Required:

45 minutes

Provided Materials:

- "Plant Student Topic List" (RS 3.3.1)—one per student pair
- "Plant Topic List" (TRS 3.3.1)
- "Plant Clipboard" (WS 3.3.1)—one per student pair
- "Informational Text" (OER 3.3.1) PowerPoint
- "Flower Power Grouping Cards" (RS 3.3.2)—cut out a pair of cards for each pair of students

Materials You Will Need to Obtain:

- Computers
- Projection device
- Pencils
- Nonfiction books, reference materials, and printed pages from Web sites about plant life

Prior to the Lesson:

Collect as many books, reference materials, and printed pages from Web sites as possible to create an interesting and informative plant research display. Use the "Plant Student Topic List" (RS 3.3.1) to guide your choices. It is recommended that you use the provided teacher resource sheet, "Plant Topic List" (TRS 3.3.1), to assist you with helping students come up with a successful research question.

Lesson Procedures:

Engagement:

1. Bring in a household plant that is not looking very healthy. Pretend that you are trying to "bring the plant to life" by watering it. Say, "I just don't understand why this plant isn't looking better!" Ask students to suggest what to do to help the

plant become healthy. Write suggestions on the board. Suggestions may include: the plant needs water, the plant needs a new container with fresh dirt, or the plant needs more or less sun.

Activity:

2. Thank students for their suggestions, and distribute the "Flower Power Grouping Cards" (RS 3.3.2). Once all the cards have been distributed, ask students to find the other student in the class who has the same flower as they do.

3. Once students have found their match, explain that this classmate will be their partner for the next activity. Student pairs should now sit together.

4. Explain to students that they will be using informational texts to find facts about plant life. Their research can focus on a wide variety of facts, and they will have options from which to choose.

5. Distribute a nonfiction plant book from the plant research display to each pair of students. Tell students to use this nonfiction book as informational text discussed in the upcoming "Informational Text" (OER 3.3.1) PowerPoint.

6. Share the "Informational Text" (OER 3.3.1) PowerPoint. While showing the title slide, ask students to name some text features that can be found in an informational text. Progress to the next slide, "Text Features." Explain each of the text features found in an informational text, and give student pairs an opportunity to find each of the text features in their nonfiction book. Ask students to share what they have found.

7. Progress through the "Informational Text" (OER 3.3.1) PowerPoint and ask students to explain the importance of using each of the following terms: "keywords," "table of contents," "glossary," and "index." Stop at the "Index" slide.

8. Explain that research begins with a researchable question that usually begins with "how" or "why." Explain that a question that begins with "what" usually limits the answer. Continue the "Informational Text" (OER 3.3.1) PowerPoint and discuss the difference between a researchable question and a dead end question.

9. Go back to the ideas the students had listed during the engagement activity. Discuss how each idea they offered is an aspect of plant life. For example, the answer "the plant needs water" could be the basis of the following research question, "How does water affect plant growth?" The answer "the plant needs a new container with fresh dirt" could also be made into a research question: "How do the components of soil help plants grow?"

Transition:

10. Display and distribute the "Plant Student Topic List" (RS 3.3.1).
11. Give students a moment to review the list in pairs and select a research topic from the list.

Activity:

Embedded AASL Skills Indicator: ___.___.___: _____

_____

12. With their partner, ask students to brainstorm and create a research question based on their topic that begins with the words "how" or "why." Instruct students to record their research question ideas on the "Plant Student Topic List" (RS 3.3.1).
13. Ask students to share their research questions and record them on the board.

Embedded AASL Skills Indicator: ___.___.___: _____

_____

14. Together as a class, work to make each research question stronger and ask for each pair of students to edit their question on their "Plant Student Topic List" (RS 3.3.1).
15. Distribute the "Plant Clipboard" (WS 3.3.1) to each pair of students.
16. Tell students to write their edited research question from their "Plant Student Topic List" (RS 3.3.1) in the appropriate space on their "Plant Clipboard" (WS 3.3.1).
17. Display a page from the "Plant Clipboard" (WS 3.3.1).

Embedded AASL Responsibilities Indicator: ___.___.___: _____

_____

18. Model writing a research question. From the available plant life display resources, demonstrate using an index and table of contents to assist in selecting a few informational texts to support the answer to the research question. Be sure and point out the spaces provided to record the resources used to locate information. Demonstrate the proper way to cite a resource with your students.
19. Students may choose which page is best suited to collect their information on the "Plant Clipboard" (WS 3.3.1).

Embedded AASL Skills Indicator: ___.___.___: _____

_____

20. Go back to the plant life information display. Read some of the titles available for this project. Explain to students that they may need to refer to several resources to fully answer their research question. Ask students to determine whether the book they hold will be of value when answering their research question. If not, invite them to return their book to the plant life research display and check another book to see if it is an appropriate resource for their particular question.

Embedded AASL Skills Indicator: ___.___.___: _____

_____

Embedded AASL Dispositions in Action Indicator: ___.___.___: _____

_____

21.   Give student pairs time to begin their research.

Embedded AASL Dispositions in Action Indicator: ___.___.___: _____

_____

Embedded AASL Self-Assessment Strategies: ___.___.___: _____

_____

22.   As students are working, walk around the class to assist students as they research their question. Check to make sure students are citing the resources they use. Provide feedback to student groups as necessary in order to help them assess their own inquiry process.

Closure:

23.   Choose one or two pairs of students who were successful in their research. Ask them to share their research question and why the resource(s) they chose assisted them in answering their research question. Ask students if they were successful immediately, or if it took several tries to locate a helpful resource. Congratulate students on their persistence. Tell students that they will have time during the next class to gather more information.

Evidence of Understanding:

Collect and assess the "Plant Clipboard" (WS 3.3.1) for information that successfully answers the research question.

Technology Integration:

Technology

NETS-S

3. Research and Information Fluency

Students apply digital tools to gather, evaluate, and use information. Students:

  b.   locate, organize, analyze, evaluate, synthesize, and ethically use information from a variety of sources and media.

Allow students time to explore plant research on Web sites that you have found. Bookmark these Web sites for ease in student use. Here are some options for you to consider:

- http://www.brainpopjr.com/science/plants/plantlifecycle/grownups.weml
- http://www.crickweb.co.uk/assets/resources/flash.php?&file=lcycles5b
- http://www.ngfl-cymru.org.uk/vtc/factors_plant_growth/eng/Introduction/default.htm
- http://www.catie.org.uk/plants_galore_page.html
- http://www.bbc.co.uk/schools/scienceclips/ages/7_8/plants_grow_fs.shtml

Extension:

1. Challenge students to keep a plant journal in which they record the name and location of a plant in their neighborhood, house, or yard. Encourage students to write a description of the plant and draw a picture to illustrate it. Mention that students may wish to look on the Internet to see if they can locate more information about the plants in their plant journal. Share the following Web site with students to assist in locating information on the Internet. My Garden Guide: http://mygardenguide.com/index.php?option=com_content&task=view&id=866&Itemid=72.

Suggested Modifications:

Students in need of modifications should be challenged to locate information on one aspect of a topic for their group. Assist the student in thinking of keywords and helping them locate information.

PLANT STUDENT TOPIC LIST

Adaptation of plants

Growing plants

Aquatic plants (plants under the sea)

Plant uses

Plant parts help a plant grow

Science of plants

PLANT TOPIC LIST

For this project, students will choose an aspect of plant growth for their research topic. Help students create a researchable question by using the following options:

1. Adaptation of plants

    a. How do plants adapt to their environment?

2. Plant parts help a plant grow

    a. Why are flowers necessary in order to create fruit?

    b. How do leaves help plants and humans?

    c. How do different parts of a plant work?

    d. How do roots work?

    e. How does the stem work?

    f. How do seeds travel?

3. Growing plants

    a. How do plants grow?

    b. How are plants different?

    c. Why is pollination important in plant growth?

4. Aquatic plants (plants under the sea)

    a. How are plants under the sea like plants on land? How are they different?

5. Plant uses

    a. How are plants used besides for eating?

    b. How do plants end up in our grocery stores?

6. Science of plants

    a. How do scientists do experiments with plants?

    b. Why does science research different ways to grow plants?

PLANT CLIPBOARD

Name: _____

Research question:

_____

_____

_____

Resource list: Be sure to list every resource you use for your project.

1.

2.

3.

4.

Notes:

_____

_____

_____

_____

_____

Notes:

_____
_____
_____
_____
_____
_____
_____
_____
_____
_____
_____
_____
_____
_____
_____

Notes:

_____

_____

_____

_____

_____

_____

_____

_____

_____

_____

_____

Add words for a glossary, or more charts, graphs, or diagrams.

FLOWER POWER GROUPING CARDS

Rose

Rose

Carnation

Carnation

Lilac

Lilac

Daffodil

Daffodil

Water Lily	Water Lily
Daisy	Daisy
Corn Flower	Corn Flower
Iris	Iris

Snap Dragon	Snap Dragon
Sunflower	Sunflower
Lavender	Lavender
Tulip	Tulip

Yarrow

Yarrow

Wax Flower

Wax Flower

Black-Eyed Susan

Black-Eyed Susan

Clematis

Clematis

3RD-GRADE LESSONS

LESSON 2: GET THE DIRT ON PLANTS

Coordinate! Students will complete their research about plants. Students will share information by putting it in a newsletter format. Each newsletter will be placed in the "Seed Packet" (WS 6.3.2) for students to refer to at a later date. *Coordinate* by sharing the "Seed Packet" (WS 6.3.2) with the classroom teacher. The teacher may be interested in placing the "Seed Packet" (WS 6.3.2) in a classroom science center for students to use to pursue personal interests.

Cooperate! After students complete their research, discuss the student created product, "Plant Newsletter" (WS 6.3.3), with the classroom teacher. Is there another product that the classroom teacher believes could assist the students more effectively? Or, are there skills necessary in the creation of the "Plant Newsletter" (WS 6.3.3) that the classroom teacher would like you to emphasize? These kinds of questions may lead to a *cooperative* activity or full collaboration.

Lesson Plan

Integrated Goals:

Language Arts

Standard 3. Students apply a wide range of strategies to comprehend, interpret, evaluate, and appreciate texts. They draw on their prior experience, their interactions with other readers and writers, their knowledge of word meaning and of other texts, their word identification strategies, and their understanding of textual features (e.g., sound-letter correspondence, sentence structure, context, graphics).

Standard 5. Students employ a wide range of strategies as they write and use different writing process elements appropriately to communicate with different audiences for a variety of purposes.

Life Science

Content Standard C: Grades K–4

As a result of activities in grades K–4, students should develop an understanding of

- The characteristics of organisms
- Life cycles of organisms
- Organisms and environments

Library Media

AASL 21st Century Standards

> **Standard 2:** Draw conclusions, make informed decisions, apply knowledge to new situations, and create new knowledge.

Standard 3: Share knowledge and participate ethically and productively as members of our democratic society.

Essential Questions:

How does an assessment rubric assist in the successful completion of a product?
How does collaboration improve your product?

CLASSROOM CONNECTIONS

Extend student's learning about plants and collaborate with the classroom teacher to plan lessons around planning a schoolyard habitat. The art teacher will also be a valuable resource as you work together to design the garden with students.

Desired Understandings:

Students will understand:

How to use a rubric as they create their product.
Collaboration contributes to a deeper understanding of information.

Integrated Objectives:

- Students will use informational text to create their own newsletter to share with their classroom or school.

Time Required:

45 minutes

Provided Materials:

- "Plant Clipboard" (WS 3.3.1)—one per pair completed from previous lesson
- "Seed Packet" (WS 3.3.2)—one copy, cut out
- "Newsletter Sample" (ORS 3.3.1)—for display
- "Plant Newsletter" (WS 3.3.3)—one per student group
- "Plant Newsletter Rubric" (RS 3.3.3)—for display and one per student group

Materials You Will Need to Obtain:

- Projection device
- Pencils
- Laptop
- Large 12 × 15 ½ manila envelope
- Students should have prior knowledge of Microsoft Word: WordArt, text boxes, font color changes, how to insert a picture and table creation—if you choose to use the electronic version of "Plant Newsletter" (OEWS 3.3.1)
- Crayons or colored pencils
- Rulers

Prior to the Lesson:

Copy the "Seed Packet" (WS 3.3.2). Cut in half and adhere the two half pages to the front and back of a 5 × 7 manila envelope to show students an example of the "Seed Packet" (WS 3.3.2). Decide whether students will be completing the "Plant Newsletter" (WS 3.3.3) electronically or with paper. Make sure you have enough computers available. Ask students to sit with their assigned partner.

Lesson Procedures:

Engagement:

1. Show students the "Seed Packet" (WS 3.3.2). Explain that their finished work will be placed inside the packet to share with other students. (You may wish to keep this in the library media center, or allow the classroom teacher to use it in the classroom for students to reference.)

Activity

2. Redistribute the "Plant Clipboard" (WS 3.3.1) to student pairs.

Embedded AASL Dispositions in Action Indicator: ___.___.___: _____

_____

3. Ask if students had difficulty locating information about their topic. Address student concerns.

Embedded AASL Skills Indicator: ___.___.___: _____

_____

4. Allow students time to finish their research.
5. Circulate and offer assistance, as needed.

Transition:

6. Display the "Newsletter Sample" (ORS 3.3.1).
7. Call students' attention to the "Newsletter Sample" (ORS 3.3.1). Explain that students will share the information they learned in a newsletter format. Each newsletter will be included in the "Seed Packet" (WS 3.3.2). Point out to students that the main headline for their newsletter should be their research question.

Activity:

8. Distribute copies of "Plant Newsletter Rubric" (RS 3.3.4) and "Plant Newsletter" (WS 3.3.3) to each pair of students.
9. Review the "Plant Newsletter Rubric" (RS 3.3.3) and make sure students are aware of the project expectations. Show students how the "Newsletter Sample" (ORS 3.3.1) meets the expectations listed on the "Plant Newsletter Rubric" (RS 3.3.3).
10. Remind students to cite their sources. Show them where they may place this information on the "Plant Newsletter" (WS 3.3.3).

Embedded AASL Skills Indicator: ___.___.___: _____

_____

Embedded AASL Dispositions in Action Indicator: ___.___.___: _____

_____

Embedded AASL Responsibilities Indicator: ___.___.___: _____

_____

11. Give students time to complete their "Plant Newsletter" (WS 3.3.3).
12. If necessary, you may wish to extend this lesson for an additional day.

Closure:

Embedded AASL Skills Indicator: ___.___.___: _____

_____

Embedded AASL Self-Assessment Strategies: ___.___.___: _____

_____

13. Ask students to swap and assess each other's work based on the "Plant Newsletter Rubric" (RS 3.3.4). Students should verbally share positive comments and suggestions for future improvement.

Evidence of Understanding:

Collect the "Plant Newsletter" (WS 3.3.3). Use the "Plant Newsletter Rubric" (RS 3.3.3) to assess student work.

Technology Integration:

Technology

NETS-S

2. Communication and Collaboration

Students use digital media and environments to communicate and work collaboratively, including at a distance, to support individual learning and contribute to the learning of others. Students:

  a. interact, collaborate, and publish with peers, experts, or others employing a variety of digital environments and media.

  Provide students with access to the electronic version of "Plant Newsletter" (OEWS 6.3.1). Have students complete the activity using the computers.

Enrichment Using Technology:

Have students share their information via podcast. Visit http://audacity.sourceforge.net or consider having students create a podcast using GarageBand or other software.

Extension:

1. Students who finish early may decorate the outside of the "Seed Packet" (WS 3.3.2) and include relevant information: "General Plant Care," "General Seed Information," and draw a picture to place in the "Our Garden" section.

2. Use curriculum connections to encourage a schoolwide collaborative project that would be of interest to your school community. Third-grade students could be responsible for a portion of the planning for a school garden. Perhaps they could plan for the care of the garden. Fourth grade could focus on creating a butterfly garden by selecting the proper plants and plant placement. Fifth grade could design the location of the garden based on their knowledge of habitat, predators, and methods of keeping our planet environmentally sound. Look to classroom teachers or to your school's green committee to help you with this activity.

Suggested Modifications:

Modify this activity by assisting students with synthesizing the information in order to contribute to the newsletter.

SEED PACKET

All About Plants
Seed Packet

Created by class:

_____

School name:

_____

General Directions for Plant Care
Plants need:

-
-
-
-
-
-
-
-

Seeds

General information about seeds:

-

-

-

-

-

Our Garden

PLANT NEWSLETTER

Name:_____

Date:_____

Volume_____, Issue_____

All About Plants

From *Destination Collaboration 1: A Complete Research Focused Curriculum Guidebook to Educate 21st Century Learners in Grades 3–5* by Danielle N. DuPuis and Lori M. Carter. Santa Barbara, CA: Libraries Unlimited. Copyright © 2011.

PLANT NEWSLETTER RUBRIC

Expectations	Not met (1)	Almost there (2)	Great job! (3)	
The newsletter includes an appropriate research question.	The students did not include an appropriate research question.	The students made an attempt at creating a research question, but the research question does not promote higher order thinking skills.	The students provided a clear and well-thought-out research question that promotes higher-order thinking skills.	
Students should address the research question and include their answer in a well-written paragraph.	Students did not form a proper paragraph and their ideas were unclear.	Students made an attempt to create a well-written paragraph. The paragraph was lacking the answer or was not well written	The students constructed a well-written paragraph and successfully addressed the research question by including their answer and supporting it with evidence.	
Students should show evidence of their research by presenting clear facts that help to answer their research question.	The students presented only one fact, or their research evidence was unclear.	The students presented a few facts and made an attempt to connect their research to the research question.	The students demonstrated a strong understanding for the subject. They included several facts, and the connections made to the research were clear.	
Students should include a picture that relates to their research question.	The students did not include a picture.	The students included a picture, but it is not apparent how this picture relates to the research question.	Students created a picture that can easily be associated with the research question.	
Students should incorporate their own ideas into the newsletter to show they have made connections to the text.	The students made no attempt to include their own ideas.	The students made an attempt to include their own ideas.	The students included their own thoughts and ideas into the newsletter, which demonstrated a new understanding for the subject.	
The work is neat, complete, and demonstrates proper spelling, punctuation, and grammar usage.	Because of the students' punctuation, spelling, and grammar mistakes, the project was difficult to interpret.	The students made an effort to include proper spelling, punctuation, and grammar. There were only a few mistakes.	The students used proper punctuation, spelling, and grammar throughout the project.	
Total points				

From *Destination Collaboration 1: A Complete Research Focused Curriculum Guidebook to Educate 21st Century Learners in Grades 3–5* by Danielle N. DuPuis and Lori M. Carter. Santa Barbara, CA: Libraries Unlimited. Copyright © 2011.

Working in Collaboration

Collaboration

Collaborate! True collaboration requires both the library media specialist and the classroom teacher to share in the design of integrated instruction. Collaboration provides you with an excellent opportunity to design inquiry-based learning activities. Here are some ideas for collaborating with the classroom teachers.

3rd Grade: Pursuing Personal Growth

Essential Question: How does a good research question guide you to satisfy your curiosity about a personal interest?

- Have students brainstorm topics of personal interest. Encourage students to design questions and locate information that satisfies the need for information based on personal interest.

For further information, please visit
www.destinationcollaboration.com

4TH-GRADE LESSONS

LESSON 1: INFORMATION METAMORPHOSIS

Coordinate! Students will use informational texts to research butterflies and butterfly gardens. *Coordinate* by sharing with the classroom teacher that students are creating their own research question about these topics. Share the Web site provided in the Technology Integration section of this lesson and show the classroom teacher the resources about butterflies and butterfly gardens available in the library media center. Consider sharing the "Uncovering Butterflies" (OER 3.4.1) photo as a model for student engagement. This photo may be changed to reflect current content objectives.

Cooperate! Plan to teach this unit when the classroom teacher is teaching the life cycle in science. During this lesson, students are reminded how to write a research question. *Cooperate* with the classroom teacher by offering to assist students in creating a research question for any upcoming class project. Share the self-assessment strategies with the classroom teacher. These questions are suitable for any inquiry-based lesson or project.

Lesson Plan

Integrated Goals:

Language Arts

Standard 7. Students conduct research on issues and interests by generating ideas and questions, and by posing problems. They gather, evaluate, and synthesize data from a variety of sources (e.g., print and nonprint texts, artifacts, people) to communicate their discoveries in ways that suit their purpose and audience.

Life Science

Content Standard C: Grades K–4

As a result of activities in grades K–4, students should develop an understanding of

- The characteristics of organisms
- Life cycles of organisms

Library Media

AASL 21st Century Standards

Standard 1: Inquire, think critically, and gain knowledge.
Standard 2: Draw conclusions, make informed decisions, apply knowledge to new situations, and create new knowledge.

SCHOOL CONNECTION

Use the facts that your students locate to share with students and staff over the morning announcements or on your Web site.

Essential Questions:

How does creating an open-ended question help to guide research?
Why is it important to use self-questioning strategies?
Why is it important to use more than one resource when answering a research question?

Desired Understandings:

Students will understand:

How to write a research question.
How to use self-questioning strategies to improve their research process.
How to locate information that answers their research question.

Integrated Objectives:

- Students will read and interpret informational text in order to answer a research question.

Time Required:

45 minutes

Provided Materials:

- "Butterfly Composition Book" (WS 3.4.1)—one per student
- "Butterfly Student Topic List" (RS 3.4.1)
- "Butterfly Topic List" (TRS 3.4.1)
- "Uncovering Butterflies" (OER 3.4.1) photograph
- "Butterfly Informational Text" (OER 3.4.2) PowerPoint—optional

Materials You Will Need to Obtain:

- Nonfiction books, reference materials, and Web sites about butterflies
- Computers available for student use
- Projection device
- Pencils
- Laptop

Prior to the Lesson:

Collect as many nonfiction books, reference materials, and Web sites as possible to create an interesting and informative butterfly research display. Use the "Butterfly Student Topic List" (RS 3.4.1) to guide your choices.

Lesson Procedures:

Engagement:

1. Display the "Uncovering Butterflies" (OER 3.4.2) photograph. Explain to students that they will be using informational texts to research a scientific topic. As you display the picture, ask students what topic they think they will be researching.

Activity:

Embedded AASL Skills Indicator: ___.___.___: _____

_____

2. Tell students that they will be using a wide variety of informational texts to find answers to questions they have about butterflies and butterfly gardens. Ask students to share what they already know about butterflies and butterfly gardens.
3. Display and record their ideas on the front board.
4. Tell students that they will be working with a partner. Explain that they will be writing a research question together in order to learn more about butterflies and butterfly gardens.
5. Ask students to recall the proper way to begin a research question. Remind students that a researchable question usually begins with "how" or "why." Explain that a question that begins with "what" usually limits the answer. Discuss the difference between a researchable question and a dead end question.
6. Place students in groups of two and have them sit together.
   - **Optional**—If students need additional reinforcement regarding informational text, share the optional "Butterfly Informational Text" (OER 3.4.2) Power-Point. Use it to remind students of text feature skills; the importance of using the index, table of contents, glossary, keywords; and techniques of writing a research question. Please note that if this option is used, the unit may need to be extended.
7. Tell students that every region of the United States has a wide variety of butterflies and flowering plants that provide the butterflies with food and shelter. Gardeners who wish to invite butterflies into their yard will make an effort to plant flowers and bushes that attract butterflies. This grouping of plants is called a butterfly garden.
8. Explain that students will have the opportunity to research butterflies and butterfly gardens. Suggestions for research topics are provided on the "Butterfly Student Topic List" (RS 3.4.1).

Transition:
9. Display the "Butterfly Student Topic List" (RS 3.4.1).
10. Allow time for each student pair to choose their topic.
11. Distribute the "Butterfly Composition Book" (WS 3.4.1) to each student.

Activity:
12. Ask students to record their names and topic on the front cover of the "Butterfly Composition Book" (WS 3.4.1). Explain that students should work in their assigned pairs to assist one another with research. Each student will be completing their own "Butterfly Composition Book" (WS 3.4.1).
13. Give students time to brainstorm some "how" or "why" research questions to go along with their topic.

Embedded AASL Dispositions in Action Indicator: ___.___.___: _____

_____

14. Ask for each pair to share their research question with the class. As each research question is presented to the class, ask for students to share their

thoughts. Is the research question a good research question, or is it a dead end question? With the class, assist each student pair in creating a good research question.

15. Ask that students record their newly edited research question on the space provided in the "Butterfly Composition Book" (WS 3.4.1).

Embedded AASL Skills Indicator: ___.___.___: _____

_____

16. Ask students to predict the answer to their research question based upon their background knowledge and record their prediction in the space provided in their "Butterfly Composition Book" (WS 3.4.1).
17. Walk around the room to check that each student group has a researchable question and is recording their prediction.
18. Choose a resource from the display to answer the question, "How do butterflies go through their life cycle?" Explain that students will probably need to look in several resources to answer their question. Show students the space provided for citing their sources. Demonstrate the inclusion of the resource you used to locate your information.
19. Instruct students to open their "Butterfly Composition Book" (WS 3.4.1) to the first page and look carefully at the rubric. Read the rubric aloud and explain that students should frequently look to the rubric to ensure proper completion of the research and project.

Embedded AASL Skills Indicator: ___.___.___: _____

_____

Embedded AASL Dispositions in Action Indicator: ___.___.___: _____

_____

20. Allow students time to collect their resources from the display and begin their research.
21. As students are researching, be available to assist them.

Embedded AASL Responsibilities Indicator: ___.___.___: _____

_____

22. Remind students to cite their sources in their "Butterfly Composition Book" (WS 3.4.1) as they use them.

Closure:

Embedded AASL Self-Assessment Strategies: ___.___.___: _____

_____

23. Ask students to complete part one of the self-assessment in the back of their "Butterfly Composition Book" (WS 3.4.1).
24. Ask students to share their self-assessments with the class.

Evidence of Understanding:

Walk around the room as student groups are working to assess their ability to complete the task and work together.

Technology Integration:

Technology

NETS-S

3. Research and Information Fluency

Students apply digital tools to gather, evaluate, and use information. Students:

b. locate, organize, analyze, evaluate, synthesize, and ethically use information from a variety of sources and media.

Students will need to access Web sites in order to find relevant information about butterflies to answer their research question. Here is one option: http://www.fieldmuseum.org/butterfly/. This Web site shares basic information about butterflies and their habitats.

Extension:

1. Read *The Life Cycle of a Butterfly* by Bobbie Kalman (New York: Crabtree Publishing 2006) to encourage students to learn more about the topic and to model for students how to find information that answers their research question in a nonfiction text.

Suggested Modifications:

Be sure to partner students in need of assistance with a peer that is on or above grade level. Preselect resources of an appropriate reading level for students in need of modification to use to assist them in answering their research question.

BUTTERFLY COMPOSITION BOOK

Composition
Book

Name:_____

_____

Topic:_____

_____

From *Destination Collaboration 1: A Complete Research Focused Curriculum Guidebook to Educate 21st Century Learners in Grades 3–5* by Danielle N. DuPuis and Lori M. Carter. Santa Barbara, CA: Libraries Unlimited. Copyright © 2011.

BUTTERFLY RUBRIC

Expectations	Not met (1)	Almost there (2)	Great job! (3)
The composition book should include an appropriate research question and prediction.	The student did not include an appropriate research question and/or prediction.	The student made an attempt at creating a research question and making a prediction, but the research question and prediction do not promote higher-order thinking skills.	The student provided a clear and well-thought-out research question and prediction that promoted higher-order thinking skills.
Students should show evidence of their research by presenting clear facts that help to answer their research question.	The student presented only one fact, or their research evidence was unclear.	The student presented a few facts and made an attempt to connect their research to the research question.	The student demonstrated a strong understanding for the subject. They included several facts and the connections made to the research were clear.
In their "My Butterfly Garden" students should write a well-constructed paragraph that includes relevant information about their topic and how it relates to a specific butterfly and plant of the local region.	The student did not form a well-constructed paragraph and their information was unclear or disconnected.	The student made an attempt to create a well-constructed paragraph. The paragraph contained accurate information, but the connections were not fully developed.	The student created a well-constructed paragraph and successfully addressed the research question by including their answer, how it related to a specific butterfly and plant of the local region, and supported their answer with evidence found in research.
Students should illustrate, color, and label their "My Butterfly Garden."	The student did not include an illustration, or the illustration was drawn in haste.	The student included an illustration but the illustration does not include color and/or a label.	The student created an illustration, complete with color and labels, clearly showing a butterfly and plant of our area.
Through self-assessment, students should demonstrate what they learned and how it can be applied.	The student did not attempt to assess their own work.	The student made an attempt to assess their own work.	The student completed each of the self-assessment questions and demonstrated a new understanding for the subject.
The work is neat, complete, and demonstrates proper spelling, punctuation, and grammar usage.	Because of the students' punctuation, spelling, and grammar mistakes, the project was difficult to interpret.	The student made an effort to include proper spelling, punctuation, and grammar. There were only a few mistakes.	The student used proper punctuation, spelling, and grammar throughout the project.
Total points			

From *Destination Collaboration 1: A Complete Research Focused Curriculum Guidebook to Educate 21st Century Learners in Grades 3–5* by Danielle N. DuPuis and Lori M. Carter. Santa Barbara, CA: Libraries Unlimited. Copyright © 2011.

Butterfly Inquiry Sheet

Research question idea:

_____

_____

Edited research question:

_____

_____

My prediction:

_____

_____

_____

_____

_____

_____

_____

_____

_____

_____

_____

_____

Notes

Source citation(s):

Notes about Native Butterflies and Plants

Native butterfly:

_____

_____

_____

_____

_____

_____

_____

Native plant:

_____

_____

_____

_____

_____

_____

_____

Source citation:

_____

_____

_____

Self-Assessment

PART 1

What did I learn today that I didn't know before?

_____

_____

What information do I still need to find?

_____

_____

What was the most helpful resource I used today and why?

_____

_____

PART 2

How have I contributed to the learning of others?

_____

_____

Did I do all that was required to successfully complete my assignment? What could I do differently next time?

_____

_____

_____

_____

_____

BUTTERFLY STUDENT TOPIC LIST

In addition to selecting a topic and writing a research question about it, you must also locate a butterfly and two plants native to our area.

STUDENT TOPIC LIST

Attracting, raising, and keeping butterflies

Butterflies common to your area

Butterfly garden

Butterfly life cycle (caterpillar to butterfly)

Butterfly or moth

Monarch butterfly's life

Plants that attract butterflies in your area

BUTTERFLY TOPIC LIST

For this project, students must choose a butterfly garden plant and butterfly native to your area. These items may be found at the following Web sites:

http://www.butterfliesandmoths.org/ (butterflies by region)

http://www.naba.org/pubs/bgh.html (Click on the .pdf file for flower types closest to your region.)

The "Butterfly Student Topic List" provides suggested topics that students may choose to research about butterflies and butterfly gardens. Students should create a research question for their chosen topic. Examples are provided.

1. Attracting, raising, and keeping butterflies

    a. How do people attract, raise and keep butterflies?

2. Butterfly garden

    a. How do you make a butterfly garden?

    b. Why do people make butterfly gardens?

3. Butterfly life cycle

    a. How does the butterfly go through its life cycle?

4TH-GRADE LESSONS

LESSON 2: INVITING ALL BUTTERFLIES!

Coordinate! Students will use their research about butterflies and butterfly gardens to create their own butterfly garden. Use extension option 1 and display student work on a bulletin board. Coordinate by inviting the classroom teachers to view the student's display. Use this opportunity to explain that students have learned about different native plants and butterflies from our area, and ask the teachers about the possibilities of creating a real butterfly garden on school property.

Cooperate! Share with classroom teachers how students have taken research and used it to create their own butterfly garden. *Cooperate* by brainstorming other ways that students could share information. Think about what other kinds of student-created products would be useful for students to demonstrate their knowledge and understanding of the subject. Consider sharing the information via podcast, blog, or wiki. Discuss these options with the classroom teacher. Think about how you can work together.

Lesson Plan

Integrated Goals:

Language Arts

Standard 8. Students use a variety of technological and information resources (e.g., libraries, databases, computer networks, video) to gather and synthesize information and to create and communicate knowledge.

Standard 12. Students use spoken, written, and visual language to accomplish their own purposes (e.g., for learning, enjoyment, persuasion, and the exchange of information).

Life Science

Content Standard C: Grades K–4

As a result of activities in grades K–4, students should develop an understanding of

- The characteristics of organisms
- Life cycles of organisms
- Organisms and environments

Library Media

AASL 21st Century Standards

Standard 1: Inquire, think critically, and gain knowledge.
Standard 2: Draw conclusions, make informed decisions, apply knowledge to new situations, and create new knowledge.

Standard 3: Share knowledge and participate ethically and productively as members of our democratic society.

Essential Questions:

Why is it important to use more than one resource when answering a research question?
How does the environment support plants and butterflies in our area?
How does a rubric assist in the successful completion of a research project?

Desired Understandings:

Students will understand:

How to locate information that answers their research question.
How plants and butterflies are supported by natural resources in their environment.
How to use a rubric to assess their own work.

Integrated Objectives:

- Students will create their own butterfly garden and present their ideas and research to the class.

Time Required:

45 minutes

Provided Materials:

- "Butterfly Composition Book" (WS 3.4.1)—one per student completed from the previous lesson
- "My Butterfly Garden" (WS 3.4.2)—one per student (print back-to-back copies)

Materials You Will Need to Obtain:

- Colored pencils and crayons
- Computers with Internet access for student use
- Access to the following Web sites: http://www.butterfliesandmoths.org/ and http://www.naba.org/pubs/bgh.html (Butterflies by Region). Click on the PDF file for flower types closest to your region. Decide whether student will access the Web sites online, or print out selected information from the sites for students to use.
- Projection device
- Pencils
- Laptop

Prior to the Lesson:

Print out a copy of "My Butterfly Garden" (WS 3.4.2) and complete a sample to share with the students. Be sure to draw in both the butterfly and flower native to your state on the front and on the inside share information that your students have learned regarding the butterfly life cycle or butterfly garden and explain how the plant and butterfly on their cover would survive in a butterfly garden.

Lesson Procedures:

Engagement:

1. Display the Web site http://www.ansp.org/museum/butterflies/new_interactive/butterflies.html, and build a virtual butterfly garden for students to view.

Activity:

2. Students should use their answers to the research questions about the butterfly life cycle and butterfly gardens from the previous class to assist them in creating the perfect environment for butterflies.

3. Explain that students will also locate information about the types of plants and butterflies native to your state.

Embedded AASL Skills Indicator: ___.___.___: _____

_____

4. Share the Web sites about native butterflies and plants from the suggested materials list. Instruct each student to select a butterfly and plant native to your state to record in their "Butterfly Composition Book" (WS 3.4.1).

Embedded AASL Skills Indicator: ___.___.___: _____

_____

Embedded AASL Responsibilities Indicator: ___.___.___: _____

_____

5. Students should work in their assigned pairs to assist one another with questions but should be completing their own "Butterfly Composition Book" (WS 3.4.1).

6. Ask students what connections they made between butterflies and plants after viewing the engagement activity (different types of plants attract different types of butterflies). Tell students they should select a butterfly and choose a plant that attracts the type of butterfly they chose.

7. Redistribute the "Butterfly Composition Book" (WS 3.4.1) completed during the previous lesson and remind students to use the rubric on the first page to assist them in the completion of the project.

8. Show students the page titled "Notes about Native Butterflies and Plants." Remind students to select a butterfly and choose a plant that attracts the type of butterfly they've chosen to research.

Embedded AASL Dispositions in Action Indicator: ___.___.___: _____

_____

9. Allow students time to finish their research. Circulate and offer assistance as needed.

Transition:

10. Show students the "My Butterfly Garden" (WS 3.4.2) worksheet you created. Explain how to complete each portion of the worksheet by using the example.

Activity:

11. Give students time to complete the "My Butterfly Garden" (WS 3.4.2) worksheet.
12. Circulate to assist students as needed and note student progress to determine if an additional day is necessary for students to successfully complete the project.

Closure:

Embedded AASL Skills Indicator: ___.___.___: _____

_____

Embedded AASL Dispositions in Action Indicator: ___.___.___: _____

_____

13. As students complete their "My Butterfly Garden" (WS 3.4.2) worksheet, invite them to present their findings with the class.

Embedded AASL Self-Assessment Strategies: ___.___.___: _____

_____

Embedded AASL Self-Assessment Strategies: ___.___.___: _____

_____

14. Instruct students to complete part two of the self-assessment in the back of their "Butterfly Composition Book" (WS 3.4.1).

Evidence of Understanding:

Collect and grade the "Butterfly Composition Book" (WS 3.4.1) and "My Butterfly Garden" (WS 3.4.2) according to the rubric.

Enrichment Using Technology:

Allow students visit the "Explore Butterflies" Web site (http://www.ansp.org/museum/butterflies/new_interactive/butterflies.html) for more information and fun.

Extension:

1. As students present their "My Butterfly Garden" (WS 3.4.2) with the class, allow them to place their completed work onto a bulletin board. Prepare the bulletin board ahead of time by creating a generic landscape with a tree for shade and a

pond or lake. Students can add their projects to the board and explain why their butterfly and plant would thrive in the location they selected.

2. Your students may be interested in creating a butterfly garden for your school. Fourth-grade students will have the knowledge of a variety of butterflies and plants that will be appropriate in your area. Work with other grade levels to create the butterfly garden.

Suggested Modifications:

Continue helping students in need of modification by assisting them in locating information and helping them find resources. Record or write for those students in need of this modification.

MY BUTTERFLY GARDEN

Directions: In the space below, record information you researched about your butterfly. Also, be sure to include information about the butterfly and plant you selected that can be found in our region and how they relate to the butterfly topic you researched. Once you have recorded this information, fold this paper in half, and in the space on the front of this worksheet, illustrate and color both the plant and butterfly you chose from our area. Label both the plant and butterfly.

From *Destination Collaboration 1: A Complete Research Focused Curriculum Guidebook to Educate 21st Century Learners in Grades 3–5* by Danielle N. DuPuis and Lori M. Carter. Santa Barbara, CA: Libraries Unlimited. Copyright © 2011.

My Butterfly Garden

Working in Collaboration

Collaboration

Collaborate! True collaboration requires both the library media specialist and the classroom teacher to share in the design of integrated instruction. Collaboration provides you with an excellent opportunity to design inquiry-based learning activities. Here are some ideas for collaborating with the classroom teachers.

4th Grade: Life Science

Essential Question: How can plants attract wildlife to your area?

- Create a schoolwide butterfly garden. Students can research what types of plants to plant in the garden, where they can be purchased, and what care they will need. Students can share their findings with the school community. Collaborate with other grade levels and parent volunteers to plan and plant a school butterfly garden.

For further information, please visit
www.destinationcollaboration.com

5TH-GRADE LESSONS

LESSON 1: GOING GREEN

Coordinate! During this lesson students will research the impact of climate change on our environment and how recycling can help. Coordinate by sharing the provided Internet links from the "Green Resource List" (RS 3.5.2) with the classroom teacher. The classroom teacher could set up a science-focused learning center at the classroom computer. Students could access these links to learn more about recycling during classroom time.

Cooperate! Think about joining the school's Green Team—or create one. *Cooperate* by sharing this lesson plan about climate change with the teacher in charge of student council. Take these opportunities to discuss how to meet curriculum objectives cooperatively. Share the self-assessment questions from the "Green Graphic Organizer" (WS 3.5.1) and share noted improvements in student learning as a result of using this strategy.

Lesson Plan

Integrated Goals:

Language Arts

Standard 8. Students use a variety of technological and information resources (e.g., libraries, databases, computer networks, video) to gather and synthesize information and to create and communicate knowledge.

Standard 12. Students use spoken, written, and visual language to accomplish their own purposes (e.g., for learning, enjoyment, persuasion, and the exchange of information)

Science in Personal and Social Perspectives

Content Standard F: Grades 5–8

As a result of activities in grades 5–8, all students should develop an understanding of

* Populations, resources, and environments

Library Media

AASL 21st Century Standards

> **Standard 1:** Inquire, think critically, and gain knowledge.
> **Standard 2:** Draw conclusions, make informed decisions, apply knowledge to new situations, and create new knowledge.
> **Standard 3:** Share knowledge and participate ethically and productively as members of our democratic society.

DISCUSSION OPPORTUNITY

After completing this lesson, have students identify other problems that need solving at the school. Have students think about what information they need to begin to solve these problems.

Essential Questions:

How does human activity effect our environment?
How can human activity improve our environment?
How can self-assessment strategies help you learn?

Desired Understandings:

Students will understand:

How our environment is affected by human activity.
How human activity can improve our environment.
How to use self-assessment strategies to improve learning.

Integrated Objectives:

- Students will use informational text to locate facts about climate change.
- Students will assess their ability to locate and use information.

Time Required:

45 minutes

Provided Materials:

- "Symbol" (ORS 3.5.1)
- "Green Graphic Organizer" (WS 3.5.1)—print back-to-back copies—one per student
- "Green Resource List" (RS 3.5.2)
- "Suggested Green Books" (RS 3.5.3)

Materials You Will Need to Obtain:

- Books about the environment and climate change—some suggestions have been provided in the "Suggested Green Books" (RS 3.5.3)
- Set of encyclopedias
- Computer
- Projection device
- Pencils
- Laptops or computer lab

Lesson Procedures:

Engagement:

1. Display the "Symbol" (ORS 3.5.1) for all students to see. Ask students to share the first word or two that comes to mind when they look at the symbol. Examples may include recycling, earth, reuse, global warming, environment, climate change, and so forth.

Activity:

2. Ask students to share why recycling is important. Record and display the student's ideas.
3. Ask students to share what they know about recycling's connection to climate change. Record and display the student's ideas.

4. Explain to students that they will be using informational text to answer the following questions about climate change: How have the effects of climate change impacted our environment? How can we make a difference?

Embedded AASL Skills Indicator: ___.___.___: _____

_____

5. Ask for students to predict the answer to the research questions and share their ideas with the class.

Embedded AASL Skills Indicator: ___.___.___: _____

_____

6. Share the Web sites from the "Green Resources List" (RS 3.5.2) with students. Explain that students can use information found on the Web sites, as well as from the book sources you have collected in order to take notes about climate change. Review school Internet policy with the students and discuss the consequences of inappropriate use.

Transition:

7. Distribute the "Green Graphic Organizer" (WS 3.5.1) to students.

Activity:

Embedded AASL Skills Indicator: ___.___.___: _____

_____

Embedded AASL Responsibilities Indicator: ___.___.___: _____

_____

8. Read the instructions out loud to the class. Discuss the words "cause" and "effect," and make sure students are aware of their definitions as they relate to the worksheet. Point out the citation space at the bottom of the "Green Graphic Organizer" (WS 3.5.1). Instruct students to cite their sources as they locate information to answer the question.
9. Instruct students to turn their papers over and look at the self-assessment questions. Explain that they will be expected to answer these questions at the end of the class.

Embedded AASL Dispositions in Action Indicator: ___.___.___: _____

_____

10. Give students access to computers, books, and encyclopedias to locate their information.

Embedded AASL Skills Indicator: ___.___.___: _____

_____

11. Give students time to read and explore and to record information into their "Green Graphic Organizer" (WS 3.5.1).

Closure:

Embedded AASL Skills Indicator: ___.___.___: _____

_____

12. Ask students for students to complete the self-assessment located on the back of the "Green Graphic Organizer" (WS 3.5.1).

Embedded AASL Self-Assessment Strategies: ___.___.___: _____

_____

13. Ask for students to share some new understandings based on their self-assessment. Have students share a resource they found to be of the most assistance as they completed their worksheet.
14. Tell students that they will use the information they found to prepare an agenda for an important meeting.

Evidence of Understanding:

Collect the "Green Graphic Organizer" (WS 3.5.1) worksheets. Check that students recorded accurate information for each question and completed the self-assessment.

Enrichment Using Technology:

Have students explore the "Waste in Place" section (http://www.cleansweepusa.org/wastein place_intro.aspx) from the Keep America Beautiful Web site. Students can play interactive games; read about composting, waste, recycling; and learn about our impact on the environment in an engaging way.

Extension:

Read aloud *Why Are the Ice Caps Melting? The Dangers of Global Warming* by Anne Rockwell (New York: Collins, 2006), and ask students to share ideas that explain how humans can change our behavior to improve our environment.

Suggested Modifications:

Preselect the materials or books to meet the appropriate reading level of students with reading/learning difficulties and make sure these students have access to the materials.

GREEN GRAPHIC ORGANIZER

Name: _____

Directions: Locate information about climate change and jot down notes that will assist you in answering the following question, "How have the effects of climate change impacted our environment, and how can we make a difference?"

Explain climate change.

_____
_____
_____
_____
_____
_____

What are the causes of climate change?

_____
_____
_____
_____
_____

What are the effects of climate change?

_____
_____
_____
_____

What does it mean to "go green?"

_____
_____
_____
_____
_____
_____
_____

Sources:

_____
_____
_____
_____

SELF-ASSESSMENT

Was my prior knowledge accurate? Explain.

_____

_____

_____

What predictions did I make about the research question?

_____

_____

_____

Were my predictions correct? Explain.

_____

_____

_____

What did I learn today that I didn't know before?

_____

_____

_____

What information do I still need to find?

_____

_____

_____

What was the most helpful resource I used today and why?

_____

_____

_____

How can I use the information I found?

_____

_____

_____

GREEN RESOURCE LIST

Use the list of Web sites below to help you locate information about the Earth's environment, global warming, and ways to "go green."

The Environmental Protection Agency's Climate Change Kids Site http://epa.gov/climate change/kids/index.html

Time For Kids—Specials—GLOBAL WARMING http://www.timeforkids.com/TFK/specials/ articles/0,28285,1114322,00.html

Stop Global Warming Web site (click in the "classroom" link in the upper right-hand corner) http://www.stopglobalwarming.org/sgw_classroom.asp

Environmental Education For Kids—Global Warming http://www.dnr.state.wi.us/org/caer/ ce/eek/earth/air/global.htm

A National Coalition for the Environment http://www.saveourenvironment.org/

Kids Saving Energy sponsored by the U.S. Department of Energy's Energy Efficiency and Renewable Energy http://www.eere.energy.gov/kids/

Energy Information Administration Kids page http://www.eia.doe.gov/kids/

SUGGESTED GREEN BOOKS

Use the suggested books below to build your library media center collection. All are extremely helpful and informative for students as they complete their "Green Bookmarks" or any other project relating to the environment.

Binns, Tristan Boyer. *A Bright Idea: Conserving Energy*. Chicago: Heinemann, 2005. Print.

Cherry, Lynne, and Gary Braasch. *How We Know What We Know About Our Changing Climate: Scientists and Kids Explore Global Warming*. Nevada City: Dawn Publications, 2008. Print.

Ganeri, Anita. *Something Old, Something New: Recycling*. Chicago: Heinemann, 2005. Print.

Ganeri, Anita, and Chris Oxlade. *Down the Drain: Conserving Water*. Chicago: Heinemann, 2005. Print.

Gore, Al. *An Inconvenient Truth: The Crisis of Global Warming Adapted for a New Generation*. New York: Viking, 2007. Print.

Hall, Julie. *A Hot Planet Needs Cool Kids*. Bainbridge Island: Green Goat Books, 2007. Print.

Spilsbury, Louise. *Changing Climate: Living with the Weather*. Chicago: Raintree, 2006. Print.

———. *Environment at Risk: The Effects of Pollution*. Chicago: Raintree, 2006. Print.

Spilsbury, Richard. *The Great Outdoors: Saving Habitats*. Chicago: Heinemann, 2005. Print.

Thornhill, Jan. *This Is My Planet: The Kids' Guide to Global Warming*. Ontario: Maple Tree Press, 2007. Print.

SUGGESTED READ-ALOUDS

Harper, Joel. *All the Way to the Ocean*. Claremont, CA: Freedom Tree Press, 2006. Print.

Rockwell, Anne. *Why Are the Ice Caps Melting? The Dangers of Global Warming*. New York: Collins, 2006. Print.

5TH-GRADE LESSONS

LESSON 2: A GREENER PLANET

Coordinate! Students will continue their research and create a meeting agenda in order to share their information. The agenda could be used at a real student council or PTA meeting. Share with the classroom teacher the importance of the students' work and the quality of the agendas. *Coordinate* by inviting the student council president or the classroom teacher to listen as various students "conduct" a meeting to share their information.

Cooperate! Have students conduct a mock meeting to share what they learned with one another and the classroom teacher. After the presentation, *cooperate* with the classroom teacher by discussing the possibility of future green projects. Begin a small project, like recycling batteries, and add more grade level team members or grades as interest grows. Students can use their new understandings regarding climate change to assist in moving the project forward.

Lesson Plan

Integrated Goals:

Language Arts

Standard 8. Students use a variety of technological and information resources (e.g., libraries, databases, computer networks, video) to gather and synthesize information and to create and communicate knowledge.

Standard 12. Students use spoken, written, and visual language to accomplish their own purposes (e.g., for learning, enjoyment, persuasion, and the exchange of information)

Science in Personal and Social Perspectives

Content Standard F: Grades 5–8

As a result of activities in grades 5–8, all students should develop an understanding of

• Populations, resources, and environments

Library Media

AASL 21st Century Standards

> **Standard 1:** Inquire, think critically, and gain knowledge.
>
> **Standard 2:** Draw conclusions, make informed decisions, apply knowledge to new situations, and create new knowledge.

SCHOOL CONNECTION

Have students talk with club leaders and share the importance of creating an agenda with different clubs and committees with the school. Post meeting agendas on your Web site.

Standard 3: Share knowledge and participate ethically and productively as members of our democratic society.

Essential Questions:

How does human activity effect our environment?
How can human activity improve our environment?
How can an agenda assist in meeting productivity?

Desired Understandings:

Students will understand:

How our environment is affected by human activity.
How human activity can improve our environment.
How to create and use an agenda in order to organize and hold a meeting.

Integrated Objectives:

- Students will use informational text to create an agenda for a Going Green meeting with community members.

Time Required:

45 minutes

Provided Materials:

- "Green Graphic Organizer" (WS 3.5.1)—completed from previous lesson
- "Agenda Sample" (RS 3.5.4)
- "Green Agenda" (WS 3.5.2)—one per student group

Materials You Will Need to Obtain:

- Books about the environment and climate change
- Gavel or crab mallet
- Set of encyclopedias
- Computer
- Projection device
- Laptops or computer lab
- Pencils

Lesson Procedures:

Engagement:

1. Hit a gavel or crab mallet on the desk and say, "I'd like to call this meeting to order. The purpose of our meeting is to inform the school and community about climate change and what can be done to help our Earth. Your job will be to use your notes from the previous class to assist you in creating a meeting agenda. Then, present your information to either the Parent Teacher Association or to the student council to inform them of your findings. This meeting is adjourned."

Activity:

2. Explain to students that you were pretending to call together a meeting. Display the "Agenda Sample" (RS 3.5.4). Explain the purpose and layout of an agenda for a meeting. Ask students if they have any questions about this kind of document.

3. Redistribute the "Green Graphic Organizer" (WS 3.5.1) completed in the previous class.
4. Have students discuss their answers as a class. As students discuss their answers, suggest they update their notes to reflect the class discussion.
5. Brainstorm some ways that students, parents, and teachers can be more environmentally friendly at school, home, work, and in the community.
6. Record and display student's answers and suggestions.

Embedded AASL Responsibilities Indicator: ___.___.___: _____

_____

7. Tell students that it will be their responsibility to help educate the school and community about climate change and to give suggestions for what they can do to help the environment. These suggestions will be conveyed by holding a "Going Green" meeting at the PTA or student council meetings. Each suggestion will be its own agenda item.

Transition:

8. Place students in groups of two to four and distribute the "Green Agenda" (WS 3.5.2) worksheets.
9. Ask students to share some suggestions for agenda items. Record and display their ideas.

Activity:

10. Tell students that they will work with the other members of their group to come up with a detailed agenda for a "Going Green" meeting. Students should complete the first part of the "Green Agenda" (WS 3.5.2) titled, "agenda."
11. Give students time to complete this portion of the activity.

Embedded AASL Skills Indicator: ___.___.___: _____

_____

Embedded AASL Responsibilities Indicator: ___.___.___: _____

_____

12. Ask students to hold a mock meeting with their group. Discuss meeting etiquette with the students such as taking turns to speak, valuing the opinions of others, giving everyone a chance to be heard, and using evidence to back up opinions. Students should use the "Topic" spaces provided on the "Green Agenda" (WS 3.5.2) to record their discussion and discussion outcomes.
13. Be sure and mention to students that they can go back and use the Web sites and books to locate more information if necessary.

Embedded AASL Skills Indicator: ___.___.___: _____

_____

14. Give students time to discuss and record their outcomes.

Embedded AASL Skills Indicator: ___.___.___: _____

_____

Embedded AASL Self-Assessment Strategies: ___.___.___: _____

_____

15. Ask for students to record ideas for a future meeting regarding climate change and how it relates to our school.

Closure:

Embedded AASL Skills Indicator: ___.___.___: _____

_____

Embedded AASL Dispositions in Action Indicator: ___.___.___: _____

_____

16. Ask each group to share the action items of their "Green Agenda" (WS 3.5.2) worksheet. Have the class select one group as their representative to a PTA or student council meeting so that they can share their ideas.

Evidence of Understanding:

Collect the "Green Agenda" (WS 3.5.2) and grade for understanding of the lesson.

Enrichment Using Technology:

Have students use the computers to design a bookmark using the tech option worksheet "Green Bookmark Tech" (OEWS 3.5.1) in Word. Students can add WordArt, graphics, pictures, borders, and so forth, to enhance the message of their bookmark.

Extension:

Have students create a bookmark that gives a fact about climate change. Have students add their own thoughts and ideas. Show the "Green

> **SCHOOL CONNECTION**
>
> Have students from your class share an environmental tip they learned on a bookmark to be shared with the school. Other students will learn what the students in your class learned when they use the bookmark.

Bookmark Sample" (EX 3.5.2) to give students an idea to complete the project. You will also need copies of the "Green Bookmark" (EX 3.5.1)—print one bookmark for each student (in keeping with the green theme of the activity, we recommend that you print the bookmarks on paper that has already been used on one side).

Suggested Modifications:

Assist students with special needs in selecting a topic of focus for their agenda.

Green Meeting Agenda

Teacher's name here.

Your name and the names of your teammates here.

Meeting called by:_____

Attendees:_____

_____

_____

Agenda:_____

_____

What do you plan on discussing at this meeting? Place them here in a list format.

Topic #1:

Presenter:

Select a topic to write about and place it here.

Discussion:

Name of the group member who will do the talking at the meeting.

Record what you talked about with your teammates here.

Conclusions:

What can you conclude? Was there anything significant that you discovered/decided as a group?

Action items:	***Person responsible:***	***Deadline:***

What else needs to be done after this meeting is over?

Who in the group will be responsible for taking care of the "action items?"

When will this be completed?

Agenda items for next meeting:

_____

_____

_____

_____

What do you plan on discussing at the next meeting? List your ideas here.

From *Destination Collaboration 1: A Complete Research Focused Curriculum Guidebook to Educate 21st Century Learners in Grades 3–5* by Danielle N. DuPuis and Lori M. Carter. Santa Barbara, CA: Libraries Unlimited. Copyright © 2011.

Green Meeting Agenda

Meeting called by: _____ Attendees: _____

_____

_____

Agenda: _____

_____

_____

_____

_____

_____

_____

_____

_____

_____

_____

_____

_____

Topic #1: _____ Presenter: _____

Discussion: _____

_____

_____

Conclusions: _____

_____

_____

_____

Action items:	Person responsible:	Deadline:

Topic #2:   Presenter:

Discussion:

_____

_____

_____

Conclusions:

_____

_____

_____

_____

Action items:	*Person responsible:*	*Deadline:*

Topic #3:   Presenter:

Discussion:

_____

_____

_____

Conclusions:

_____

_____

_____

Action items:	*Person responsible:*	*Deadline:*

Agenda items for next meeting:

_____

_____

_____

_____

GREEN BOOKMARK

Directions: Use the bookmark template below to record one fact about the effects of climate change. Be sure and include a suggestion for how this can be corrected or changed. Decorate and color your bookmark to make it attractive. When you are finished, cut out your bookmark and put your name on the back.

Directions: Use the bookmark template below to record one fact about the effects of climate change. Be sure and include a suggestion for how this can be corrected or changed. Decorate and color your bookmark to make it attractive. When you are finished, cut out your bookmark and put your name on the back.

GREEN BOOKMARK SAMPLE

You are using energy even when you aren't using your electric products. Did you know that a plasma TV consumes

1,452 kilowatts

a year, just by being plugged in and turned off?

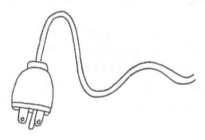

Cut energy costs and save valuable resources—unplug electronic items in your home when they aren't in use such as cell phone and game chargers, TV's Game consoles, and computers. If you want to make things easier—plug these items into a power strip and just turn off the power strip!

Source: "Vampire Energy." *GOOD Worldwide*. 3 Dec. 2007. Web. 23 Jan. 2010. ‹http://www.good.is/post/vampire-energy-2/›.

Working in Collaboration

Collaborate! True collaboration requires both the library media specialist and the classroom teacher to share in the design of integrated instruction. Collaboration provides you with an excellent opportunity to design inquiry-based learning activities. Here are some ideas for collaborating with the classroom teachers.

5th Grade: Science in Personal and Social Perspectives

Essential Question: Why are global warming and climate change controversial topics of our time?

- Students can research all avenues of climate change: research, speculation, and theory. Collaborate with the classroom teachers to set up a student debate regarding climate change. Plan a schoolwide event and invite public officials and community members.

Essential Question: How can humans improve the Earth's environment?

- Students can research the cause and effect of human impact on the Earth's environment. Collaborate with the classroom teachers to have students design 60-second commercials in which they promote positive ways students, teachers, and community members can change human behavior to help the environment. Share the commercials with the school or on your local school television network.

For further information, please visit
www.destinationcollaboration.com

Bibliography

Works Cited

American Association of School Librarians. *Standards for the 21st-Century Learner in Action*. Chicago: American Association of School Librarians, 2009. Print.

Eisenberg, Michael B. "Information Literacy: Essential Skills for the Information Age." *DESIDOC Journal of Library & Information Technology* 28.2 (2008): 39–47. Print.

Kletzien, Sharon Benge, and Mariam Jean Dreher. *Informational Text in K-3 Classrooms: Helping Children Read and Write*. Newark: International Reading Association, 2004. Print.

Miller, Katherine. "Novice Teachers' Perceptions of the Role of the Teacher-Librarian in Information Literacy." *School Libraries in Canada* 24.3 (2005): 1–45. Print.

Suggested Print Resources

Kalman, Bobbie. *The Life Cycle of a Butterfly*. New York: Crabtree, 2006. Print.

Moffett, Mark. W. *Face to Face With Frogs*. Washington, D.C.: National Geographic, 2008. Print.

Walton, Rick. *There Once Was a Bullfrog*. Salt Lake City: Gibbs Smith, 1995. Print.

Suggested Web Resources

Audacity. 2008. Web. 20 Nov. 2008. <http://audacity.sourceforge.net>.

"Butterflies at the Field Museum." *The Field Museum*. 2007. Web. 28 Nov. 2009. <http://www.fieldmuseum.org/butterfly/>.

"Butterfly Gardens and Habitats." *North American Butterfly Association*. 12 Dec. 2006. Web. 20 Nov. 2008. <http://www.naba.org/pubs/bgh.html >.

"Clean Sweep USA." *Keep America Beautiful*. U.S. Department of Education. 2007. Web. 23 Nov. 2008. <http://www.cleansweepusa.org/wasteinplace_intro.aspx>.

"Climate Change Kids Site." *United States Environmental Protection Agency*. 30 Oct. 2008. Web. 23 Nov. 2008. <http://epa.gov/climatechange/kids/index.html>.

"Energy Kid's Page." *Energy Information Administration*. Department of Energy. Web. 23 Nov. 2008. <http://www.eia.doe.gov/kids/>.

"Explore Butterflies." *Academy of Natural Sciences*. Natural History Museum in Philadelphia. 2008. Web. 23 Nov. 2008. <http://www.ansp.org/museum/butterflies/new_interactive/butterflies.html>.

"Factors Affecting Plants." *NGfL CMYRU*. 2003. Web. 20 Nov. 2008. <http://www.ngfl-cymru.org.uk/vtc/factors_plant_growth/eng/Introduction/default.htm>.

"Global Warming Is Hot Stuff." *Environmental Education for Kids!* Wisconsin Department of Natural Resources. Web. 23 Nov. 2008. <http://www.dnr.state.wi.us/org/caer/ce/eek/earth/air/global.htm>.

"Helping Plants Grow Well." *BBC—School Science Clips*. BBC. Web. 20 Nov. 2008. <http://www.bbc.co.uk/schools/scienceclips/ages/7_8/plants_grow_fs.shtml>.

"Kids Saving Energy." *Energy Efficiency and Renewable Energy*. United States Department of Energy. 29 Aug. 2008. Web. 23 Nov. 2008. <http://www.eere.energy.gov/kids/>.

The New York Times Learning Network. The New York Times Company. 2008. Web. 23 Nov. 2008. <http://www.nytimes.com/learning/>.

Opler, Paul A, et al. "Butterflies and Moths of North America." *Bozeman, MT.* NBII Mountain Prairie Information Node. 2006. Web. 20 Nov. 2008. <http://www.butterfliesand moths.org/>.

"Plant Encyclopedia." *My Garden Guide.* Environmental News Network. 2008. Web. 23 Nov. 2008. <http://mygardenguide.com/index.php?option=com_content&task=view&id= 866&Itemid=72>.

"Plant Life." *CATIE for Schools and Colleges.* CATIE. 2002. Web. 20 Nov. 2008. <http://www. catie.org.uk/plants_galore_page.html>.

"Plant Life Cycle." *BrainPOP Jr.* 2008. FWD Media, Inc. Web. 20 Nov. 2008. <http://www. brainpopjr.com/science/plants/plantlifecycle/grownups.weml>.

"Plant Life Cycles." *Crickweb.* V2V Training Ltd. 2008. Web. 20 Nov. 2008. <http://www. crickweb.co.uk/assets/resources/.php?&file=lcycles5b>.

Save Our Environment. 23 Nov. 2008. <http://www.saveourenvironment.org/>.

Scholastic News Online. Scholastic. 2008. Web. 23 Nov. 2008. <http://www2.scholastic. com/browse/scholasticNews.jsp?FromBrowseMod=true&Ns=Pub_Date_Sort1&Curr Page=scholasticNews.jsp&TopicValue=Scholastic%20News>.

SI Kids. Sports Illustrated KIDS. 2007. Web. 23 Nov. 2008. <http://www.sikids.com>.

"Special Report Global Warming." *Time For Kids.* Time Inc. 2008. Web. 23 Nov. 2008. <http:// www.timeforkids.com/TFK/specials/articles/0,28285,1114322,00.html>.

"Take Action at School." *Stop Global Warming.* 2008. Web. 23 Nov. 2008. <http://www.stop globalwarming.org/sgw_classroom.asp>.

Time For Kids. Time, Inc. 2008. Web. 23 Nov. 2008. <http://www.timeforkids.com/TFK/>.

Zoobooks Magazine. Zoobooks. 2008. Web. 23 Nov. 2008. <http://www.zoobooks.com>.

Chapter 4

Online Resources: Locating Information

Introduction

Digital citizenship is a key component of working, teaching, and learning online. Library media specialists teach elementary students how to locate, select, evaluate, and use print, audio, visual, and digital information found within the library media center, on the Internet, and on subscription online databases. Elementary students frequent the Internet and virtual worlds from home, often without a roadmap or the digital skills required to do so securely or effectively. Schools heavily filter Internet content and some even restrict the use of search engines like Google, Yahoo, or Bing in order to keep students from finding inappropriate Internet content. Students may be left to their own devices at home. Learning about Internet safety and online searching techniques at school with very limited opportunity to practice their skills in real time is an unfortunate consequence of filtering. This is not the optimum situation to educate a digital citizen for digital responsibility in the 21st century. In this book, opportunities are available to assist students in learning about digital responsibility in safe online environments. Through the use of Google sites and Google custom search engines to replicate authentic online environments, students will learn and practice safe searching and authentic digital communication. Teaching students how to search the Internet safely and behave ethically is the only way to educate a responsible, ethical, and safe 21st century digital citizen.

From Year to Year

Being responsible in the navigation and use of digital information is a valuable skill required of all 21st century learners. The lessons in this chapter will build on the understandings from the previous year. The 3rd-grade lessons begin with the basics of browsing a Web site and discuss proper terminology and Internet safety precautions. A large portion of the lessons focus on evaluating Web sites to determine whether they are accurate and reliable. The 4th-grade lessons build on the concept of online safety and place a large emphasis on social networking and digital footprints. Students will examine their own online habits to determine what type of digital footprint they are leaving behind for others to find. The 5th-grade lessons are designed to take digital responsibility to the next level. The focus of these lessons is communication, and how to communicate effectively. Students explore a number of scenarios to determine the best communication method for each scenario, and then they share their thoughts in a collaborative online environment to expand their understanding and ideas with one another. Students need to locate information *and* evaluate what they find, and then they must successfully communicate their understandings to others. With these exercises, students will be prepared for whatever the digital world has to explore.

Information Literacy in the Library

Information is immediately available through a variety of digital tools, and the formats in which information is presented is changing at an extremely fast pace. When writing a bibliography for a report in the year 1999, citations would primarily consist of book resources, databases, and Web sites. Now, the variety of formats posted to the Internet seems endless. Students have more variety, choices, and formats from which to choose when searching for and selecting information than ever before, and it appears to be a growing trend. Students have many avenues to explore when completing a class project or pursuing a personal interest. However, it is also true that there are many inappropriate, inaccurate, and irrelevant Web sites and digital resources in cyberspace. Because students may not have an adult present at home when they complete their homework or when they are going online to network, it is extremely important that educators share and demonstrate how to communicate and explore digital resources in a safe, appropriate, and effective way.

Students have a natural curiosity to learn more about topics of interest to them. Library media specialists should play an active role in helping students explore topics of interest safely. To do this, library media specialists can provide lists of reputable Web sites, links to games, and reliable resources from the school's Web site. This will help students as they pursue various informational needs. If the local public library offers homework help, place a link to this information from the school Web site as well. Providing students with as many reliable and relevant resources as possible will ensure students have a wealth of information from which to choose. Students will also gain valuable practice and experience using these digital resources. Practice and experience can prepare students to be able determine on their own when a resource is unreliable because they will have had plenty of good examples in their repertoire. This is a beginning step for working toward more interactive online endeavors.

Web 2.0 requires library media specialists to give students access not only to the Internet but also to information and one another. Consider creating a personal learning network where students can post their work and react and respond to the work of others in positive and effective ways. Blogs, wikis, and podcasts are a great place to begin. Students can also post their work to an electronic portfolio or Web site of their own to keep from grade to grade and year to year. This documentation of their work will provide students with the necessary proof and experience to move forward as they apply their skills to achieve their desired goals.

Self-Assessment Strategies

Due to the reality that the ways in which information is displayed and shared is rapidly changing, it is imperative for students to question the resources they use. Throughout this chapter, students are asked to stop and assess the way they look for information, as well as the relevancy of the information, and the way they share and communicate new information with their peers, parents, and teachers. Self-assessment is required in order for students to cognitively acknowledge how they will change their methods in the future in order to improve their ability to become information literate. Each self-assessment question provides students with an opportunity to examine their own learning style and methods, and to really take an active role in their own learning process. It is through self-assessments that students can recognize their own strengths and weaknesses, determine how they can benefit from working with others, and realize their full potential as 21st century learners and leaders.

Relevancy

Teaching digital natives how to navigate the world in which they already reside is the responsibility of all educators, but the task is generally accomplished through library media specialists and technology leaders. In order to become information and technology literate, students must learn and understand the skills, dispositions, and responsibilities required to develop into effective digital citizens of the global economy. Teaching these important skills within the highly restrictive environment of an elementary school setting is challenging. The information in this chapter will assist you in breaking barriers and finding other avenues to teach necessary online learning skills in any environment.

Technology is advancing at a rapid pace. Be sure to seek out every opportunity to learn how to create, display, and share information using digital tools in an online environment. Learning to apply your experience in information literacy and student learning while leveraging the use of technology to share what you know will assist you in being seen as a technology leader in your school. The time to be a leader in the school library is now. Create you own personal learning network through the use of Google reader, Google groups, and blogging, and become part of the interactive, online discussion and share your knowledge and understandings globally. This is one of the most incredibly exciting times for information development and sharing. Let your voice be heard.

Working in Isolation

This unit will provide students with real world application of digital resources, tools, and communication methods. Students will learn how to navigate the Internet, practice valuable safety measures in regards to technology, and communicate appropriately and effectively using technology and digital tools. The products necessary for the successful completion of these units have already been provided for you. Use these products and change them to suit your needs, as well as the needs of students and teachers. Share these ideas with the classroom teacher to encourage a discussion that could lead to coordination, cooperation, and collaboration.

In order to support the classroom teacher in regards to this lesson, keep an up-to-date digital file or bookmark sites of various safe and reliable Web resources for both teachers and students to use. Another way to share select resources is to create print bookmarks or pamphlets with instructions for how students, teachers, and parents can access this information.

Seek technology education professional development opportunities to ensure that you are seen as a technology leader in your school. Keeping up to date on new digital tools and resources will ensure the necessity of your job as a library media specialist.

3RD-GRADE LESSONS

LESSON 1: WEB BASICS

Coordinate! Students will learn how to navigate and evaluate information found on a Web site. Once students have completed their "Internet Scavenger Hunt Notebook" (WS 4.3.1), *coordinate* by sharing the notebook with the classroom teacher. Discuss students' abilities to locate and evaluate information on a Web site. With the classroom teacher, discuss the possibility of including Web site evaluation as part of an upcoming research project.

Cooperate! Students are often asked to find information on the Internet for classroom research projects. *Cooperate* with the classroom teacher by offering to assist students during the research process in the library media center. Discuss creating a Web site evaluation tool for students to use during the research process for classroom projects.

Lesson Plan

Integrated Goals:

Language Arts

Standard 3. Students apply a wide range of strategies to comprehend, interpret, evaluate, and appreciate texts. They draw on their prior experience, their interactions with other readers and writers, their knowledge of word meaning and of other texts, their word identification strategies, and their understanding of textual features (e.g., sound-letter correspondence, sentence structure, context, graphics).

Library Media

AASL 21st Century Standards

Standard 1: Inquire, think critically, and gain knowledge.

Technology

NETS-S

5. Technology Research Tools

Students use technology to locate, evaluate, and collect information from a variety of sources. Students:

b.   locate, organize, analyze, evaluate, synthesize, and ethically use information from a variety of sources and media.

Essential Questions:

How do we know if information on the Internet is accurate?
How is finding information on the Internet different than printed text?

Desired Understandings:

Students will understand:

How to use text features when locating information.
How to use the back button and hyperlinks to navigate through a Web site.
How to evaluate a Web site for accuracy.

Integrated Objectives:

- Students will evaluate a Web site.
- Students will navigate through a Web site using hypertext links and the back button.

Time Required:

45 minutes
   This lesson may require a second day depending upon the background knowledge of the students and their ability to use PowerPoint.

Provided Materials:

- "Internet Scavenger Hunt Notebook" (WS 4.3.1)—one per student printed and folded to look like a notebook
- "Internet Basics" (OER 4.3.1) PowerPoint
- Access to the Google Internet Scavenger Hunt Web site (http://sites.google.com/ site/dcinternetscavengerhunt/)
- "Scavenger Hunt" (OER 4.3.2) PowerPoint
- "Matching Vocabulary" (MN 4.3.1)—optional

Materials You Will Need to Obtain:

- Projection device
- Pencils
- Computers

   Prior Knowledge: Prior to this lesson, review or explain the following vocabulary words: e-mail, text features, hyperlinks, back button, curser, evaluate, publisher, file extension, author, bias, in-depth, cross-checking, and up-to-date. Knowledge of these vocabulary words will assist students in gaining a better understanding of the lesson. Use the "Matching Vocabulary" (MN 4.3.1) as an optional way to review these terms and definitions.

Prior to the Lesson:

Decide whether students will complete their "Internet Scavenger Hunt Notebook" (WS 4.3.1) in pairs or groups, and plan accordingly. Also, locate an image of a spider web and place it into the second slide on the "Internet Basics" (OER4.3.1) PowerPoint.

Lesson Procedures:

Engagement:

Embedded AASL Skills Indicator: ___.___.___: _____

_____

1. Display the second slide of the "Internet Basics" (OER 4.3.1) PowerPoint with the photograph of the spider's web. Ask students why they think the World Wide Web is often described as "the web." Accept all appropriate answers. Explain to students that each intersection of the spider's web resembles how computers and servers around the world are connected so they can communicate quickly and easily with one another. Tell students they will be learning how to use the Internet as a resource and how to evaluate the results of their research for accuracy.

2. Ask students to raise their hands if they have ever used the Internet to find information. Ask the following questions: How did they access the Internet? Did they find the information they needed? Was it easy? Difficult? Was the information accurate? Choose a few students to share their experiences.

Activity:

3. Ask students to describe how information is shared on the Internet.

4. Progress through the "Internet Basics" (OER 4.3.1) PowerPoint and discuss each slide with the students by using the "notes" section as a guide. Throughout the PowerPoint, have students discuss the methods used to share and display information on the Internet.

Embedded AASL Dispositions in Action Indicator: ___.___.___: _____

_____

Embedded AASL Self-Assessment Strategy Indicator: ___.___.___: _____

_____

5. On the final slide of the "Internet Basics" (OER 4.3.1) PowerPoint, ask students to share how information on the Internet is different from printed information. Encourage students to discuss the ways in which digital information is more interactive and offers a wider variety of formats from which to learn.

Transition:

Embedded AASL Self-Assessment Strategy Indicator: ___.___.___: _____

_____

6. Divide students into pairs or groups.

7. Distribute the "Internet Scavenger Hunt Notebook" (WS 4.3.1) to each student. Instruct students to turn to page 1.

8. Tell students to reflect and answer the question, "What do I know or think I know about evaluating Web sites?"

9. Give students time to answer the question on page 1 of their "Internet Scavenger Hunt Notebook" (WS 4.3.1).

Activity:

10. Tell students they will be watching a short video from BrainPop, which will explain six items to consider when evaluating a Web site for accurate information. Briefly explain what elements of the Web site students should consider (e.g., Web site extensions to determine the publisher [.org, .gov, .com, etc.], author of the Web site, bias of the Web site, amount of in-depth information available). Note that cross-checking information and checking that information is up-to-date are two effective ways to determine the accuracy of a Web site.

11. Display the "Internet Scavenger Hunt" Google site (http://sites.google.com/site/dcinternetscavengerhunt/).

12. Read the directions on the home page and then click on the link to the BrainPop movie about online sources.

13. After the video, write and display the six checklist items. Discuss these items and ask students to record the six items into their notebooks.

Embedded AASL Self-Assessment Strategy Indicator: ___.___.___: _____

_____

14. Ask students, "How does this new information change the way you will evaluate the accuracy of Web sites?" Instruct students to write their reflection at the bottom of page 1 in their notebooks.

15. Show students how to navigate through the Internet Scavenger Hunt Google site.

Transition:

Embedded AASL Skills Indicator: ___.___.___: _____

_____

Embedded AASL Skills Indicator: ___.___.___: _____

_____

Embedded AASL Dispositions in Action Indicator: ___.___.___: _____

_____

Embedded AASL Responsibilities Indicator: ___.___.___: _____

_____

16. Tell students that the search numbers on the Web site correspond with the search numbers in the "Internet Scavenger Hunt Notebook" (WS 4.3.1). Explain that

students will be locating information on Web sites to answer the questions in their notebooks. They will be using the six checklist items in order to evaluate the accuracy of the Web sites needed to answer the questions. Complete the first question together.

Activity:

17. Allow students to work in pairs on the computers.
18. Give students time to complete the activity.

Embedded AASL Dispositions in Action Indicator: ___.___.___: _____

_____

19. As students are working, circulate around the room and assist students as needed.

Embedded AASL Self-Assessment Strategy Indicator: ___.___.___: _____

_____

20. When students are finished, ask students to reflect on the last page of their notebook about their experiences. Students will be answering the following questions: How do I know the information I find on a Web site is accurate? How is searching for information on the Internet different than searching in a printed text?
21. Ask students to share their reflections with the class.

Closure:

Embedded AASL Self-Assessment Strategy Indicator: ___.___.___: _____

_____

22. Ask students to share how the day's lesson will help them evaluate Web sites in the future. Encourage students to discuss the process of identifying the publisher, author, and possible bias, as well as the importance of cross-checking facts and checking to make sure that the Web site is up to date.

Evidence of Understanding:

Collect the "Internet Scavenger Hunt Notebook" (WS 4.3.1). Check that students have included accurate information and have successfully answered the scavenger hunt questions.

Enrichment Using Technology:

To extend students' knowledge of using the Internet, allow them to visit and work through the Welcome to the Web Web site(http://www.teachingideas.co.uk/welcome/). This Web site encourages students to learn about the Web in a fun, interactive way.

Extension:

1. Provide students with a Web site to evaluate. One fun Web site for students to evaluate is: http://zapatopi.net/treeoctopus/.

Suggested Modifications:

Students in need of modifications should be paired with stronger students. Assist students in need of assistance as they find information on the Web sites and toggling back and forth between the PowerPoint and the Internet.

INTERNET SCAVENGER HUNT NOTEBOOK

Internet Scavenger Hunt Notebook

Name: _____

Grade: 3

Class: _____

Reflections:

How can I be sure the information I find on a Web site is accurate? _____

_____

_____

_____

_____

How is searching for information found on the Internet different than searching in a printed text?

_____

_____

_____

_____

_____

_____

7

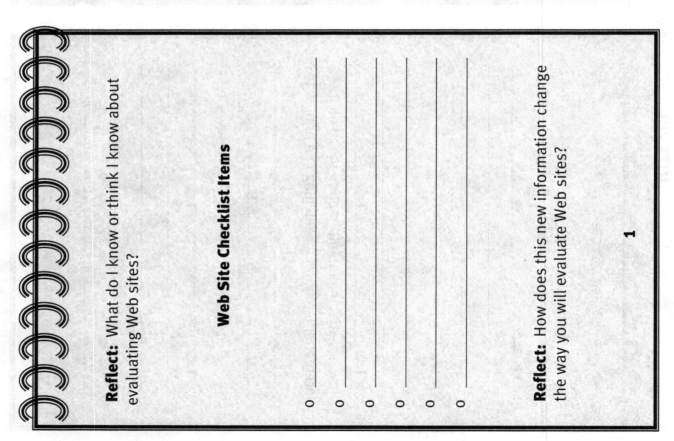

Search 6: Is the Web site up-to-date?

Web site #1: What is the Web site extension? _____

Who is the publisher? _____

Does the information appear accurate? Explain.

_____

_____

When was this Web site last updated?

Web site #2: What is the Web site extension? _____

Who is the publisher? _____

Does the information appear accurate? Explain.

_____

_____

When was this Web site last updated?

6

Reflect: What do I know or think I know about evaluating Web sites?

Web Site Checklist Items

○ _____
○ _____
○ _____
○ _____
○ _____
○ _____

Reflect: How does this new information change the way you will evaluate Web sites?

1

Search 1: Checking for the publisher

1. President John F. Kennedy's children had what unusual pet? _____

2. Who is the publisher of Web site? _____

What is the URL address? _____

What can you tell from the Web site extension? _____

Search 2: Who created the Web site?

Beverly Clearly learned to love books by: _____

Who is the creator of the Web page? _____

What is the contact information for the creator of this Web site? _____

2

Search 5: Cross-check your facts!

Sesame Street Web site:

When did Kermit the Frog first appear on television? _____

Kermit the Frog was originally made from what kind of materials? _____

Wikipedia Web site:

When did Kermit the Frog first appear on television? _____

Kermit the Frog was originally made from what kind of materials? _____

Do both Web sites seem accurate? Explain. Which one do you think is more reliable? Why? _____

5

Search 4: Does this Web site cover the topic in-depth?

This Web site has lots of information. I see information about (list a few topics):

- _____

- _____

- _____

Is the information easy to find? Why/Why not?

_____

_____

Find and click on the site map. What topics do you see? (list a few topics)

- _____

- _____

- _____

How does the site map help you find information?

_____

_____

4

Search 3: Is this Web site biased?

This company helps with water conservation by:

_____

_____

_____

Could this resource be biased? Explain.

_____

_____

_____

_____

3

MATCHING VOCABULARY

Directions:

Print these "Matching Vocabulary" cards onto card stock, cut out and laminate. Make one set to use with the entire class, or make multiple sets for students to use in a paired or group activity.

bias	To try to influence someone or something in an unfair way.
e-mail	Electronic mail is one way to send a message to another person on the Internet.

text features

A way to attract attention to information. Examples can include bold print, italicized print, or diagrams.

hyperlink

This link allows the computer user to move from one Web page to another.

back button

This button allows the computer user to view the previous Web page.

 From *Destination Collaboration 1: A Complete Research Focused Curriculum Guidebook to Educate 21st Century Learners in Grades 3–5* by Danielle N. DuPuis and Lori M. Carter. Santa Barbara, CA: Libraries Unlimited. Copyright © 2011.

cursor

The moving pointer on the computer screen.

evaluate

The process of judging whether a Web site will be valuable in answering your information need.

publisher

The company or person who pays for the Web site to be placed on the Internet.

Web site address	The address of the Web page on the Internet. Also known as the URL (uniform resource locator)
author	The writer or creator of the Web page.
in-depth	Thorough.

cross-checking

The process of looking in more than one resource to check a fact.

up-to-date

The most recent resource available.

3RD-GRADE LESSONS

LESSON 2: SEARCHING FOR INTERNET SAFETY

Coordinate! Students will learn how to do a simple search on the Internet and read the "hits" to find the most appropriate Web site for their information need. Students will also learn about the importance of Internet safety. *Coordinate* by sharing the URLs for the Internet safety sites with the classroom teacher. Discuss students' abilities to locate information through appropriate Web sites on the Internet.

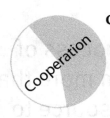

Cooperate! Students are often asked to find information on the Internet for classroom research projects. *Cooperate* with the classroom teacher by offering to assist students during the research process in the library media center. Discuss creating a Google custom search engine for students to use during a class research project.

Lesson Plan

Integrated Goals:

Language Arts

Standard 3. Students apply a wide range of strategies to comprehend, interpret, evaluate, and appreciate texts. They draw on their prior experience, their interactions with other readers and writers, their knowledge of word meaning and of other texts, their word identification strategies, and their understanding of textual features (e.g., sound-letter correspondence, sentence structure, context, graphics).

Library Media

AASL 21st Century Standards

Standard 1: Inquire, think critically, and gain knowledge.

Essential Questions:

How do we know if information on the Internet is accurate?
How is finding information on the Internet different than printed text?
How do we stay safe while searching on the Internet?

Desired Understandings:

Students will understand:

How to search for information on the Internet.
How to use search engines, read URLs, and determine which Web sites on a list will provide the best information to answer a question.
How to use simple measures to stay safe while searching on the Internet.

Integrated Objectives:

- Students will use a Google custom search to conduct a simple search on the Internet.
- Students will practice Internet safety while searching the Internet.

Time Required:

45 minutes

Provided Materials:

- Google Custom Search Engine: Internet Safety for Kids (http://www.google.com/cse/home?cx=006210179467973393198:kqmasc-8dus)
- "How to Search" (OER 4.3.2) PowerPoint
- "Pardon Me" (OER 4.3.3) PowerPoint
- "Tedd E. FAX" (ORS 4.3.1)—one per student pair
- "Bearberry Notes" (WS 4.3.2)—one per student pair copied back to back

Materials You Will Need to Obtain:

- Projection device
- Pencils
- Computer
- Computers for student use

Prior to the Lesson:

Have both the "How to Search" (OER 4.3.2) and "Pardon Me" (OER 4.3.3) PowerPoint presentations open and ready to show. Minimize the "Pardon Me" (OER 4.3.4) Power-Point. Be ready to play the "Pardon Me" (OER 4.3.3) PowerPoint once the last slide of the "How to Search" (OER 4.3.2) PowerPoint is revealed to make it look as if the "Pardon Me" (OER 4.3.3) PowerPoint is interrupting your class.

Lesson Procedures:

Engagement:

Embedded AASL Skills Indicator: ___.___.___: _____

_____

> **CLASSROOM CONNECTIONS**
>
> Use the Google custom search in this lesson as a starting point for creating custom search engines for students relating to various areas of the curriculum. Post links to these searches on the school Web site to encourage safe searching from home.

1. As students arrive, shuffle papers in your hand and appear confused. Tell students that a classroom teacher has asked you to find information about dolphins. Display a Google search page (http://www.google.com). Type "dolphin" in the search box and show the number of "hits" that appear for "dolphin." Act confused as to whether the teacher wanted to learn more about the Miami Dolphins or the mammal. Look at the papers again and say, "Oh, I see, we need to find facts about the bottlenose dolphin that would be suitable for kids!" Type "bottlenose dolphins facts for kids" into the search box. Show students the number "hits." Ask students why they think the number has become lower. Show

students the link http://kids.nationalgeographic.com/Animals/CreatureFeature/Bottlenose-dolphin.

2. Ask students if they think this Web site will satisfy the classroom teachers request. Thank the students for their help and appear relieved. Explain to students that today they will be learning how to search the Internet safely.

Activity:

4. Display the "How to Search" (OER 4.3.2) PowerPoint. Using the "notes" section of the PowerPoint as a guide, discuss each slide with the students.

5. On the last slide of the "How to Search" (OER 4.3.2) PowerPoint, pretend there are computer connection problems and then display the "Pardon Me" (OER 4.3.3) PowerPoint *before* clicking on the "Internet" link.

6. Progress through the entire "Pardon Me" (OER 4.3.3) PowerPoint. Read each line aloud on the Bearberry, and pretend to type in a response to Tedd E. Brownstone. If students question the interaction and suggest that talking to a stranger on a "bearberry" is wrong, explain that this is part of a library media lesson and Tedd E. Brownstone is a fictional character whose purpose is to make the lesson more enjoyable. Be sure to play along with the dialogue between the class and Tedd E. Brownstone. Ask students how to answer and lead them to the text that is embedded in the "Pardon Me" (OER 4.3.3) PowerPoint.

Transition:

7. Encourage students to want to help Tedd E. Brownstone. Return to the last slide of the "How to Search" (OER 4.3.2) PowerPoint.

8. Divide students into pairs.

9. Distribute the "Tedd E. FAX" (ORS 4.3.1) and the "Bearberry Notes" (WS 4.3.2) to each student pair.

10. Ask students to record both of their names on the cover of the "Bearberry Notes" (WS 4.3.2).

Activity:

Embedded AASL Dispositions in Action Indicator: ___.___.___: _____

_____

11. Explain to students that they will be finding the answers to Tedd E. Bearstone's questions listed on the "Tedd E. FAX" (ORS 4.3.1). Students should record the answers they find on their "Bearberry Notes" (WS 4.3.2) worksheet.

12. Give students access to the Google custom search "Internet Safety for Kids" by providing them with a computer and the link listed in the materials section of this lesson.

13. Read the first question on the "Tedd E. FAX" (ORS 4.3.1).

14. Click on the "Internet" button on the last slide of the "How to Search" (OER 4.3.2) PowerPoint. The button links to the Google custom search. Please note that you must be in "slide show" view for the link to work.

15. Demonstrate how to conduct a search for the students by using search terms to locate the first answer in the "Bearberry Notes" (WS 4.3.2) worksheet. Share your thinking as you determine which Web site will have the answer to the ques-

tion. Tell students to turn to page one of their "Bearberry Notes" (WS 4.3.2) and explain how to record the answer in their Bearberry.

Embedded AASL Skills Indicator: ___.___.___: _____

_____

Embedded AASL Dispositions in Action Indicator: ___.___.___: _____

_____

16. Give students time to complete the activity.
17. Walk around the room and assist students as needed.
18. When students are finished, display the last slide of the "Pardon Me" (OER 4.3.3) PowerPoint and display Tedd E. Bearstone's thank you message.

Embedded AASL Dispositions in Action Indicator: ___.___.___: _____

_____

Embedded AASL Self-Assessment Strategy Indicator: ___.___.___: _____

_____

19. Ask students, "Were you and your partner successful in searching for information on the Internet using search terms?" Discuss students' answers. Instruct students to write their group reflections on the last page of the "Bearberry Notes" (WS 4.3.2) worksheet.
20. Ask students to share their reflections with the class.

Closure:

Embedded AASL Responsibilities Indicator: ___.___.___: _____

_____

21. Ask students to share how the day's lesson will help them search for information safely on the Internet.

Evidence of Understanding:

Collect and assess the "Bearberry Notes" (WS 4.3.2). Check that students have included accurate information that successfully answers the questions, proper search terms, and URL identification.

Enrichment Using Technology:

To extend students' knowledge of using the Internet, allow them to visit and work through Welcome to the Web (http://www.teachingideas.co.uk/welcome/). This Web site encourages students to learn about the Web in a fun, interactive way.

Extension:

1. Ask students to write a letter explaining the importance of Internet safety to the 3rd-grade student featured in today's lesson scenario. Use http://www.readwrite think.org/classroom-resources/student-interactives/letter-generator-30005.html as a way to integrate technology into this extension.

Suggested Modifications:

Students in need of modifications should be paired with stronger students. Assist students in need of assistance as they find information on the Web sites.

BEARBERRY NOTES

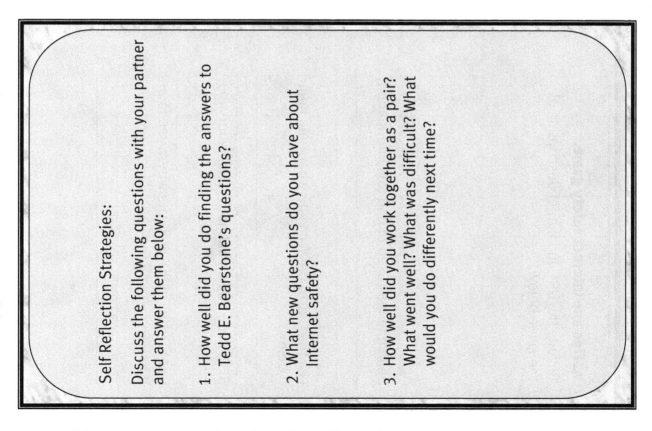

BEARBERRY

OUR BEARBERRY NOTES

NAMES:

Send

Self Reflection Strategies:

Discuss the following questions with your partner and answer them below:

1. How well did you do finding the answers to Tedd E. Bearstone's questions?

2. What new questions do you have about Internet safety?

3. How well did you work together as a pair? What went well? What was difficult? What would you do differently next time?

1. Internet safety guide tips:

Do not give out this personal information:

1.

2.

3.

4.

5.

Treat anyone online as if they are a

Never agree to _____ a person you
have met online.

Never send anyone online _____
of yourself.

Search terms I used to find this information:

_____

The Web site's URL where I found this
information is:

_____

_____

1

4. Find one Internet safety game.

Include the URL and a brief description of
the game below.

Search terms I used to find this information:

_____

List the URL of the Web site where you found
it below:

_____

5. Did you find an online certificate for
Internet safety?

List the URL of the Web site where you found
it below:

_____

4

3. FauxPaw the Techno Cat's video shows why

it is important to use safety on the Internet. Some tips from the video are:

1.

2.

3.

Would you recommend this video? Why or why not?

_____

_____

_____

Search terms I used to find this information:

_____

The Web site's URL where I found this information is:

_____

3

2. McGruff's advice to stay safe online:

If you see anything online that makes you feel unsafe or uncomfortable what should you do?

_____

When you get an e-mail from someone you don't know what should you do? Why?

_____

_____

Should you ever buy anything online?

_____

What should you do before you download any songs or movies?

_____

Search terms I used to find this information:

_____

The Web site's URL where I found this information is:

_____

2

Working in Collaboration

Collaboration

Collaborate! True collaboration requires both the library media specialist and the classroom teacher to share in the design of integrated instruction. Collaboration provides an excellent opportunity to design inquiry-based learning activities. Here are some ideas for collaborating with the classroom teachers.

3rd Grade: Social Studies

Essential Question: How has technology changed the roles and responsibilities of citizens in the global community?

- Have students discuss ways to be a responsible online citizen. Students can brainstorm, design, and create a national symbol that represents the 21st century online citizen.

For further information, please visit
www.destinationcollaboration.com

4TH-GRADE LESSONS

LESSON 1: DIGITAL NETIQUETTE

Coordinate! Students will learn about digital footprints and how they can affect students each time they send an electronic message, upload a photo, or visit a Web site. *Coordinate* by informing the classroom teacher of the student survey results from the "Footprint Survey" (WS 4.4.1). The teacher may be interested to learn how much or how little students are navigating the Internet and the digital trail they are leaving behind.

Cooperate! During this lesson, students learn about the impact of their digital footprint. *Cooperate* with the classroom teacher by sharing the "Footprint Data" (ORS 4.4.2) Excel spreadsheet completed in media class. Offer to assist in making a new survey relating to the digital "netiquette" lesson. The classroom teacher may wish to have students compare and contrast the data from each spreadsheet.

Lesson Plan

Integrated Goals:

Language Arts

Standard 4. Students adjust their use of spoken, written, and visual language (e.g., conventions, style, vocabulary) to communicate effectively with a variety of audiences and for different purposes.

Library Media

AASL 21st Century Standards

Standard 2: Draw conclusions, make informed decisions, apply knowledge to new situations, and create new knowledge.

Standard 3: Share knowledge and participate ethically and productively as members of our democratic society.

Essential Questions:

Why is it important to use precautions when using the Internet?

How can a person's "digital footprint" affect their future?

How can students demonstrate safe behavior on the Internet?

Desired Understandings:

Students will understand:

> **SCHOOL CONNECTION**
>
> Create an electronic survey on the topic of digital footprints and send it out to all of your students and parents. Students can assist in the gathering and displaying of data. Share the results with the school community.

How to safely navigate the Internet.

How to leave an appropriate "digital footprint."

How to behave appropriately when using the Internet.

Integrated Objectives:

- Students will share information with their classmates through a survey.
- Students will assess their own "digital footprint."

Time Required:

45 minutes

Provided Materials:

- "Footprint" (TRS 4.4.1)
- "Digital Footprint" (OER 4.4.1) PowerPoint
- "Digital Footprint" (OER 4.4.2) QuickTime Movie
- "Footprint Survey" (WS 4.4.1)—one per student
- "Footprint Data" (ORS 4.4.1) Excel spreadsheet

Materials You Will Need to Obtain:

- Computer
- Projection device
- Pencils
- Computers for student use

Lesson Procedures:

Engagement:

1. Display the "Footprint" (TRS 4.4.1). Ask students to share the definition of a footprint. Explain that we leave footprints behind as we walk, which show others where we have been. Tell students that today they will learn about digital footprints and how to leave a responsible digital footprint behind. Make the connection that digital footprints leave behind a trail showing others where we have been online, or through other means of digital communication.

Activity:

2. Explain to students that before moving forward in the lesson, students will have to take a survey to share information about themselves with the class. Explain to students the point of the survey is to gather data from the class about how they use the Internet and other digital tools.
3. Distribute copies of the "Footprint Survey" (WS 4.4.1).
4. Allow students time to complete the survey on the first page.
5. Tell students that you would like to display all of the information from each student survey to show the size of the class' digital footprint. Ask for students to share their ideas for the best method to share this type of survey data.
6. Display a copy of the "Footprint Data" (ORS 4.4.1).
7. Read each question of the "Footprint Survey" (WS 4.4.1) aloud. As you read each possible response, ask students to raise their hands to share how they answered.

Take a quick hand count, and record the results into the "Footprint Data" (ORS 4.4.1) spreadsheet.

8. Once all of the data has been collected, graph the results of the survey by following the directions on sheet 2 of the "Footprint Data" (ORS 4.4.1) spreadsheet titled "Instructions" to show the impact of the class' digital footprint. The more "yes" responses gathered from students, the larger the digital footprint.

Transition:

9. Use the data displayed as an introduction to discuss digital footprints.

Activity:

10. Display the "Digital Footprint" (OER 4.4.1) PowerPoint.

Embedded AASL Responsibilities Indicator: ___.___.___: _____

_____

11. Follow the directions on each slide to help students understand their impact as they use, explore, and share information on the Internet. Pause the "Digital Footprint" (OER 4.4.1) PowerPoint at slide 4 and share the "Digital Footprint" (OER 4.4.2) Quicktime Movie before discussing each of the eight scenarios from the movie.
12. After viewing and discussing the entire "Digital Footprint" (OER 4.4.1) Power-Point, go back to the data previously gathered and placed in the chart on the "Footprint Data" (ORS 4.4.2) spreadsheet.

Embedded AASL Skills Indicator: ___.___.___: _____

_____

Embedded AASL Dispositions in Action Indicator: ___.___.___: _____

_____

13. Ask students to turn to the person sitting next to them, or others at their table, and using what they already know about digital footprints, discuss what the data in the "Footprint Data" (ORS 4.4.1) spreadsheet chart shows about the class. Does the data show that the class has already left a large digital footprint? Or, perhaps the data shows that the class has not shared any information on the Internet at all. Ask students to explain how the class can work towards making a responsible digital footprint.

Closure:

Embedded AASL Skills Indicator: ___.___.___: _____

_____

14. Ask students to complete the self-assessment on the back of the "Footprint Survey" (WS 4.4.1).

Embedded AASL Self-Assessment Strategy Indicator: ___.___.___: _____

_____

15. Give students time to complete their self-assessment.
16. Ask students to share their self-assessments with the class and address any questions students may have.

Evidence of Understanding:

Check for understanding as students participate in discussions related to digital footprints and responsible Internet behavior.

Technology Integration:

Technology

NETS-S

3. Research and Information Fluency

Students apply digital tools to gather, evaluate, and use information. Students:

  b. locate, organize, analyze, evaluate, synthesize, and ethically use information from a variety of sources and media.

   Students can listen to and view advice and tips regarding digital footprints through the following Web site: http://www.kidsmart.org.uk/digitalfootprints/. Students can use the advice and ideas from the site to assist in completing their self-assessment.

Extension:

  1. Challenge students to discuss the positive and negative impact of digital footprints with their family. Together with either their family or teachers, students can create an action plan for creating a responsible digital footprint.

Suggested Modifications:

For students who will need an additional visual aid of the information shared in the "Digital Footprint" (OER 4.4.1) PowerPoint, print out the slides in the "notes" view format so that students can record their thoughts or follow along as they view the "Digital Footprint" (OER 4.4.2) Quicktime Movie.

FOOTPRINT

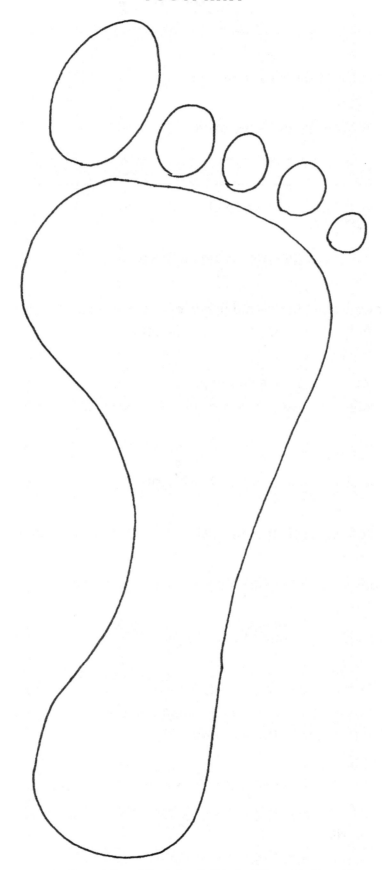

FOOTPRINT SURVEY

Name: _____

1. Have you ever gone on a Web site before?

   ☐ Yes   ☐ No

   If yes, list one or two that you have used.

   _____

   _____

2. Have you ever downloaded pictures off of the Internet?

   ☐ Yes   ☐ No

3. Have you ever uploaded pictures to the Internet?

   ☐ Yes   ☐ No

4. Have you ever participated (even if it was only once) on a social networking site such as Club Penguin, Facebook, Myspace, or something similar?

   ☐ Yes   ☐ No

Name a social networking site have you used. _____

5. Have you ever submitted your name, or other personal information to enter an online contest?

   ☐ Yes   ☐ No

6. Have you ever downloaded music off the Internet?

   ☐ Yes   ☐ No

7. Have you ever sent or received an e-mail?

   ☐ Yes   ☐ No

8. Do you have your own e-mail account?

   ☐ Yes   ☐ No

9. Have you ever posted a comment to a blog?

   ☐ Yes   ☐ No

10. Have you ever played a video game in which you have communicated to someone else virtually? (through a video game console connected to the Internet, an online game, or an app through a phone or MP3 player?)

    ☐ Yes   ☐ No

11. Have you ever purchased anything online before? (e.g., ringtone, music, graphics, games, etc.)

    ☐ Yes   ☐ No

SELF-ASSESSMENT

How can I share what I have learned with others? _____

_____

_____

_____

_____

How did sharing our classroom data using Excel help me to better understand the lesson?

_____

_____

_____

How can I apply what I learned today to my future actions? _____

_____

_____

_____

What questions do I still have about digital footprints? _____

_____

_____

_____

Where could I go/who could I ask for answers? _____

_____

_____

_____

How have I helped others to understand this lesson better during group discussions?

_____

_____

_____

4TH-GRADE LESSONS

LESSON 2: ONLINE COMMUNICATION

Coordinate! Students will learn how to communicate responsibly and effectively in an online setting. *Coordinate* with the classroom teacher by sharing the National Educational Technology Standards for Teachers (http://www.iste.org/Content/NavigationMenu/NETS/ForTeachers/NETS_for_Teachers.htm) to promote and model digital citizenship and responsibility. Point out that this set of standards is a helpful guide for teachers as they plan technology-related lessons and consider their own professional development.

Cooperate! Students will determine how the actions they perform in a digital setting will have an impact on their present and future endeavors. Students will share their new knowledge in the form of a letter to their parents. *Cooperate* with the classroom teacher to alter the letter slightly to meet all the necessary school and classroom rules in regards to using technology and online communication tools responsibly. Teachers can create a poster-sized version of the letter for the classroom and have all the students sign it as a responsible student contract for online communication practices.

Lesson Plan

Integrated Goals:

Language Arts

Standard 4. Students adjust their use of spoken, written, and visual language (e.g., conventions, style, vocabulary) to communicate effectively with a variety of audiences and for different purposes.

Library Media

AASL 21st Century Standards

Standard 1: Inquire, think critically, and gain knowledge.
Standard 2: Draw conclusions, make informed decisions, apply knowledge to new situations, and create new knowledge.
Standard 3: Share knowledge and participate ethically and productively as members of our democratic society.

Technology

NETS-S

3. Communication and Collaboration

Students use digital media and environments to communicate and work collaboratively, including at a distance, to support individual learning and contribute to the learning of others. Students:

a. interact, collaborate, and publish with peers, experts, or others employing a variety of digital environments and media.

d. contribute to project teams to produce original works or solve problems.

Essential Questions:

How can a person's "digital footprint" affect their future?

How can people communicate effectively in a digital world?

How can students maintain a responsible digital footprint?

Desired Understandings:

Students will understand:

How to leave a responsible "digital footprint."

What precautions to use when sharing information digitally.

How a digital footprint can affect a person positively or negatively.

Integrated Objectives:

- Students will use digital tools to communicate safely and effectively and share their knowledge and understanding with parents and teachers.

Time Required:

45 minutes

Provided Materials:

- "Information Sharing" (OER 4.4.3) PowerPoint
- "Digital Collaborative Document" (ORS 4.4.2)
- "Response Cards" (MN 4.4.1)—Consider using this option for students who require kinesthetic learning options—optional
- "Digital Notes" (WS 4.4.2)—one per student
- "Footprint" (TRS 4.4.1)

Materials You Will Need to Obtain:

- Computers with Internet access for each student pair to use
- An account through Wikispaces, http://www.wikispaces.com/ (for directions on how to set up and use view the "For Teachers" section: http://www.wikispaces.com/site/for/teachers) or Google Apps for Education, http://www.google.com/a/edu (for directions on how to set up and use view the "Resource Center" section, http://www.google.com/a/help/intl/en/edu/resource_center.html), or access to a digital collaborative learning space for students to use safely such as SubEthaEdit.
- Access to Cybersmart (http://www.cybersmart.gov.au/Kids/Tips%20to%20stay%20safe%20and%20cybersmart/Your%20digital%20footprint.aspx) and KidSmart (http://www.kidsmart.org.uk/digitalfootprints/). *Note that you should bookmark these two sites or place the links in an online document for easy student access.
- Computer
- Projection device
- Pencils

Prior to Student Arrival:

Digitally compile both the Cybersmart and KidSmart links listed in the "Materials You Will Need to Obtain" section above. Have them readily available for students to access. Follow the directions in the "Digital Collaborative Document" (ORS 4.4.2) to prepare the digital document necessary to complete this lesson.

Lesson Procedures:

Engagement:

1. Display the "Footprint" (TRS 4.4.1) used in the previous lesson. Ask students to recall what they learned in that lesson and share with the class.
2. Explain that students will expand and collaborate on this knowledge during the day's lesson.

Activity:

3. Explain to students that oftentimes others may be unaware of just how much their digital footprint may affect their lives—whether in a good or bad way. Remind students that in the previous class, they discussed ways that information is shared digitally.
4. If using the optional "Response Card" (MN 4.4.1), distribute the cards to each student.
5. Display the "Information Sharing" (OER 4.4.3) PowerPoint.
6. As you share the "Information Sharing" (OER 4.4.3) PowerPoint with students, tell students that the scenarios shared on the PowerPoint can either have a positive or negative impact on students.
7. It will be up to students to decide if the scenario is either "good" or "bad." They should reflect their decision by a show of a "thumb's up," "thumb's down," or hold up the appropriate side of their "Response Card" (MN 4.4.1) to share their answer with the rest of the class. Use the student responses to prompt a conversation about how information shared on the Internet can have either a positive or negative impact on an individual's future. Discuss ways in which the negative responses can be changed to reflect a more positive outcome.

Embedded AASL Skills Indicator: ___.___.___: _____

_____

8. Record and display the student's ideas as they are shared.

Embedded AASL Responsibilities Indicator: ___.___.___: _____

_____

9. Distribute copies of "Digital Notes" (WS 4.4.2) and explain that students will be investigating other tips about online information sharing on their own. They should record their ideas on the provided worksheet, "Digital Notes" (WS 4.4.2), and they will have an opportunity to share, discuss, and elaborate on their ideas together later in the class.

Transition:

10. Display the Cybersmart and KidSmart links you embedded from the "Materials You Will Need to Obtain" section of this lesson.
11. Show students how to access the sites and allow students a few moments to become familiar with the Web sites and the types of information they can find there.

Activity:

Embedded AASL Skills Indicator: ___.___.___: _____

_____

12. Allow students time to complete the activity individually.
13. Explain to students that one of the biggest problems with online safety and sharing information digitally is that others may be unaware of how it will affect them in both the short and long term. It will be important for students to make a commitment to sharing information appropriately and responsibly.
14. In order to share what they know, and to also make a commitment about their future in the digital world, explain that students will be responsible for writing a letter to their parents and teacher which informs them of what they learned and acts as an action plan for their future in the digital world.

Embedded AASL Dispositions in Action Indicator: ___.___.___: _____

_____

15. Display the online environment created using a wikispace, GoogleDoc, or document on SubEthaEdit. Tell students that a digital collaborative document is a place where information can be shared in real time. Once a document is posted, others who have access to the document can not only read it but they can also edit, add, and make changes to it. This will allow students to share their ideas together to create a collaborative letter.
16. Demonstrate how to add information to the online document.
17. Place students into pairs and allow them time to share their thoughts in the space provided in the online document.

Embedded AASL Skills Indicator: ___.___.___: _____

_____

Embedded AASL Skills Indicator: ___.___.___: _____

_____

Closure:

Embedded AASL Self-Assessment Strategy Indicator: ___.___.___: _____

_____

18. Once students have entered their information into the collaborative digital space, read aloud the thoughts they have compiled. Together as a class, have students contribute to the writing of the letter and make their editing suggestions.

19. Edit the student's suggestions and print copies of the completed letter for students to take and share with their teacher and parents. As an extra reminder for students to be responsible with the type of information they share digitally, have students sign a copy of the letter along with their parents and teacher.

Evidence of Understanding:

Check that students are actively participating in the class discussions as well as paired activities. Collect the "Digital Notes" (WS 4.4.2) and check that students demonstrated understanding through the answers they provided.

Enrichment Using Technology:

Using the letter created in class, have students compose an e-mail (if this is available as an option for students) to their parent/guardian or teacher, explaining what they learned about digital footprints.

Extension:

1. After some time has passed (a week or two) after completing this lesson, have students complete the "Future Footprint Survey" (EX 4.4.1; one sheet per student) and place the data gathered from the survey into the "Future Footprint Data" (OEX 4.4.2) spreadsheet. Compare the results of this data with that of the previous "Footprint Data" (ORS 4.4.1) data chart to determine whether students are being more responsible in regards to their digital footprint.

2. Read the book *That's Good! That's Bad!* by Margery Cuyler (New York: Henry Holt, 1993) to coincide with the structure of the "Information Sharing" (OER 4.4.3) PowerPoint. Students will enjoy participating in the story by shouting back "That's Good!" or "That's Bad!"

Suggested Modifications:

Students in need of modifications can be placed into pairs prior to students beginning the "Digital Collaborative Document" (ORS 4.4.3). Students can share the workload of the "Digital Notes" (WS 4.4.2) worksheet, or offer them the modified worksheet "Digital Notes" (MOD 4.4.1) to complete individually.

RESPONSE CARDS

That's Good! That's Bad!

That's Good! That's Bad!

That's Good! That's Bad!

That's Good! That's Bad!

That's Good! That's Bad!

That's Good! That's Bad!

271

DIGITAL NOTES

Name: _____

Directions: Use what you have already learned about digital footprints, along with evidence from the Webs ites about digital footprints to take notes in your own words and draw conclusions about the following questions. Be sure and cite the Web site(s) you used at the bottom of the paper.

1. How can you protect your personal information when you are online?

   _____

   _____

   _____

   _____

   _____

2. Knowing that universities and future employers are watching you, what types of activities should or shouldn't you be doing to build a responsible digital footprint?

   _____

   _____

   _____

   _____

   _____

3. What should you do if you are online and are contacted by someone you don't know?

   _____

   _____

   _____

   _____

4. What is an IP address and how is it related to digital footprints?

   _____

   _____

   _____

   _____

   _____

5. Create one or two tips or suggestions for you and your classmate to use when you share information digitally.

_____

_____

_____

_____

_____

Source citations: _____

_____

_____

_____

_____

FUTURE FOOTPRINT SURVEY

Name: _____

1. After learning about digital footprints, are you now more careful when sharing information on the Internet?

    ☐ Yes   ☐ No

2. If you have an account with a social networking site such as Club Penguin, Facebook, Myspace, or something similar, have you changed your privacy settings since learning about digital footprints?

    ☐ Yes   ☐ No

3. Are you more aware and cautious about the information you share on the Internet?

    ☐ Yes   ☐ No

4. Have you discussed with your parents how and when you should be using the Internet?

    ☐ Yes   ☐ No

5. Do you have a plan in place for what to do in case you are ever in an unsafe situation in regards to the Internet?

    ☐ Yes   ☐ No

DIGITAL NOTES

Name: _____

Directions: Use what you have already learned about digital footprints, along with evidence from the Web sites about digital footprints to take notes in your own words and draw conclusions about the following questions. Be sure and cite the Web site(s) you used at the bottom of the paper.

1. How can you protect your personal information when you are online?

   _____
   _____
   _____
   _____
   _____

2. How can you build a responsible digital footprint?

   _____
   _____
   _____
   _____
   _____

3. What should you do if you are online and are contacted by someone you don't know?

   _____
   _____
   _____
   _____
   _____

   Source citations: _____

   _____
   _____
   _____
   _____

Working in Collaboration

Collaboration

Collaborate! True collaboration requires both the library media specialist and the classroom teacher to share in the design of integrated instruction. Collaboration provides you with an excellent opportunity to design inquiry-based learning activities. Here are some ideas for collaborating with the classroom teachers.

4th Grade: Social Studies

Essential Question: How can technology be monitored to protect the rights of individuals?

- Create a debate on ways technology is currently being monitored. Students can probe deeper into the subject and explore computer filters and how they are used in school systems. Students can debate the pros and cons of using filters in the school system. Students could create suggestions for how these sensitive issues would best be handled and share their ideas in a letter to the school superintendent or principal.

Essential Question: How can an acceptable use policy help or hinder students when working on the Internet?

- Explore your school system's "Acceptable Use of Computer Technology" policy. Students can discuss how the policy ideas either help or hinder overall student achievement. Students could design a plan of action that outlines how the policy could be improved. Students could incorporate what they learned from this unit into their plan of action.

For further information, please visit
www.destinationcollaboration.com

5TH-GRADE LESSONS

LESSON 1: PRACTICAL COMMUNICATION

 **Coordinate!** During this lesson students will learn how to choose between communication methods. These methods include: face to face, telephone, letter writing, texting, instant messaging, and social network. Coordinate by offering to teach these lessons when classroom teachers are discussing letter writing, essay writing, or other writing techniques in classroom work.

Cooperate! Students will compare class data with national data in regards to communication methods. *Cooperate* with the classroom teacher by sharing the "Communication Survey Data" (ORS 4.5.1) Excel spreadsheet (data are from Lenhart [2009]). Discuss how this spreadsheet can be edited to meet other objectives or needs regarding technology use. Create a new survey together, survey multiple classes, and have students chart, compare, and share the results using a specific practical communication method. Also consider sharing the "Ways to Communicate" (OER 4.5.1) PowerPoint with the classroom teacher and offer the use of the PowerPoint for a classroom debate about 21st century communication options. Debate topics could include students respecting the ideas of others and how to communicate responsibly.

Lesson Plan

Integrated Goals:

Language Arts

Standard 12. Students use spoken, written, and visual language to accomplish their own purposes (e.g., for learning, enjoyment, persuasion, and the exchange of information).

Library Media

AASL 21st Century Standards

Standard 1: Inquire, think critically, and gain knowledge.
Standard 2: Draw conclusions, make informed decisions, apply knowledge to new situations, and create new knowledge.
Standard 3: Share knowledge and participate ethically and productively as members of our democratic society.

Essential Questions:

How do communication tools help or hinder our contact with others?
What are the preferred communication methods of students?
When is it appropriate to use informal vs. formal writing?

> **DISCUSSION OPPORTUNITY**
>
> Use this lesson as an opportunity to discuss ways in which students communicate with one another. Asking students why we have so many ways to communicate with one another is a great discussion starter.

Desired Understandings:

Students will understand:

How to communicate effectively.
How the class's use of communication compares with that of the nation.
How to use communication tools appropriately.

Integrated Objectives:

- Students will determine appropriate ways to communicate information to meet a variety of different purposes.
- Students will compare the ways in which they communicate with the national average.
- Students will understand when it is appropriate to use formal vs. informal communication.

Time Required:

45 minutes

Provided Materials:

- "Text Message" (RS 4.5.1)
- "Ways to Communicate" (OER 4.5.1) PowerPoint
- "Communication Survey" (RS 4.5.2)
- "Communication Survey Data" (ORS 4.5.1) Excel spreadsheet
- "Communication Conundrum" (WS 4.5.1)—one per student

Materials You Will Need to Obtain:

- Computer
- Projection device
- Pencils
- Cell phone

Lesson Procedures:

Engagement:

1. Have your cell phone in the classroom and pretend as though you are receiving a text message. Share the "Text Message" (RS 4.5.1) with the students.
2. Ask a student to read the message aloud.

Activity:

Embedded AASL Skills Indicator: ___.___.___: _____

_____

3. Ask students to share when it is appropriate to use text messaging. (texting with friends, sending quick messages, etc.).
4. Ask students to share when it wouldn't be appropriate to use text messaging to communicate with someone else (e.g., when you want to have a long conversation or when you want to have a conversation with someone in real time).

5. Explain to students that they will be learning about appropriate ways to use different forms of communication.
6. Display the "Ways to Communicate" (OER 4.5.1) PowerPoint and use the "notes" section of the PowerPoint to guide the instruction.
7. Progress through the "Ways to Communicate" (OER 4.5.1) PowerPoint and engage students in a discussion about ways to communicate information.
8. Stop the PowerPoint on slide 8. Explain to students that the next slide contains statistics, which shows the average communication methods of teenagers.

Embedded AASL Skills Indicator: ___.___.___: _____

_____

9. Tell students it would be interesting to compare the national data with data from the class to determine how students in the class communicate with one another in comparison with the national average.

Transition:

10. Ask students the survey questions from the "Communication Survey" (RS 4.5.2).
11. Record their answers in the "Communication Survey Data" (ORS 4.5.1) Excel spreadsheet.

Activity:

12. Once the answers have been recorded in the spreadsheet, compare the class results with those of the national average.
13. Distribute copies of "Communication Conundrum" (WS 4.5.1) to each student.

AASL Self Assessment Strategy Indicator: ___.___.___: _____

_____

AASL Dispositions in Action Indicator: ___.___.___: _____

_____

AASL Responsibilities Indicator: ___.___.___: _____

_____

14. Have students complete the self-assessment, which asks for students to share why they use the communication methods they use as opposed to other communication methods.
15. Give students time to complete the self-assessments.

16. After students have completed their self-assessment, ask students to read the scenario on the back of the "Communication Conundrum" (WS 4.5.1) worksheet and record the best communication method for the scenario and explain why the method they chose is the best communication option.

Closure:

Embedded AASL Skills Indicator: ___.___.___: _____

_____

17. Have students share the communication method for the scenario on the "Communication Conundrum" (WS 4.5.1) worksheet and the reasons why they selected that method. Discuss the answers together as a class.

Evidence of Understanding:

Collect the "Communication Conundrum" (WS 4.5.1) worksheets. Check that students completed the self-assessment and applied what they learned from the lesson to demonstrate new understandings.

Enrichment Using Technology:

Have students access Read, Write, Think's Web page and practice creating a profile online. Take this opportunity to discuss appropriate information to share online (http://www.readwritethink.org/classroom-resources/student-interactives/profile-publisher-30067.html).

Extension:

Have students complete the "Communication AdLib" (EX 4.5.1). Students will enjoy reading the story and filling in the blanks.

Suggested Modifications:

Consider having students work in small groups or pairs rather than individually.

TEXT MESSAGE

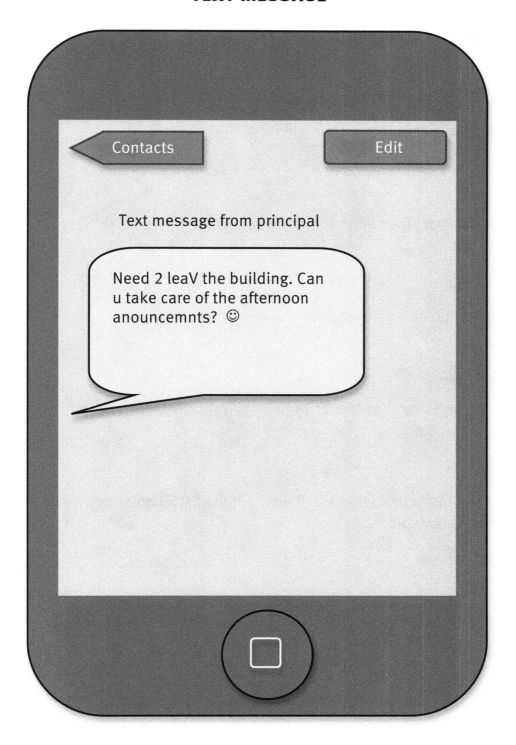

COMMUNICATION SURVEY

1. Do you spend time with friends face to face?

2. Do you talk to your friends on a landline?

3. Do you talk to your friends on your cell phone?

4. Do you communicate with friends by sending them email?

5. Do you send messages to friends through social networking sites?

6. Do you send instant messages to friends through MSN messenger, AIM, GoogleChat, or another IM feature?

7. Do you send text messages to friends?

COMMUNICATION CONUNDRUM

Name: _____

SELF-ASSESSMENT

Directions: Look at the results of the Communication Survey on display. Looking at how you and your classmates communicate, how does it compare with the National average? How is it the same or different, and why?

_____

_____

_____

_____

Is there one communication method you prefer over another? What is it and explain why you prefer this method compared to other methods. Be specific.

_____

_____

_____

_____

What communication tools would you like to use in school? How would they help you learn?

_____

_____

_____

_____

What do you think would be the best way to communicate with your friends and family members? Be as creative as you like—perhaps your idea hasn't been invented yet.

_____

_____

_____

_____

ACTIVITY

Directions: Read the scenario below. Then answer the question below the scenario.

COMMUNICATION SCENARIO

It's a Friday afternoon. You are home from school and get online to check your e-mail. Whoa! In your e-mail is a message from the Young Artists Organization. You had sent your watercolor landscape to them in a contest they were holding a month ago. You've been selected as a finalist! The e-mail states that your work has been posted Online. Young Artists has provided you with a link to the work and now it is up to the people who visit the website to vote on your work. You have three days to get as many votes as you can. If your art gets the most votes, you will receive a round trip vacation for you and 3 other people to the Eric Carle museum of Picture Book Art in Massachusetts. Now it's up to you to contact as many people as you know, as quickly as you can, and to provide them with the information. Take a look at the list of your friends and family below and record the communication method you would use to contact them, and explain why.

Grandparents: Your grandparents live in a very small town in Maine. They don't believe in cell phones or the Internet. How would you communicate with them? Explain why this is the method you chose. _____

_____
_____
_____

Parents and Sibling: You live with your parents and older brother and see them everyday. How would you communicate with them? Explain why this is the method you chose.

_____
_____
_____

Friends: You have quite a few friends at school, and could tell them on Monday. But it is Friday and by the time you tell your friends about the contest on Monday, it will be too late. How would you communicate with them? What would you say? Explain why this is the method you chose. _____

_____
_____
_____

COMMUNICATION ADLIB

Name: _____

Directions: Work with a partner to complete the AdLib below. Don't read the paragraph until after you have asked your partner to provide you with all of the words in the blank spaces. For example; the first blank line asks for a person's name. Ask your partner for a person's name and fill in the blank with the word they provide. After you ask your partner for all of the required words to fill in the blanks, read your story aloud.

One day, _____ received a text message from
person's name (person A)

_____ about _____. However,
person's name (person B)   school subject

the text message was confusing because all the letters were squished together,

so _____ didn't know what the message said. Not
person's name (person A)

thinking it was a big deal, _____ packed up their
person's name (person A)

backpack, making sure to pack their _____, _____,
noun   noun

and _____. Meanwhile, _____
noun   person's name (person B)

was tapping their _____, waiting for a response. Not sure where
body part

_____ was, _____ decided
person's name (person A)   person's name (person B)

to send an e-mail. While waiting for a response, _____
person's name (person B)

ate some _____. After waiting _____ minutes
food product   number

without hearing anything, _____ decided to call from
person's name (person B)

their _____ cell phone. _____
color   person's name (person A)

answered on the _____ ring. "Where have you been!?" said
number

_____. "I tried texting and e-mailing you, but
person's name (person B)

I couldn't get a hold of you."

"Well, said _____, I _____
person's name (person A)   verb in the past tense

home from school as fast as I could, but on the way I ran into a _____
adjective

_____, a _____ _____, and
noun   adjective   noun

a _____ _____!"
adjective   noun

"Wow! That does sound pretty _____! Do you have time to help me
adjective

with my homework question now?" asked _____.
person's name (person B)

"Well," said _____, "that might be a problem. . . . I think
person's name (person A)

I think I left it at school! I think we will need to _____ the
method of communication

teacher and find out what we missed!"

5TH-GRADE LESSONS

LESSON 2: EFFECTIVE COMMUNICATION

Coordination

Coordinate! Students will determine the most effective ways to communicate information and provide their reasons for why the method they selected is the most effective. Use this lesson to *coordinate* with the classroom teacher on how to teach students about effective communication in relation to school. Students could brainstorm ways they communicate information and create a new set of "Communication Cards" (MN 4.5.1) to use with their class.

Cooperation

Cooperate! Students will communicate responsibly, ethically, and effectively with one another on a blog, wiki, or Google group space. Use this as an opportunity to *cooperate* with the classroom teacher. Share the information students have posted in the online space and offer to set up another collaborative space for students to share and discuss topics of interest in the classroom. This is a great way to encourage students to communicate outside of the classroom about school-related topics and to do it in a safe and responsible manner.

Lesson Plan

Integrated Goals:

Language Arts

Standard 4. Students adjust their use of spoken, written, and visual language (e.g., conventions, style, vocabulary) to communicate effectively with a variety of audiences and for different purposes.

Standard 12. Students use spoken, written, and visual language to accomplish their own purposes (e.g., for learning, enjoyment, persuasion, and the exchange of information).

Library Media

AASL 21st Century Standards

Standard 1: Inquire, think critically, and gain knowledge.
Standard 2: Draw conclusions, make informed decisions, apply knowledge to new situations, and create new knowledge.
Standard 3: Share knowledge and participate ethically and productively as members of our democratic society.

Essential Questions:

How do different communication tools meet different communication needs?

> **SCHOOL CONNECTION**
>
> Have students share what they learned in this lesson in the form of a public service announcement to the entire school during morning or afternoon announcements.

When is it appropriate to use informal vs. formal writing?
What is considered "appropriate" online behavior?

Desired Understandings:

Students will understand:

How to communicate effectively.
How to use communication tools appropriately.
How to communicate appropriately and responsibly online.

Integrated Objectives:

- Students will determine appropriate ways to communicate information to meet a variety of different purposes.
- Students will understand when it is appropriate to use formal vs. informal communication.
- Students will communicate with one another online in a responsible and respectful manner.

Time Required:

45 minutes

Provided Materials:

- "Communication Cards" (MN 4.5.1)—one set per student group
- "Effective Communication" (OER 4.5.2) PowerPoint
- "Online Instructions" (TRS 4.5.1)
- "Communicating Effectively" (OER 4.5.3) PowerPoint—optional—Technology has already been integrated into this lesson through the use of a blog, wiki, or Google group. However, if this is not an option well suited for the class, use the "Communicating Effectively" (OER 4.5.3) PowerPoint for students to share what they learned. Give students access to this PowerPoint and have each student add a slide to the PowerPoint to show what they learned. Display the slides and use them to prompt further discussion in regards to effective communication methods.

Materials You Will Need to Obtain:

- Computer
- Projection device
- Pencils
- Computers for student use

Prior to Student Arrival:

Use the "Online Instructions" (TRS 4.5.1) to create a blog, wikispace, or Google group to which your students can access and add their input during this lesson.

Lesson Procedures:

Engagement:

1. Have students sit in groups of two to four.
2. Distribute the "Communication Cards" (MN 4.5.1) sets to each group.

Embedded AASL Skills Indicator: ___.___.___: _____

_____

3. Explain that students should spread out the cards, read them aloud, and work with the other members of their group to match up the situation to the appropriate form of communication. Students should communicate with each other to explain their reasons for selecting the communication method they did, and why.

Activity:

4. Give students time to complete the activity.
5. Ask for each student group to share one or two of the matches they made. Students should also share how their group determined that the communication method they selected was the best method for the situation.

Transition:

6. Explain to students that there is a time and place for everything and determining the appropriate method to communicate information depends on who is involved and what type of information is being communicated.
7. Display the "Effective Communication" (OER 4.5.2) PowerPoint.

Activity:

8. Follow the directions and prompts in the "notes" section of the "Effective Communication" (OER 4.5.2) PowerPoint to guide the discussion and encourage student participation in the lesson.
9. After discussing all of the slides in the "Effective Communication" (OER 4.5.2) PowerPoint, display the blog, wiki, or Google group you created using the "Online Instructions" (TRS 4.5.1) for this lesson.

Embedded AASL Skills Indicator: ___.___.___: _____

_____

10. Read the directions aloud and explain that students will now synthesize what they learned to communicate with one another in a responsible and effective manner online.

Transition:

11. Give students access to computers and the site created for this lesson. Students may work individually or in pairs to complete the assignment.

Activity:

Embedded AASL Skills Indicator: ___.___.___: _____

_____

12. Give students time to complete the activity.
13. Display the site so that students can see their responses posted in real time.

Embedded AASL Dispositions in Action Indicator: ___.___.___: _____

_____

Embedded AASL Responsibilities Indicator: ___.___.___: _____

_____

14. Once students have made their initial comments, redirect them to now make comments about what other students had to say on the site. Students should be thoughtful and considerate when posting responses and should practice effective communication skills they learned from the "Effective Communication" (OER 4.5.2) PowerPoint earlier in the lesson.
15. Read several of the comments and responses aloud and provide insight for how the comments demonstrated effective communication. Provide suggestions for improvement if needed.

Closure:

Embedded AASL Responsibilities Indicator: ___.___.___: _____

_____

Embedded AASL Self-Assessment Strategy Indicator: ___.___.___: _____

_____

16. Ask students to share what they learned from this lesson. Questions to use for discussion could include but are not limited to: How has this lesson helped you to become more effective when communicating with others? How will you use the information you learned in this lesson to communicate effectively in the future?

Evidence of Understanding:

Check for student participation throughout the lesson. View and monitor the student responses on the blog, wiki, or Google group site you created.

Enrichment Using Technology:

1. The library media specialist can visit the Unabridged Instant Text Message Dictionary (http://www.net-comber.com/acronyms.

SCHOOL CONNECTION

Using the school newsletter as a communication tool, have students share what they learned about effective communication. Students can even take a poll about communication methods used by community members and post the results in the next newsletter.

html) or the Text Message Translator (http://www.lingo2word.com/index.php). Use these sites for reference to create an appropriate text message for students to rewrite as a personal letter using correct spelling and punctuation. Note that these sites are for library media specialists reference only in order to locate and use acronyms for students to rewrite as a personal letter using correct spelling and punctuation. With students, discuss the importance of not using text messaging shortcuts in formal writing.

Extension:

Have students complete the "Muddled Messages" (EX 4.5.2) in which students have to decipher text messages and write them in the proper way if they were sending them in proper English. Use the "Muddle Messages Key" (EX 4.5.3) as a key for deciphering the text messages.

Suggested Modifications:

For students in need of modification, print the "Communicating Effectively" (OER 4.5.3) PowerPoint notes view with one slide per page. Students can write their ideas on the page as opposed to typing their answers on the PowerPoint or on the blog, wiki, or Google group.

COMMUNICATION CARDS

Directions: Copy and cut out one set of "Communication Cards" for each student group. Laminate the cards to prolong their use from class to class and year to year.

Communication	Situation
Text Message	You want to tell everyone in your family contact list that you got an "A" on your math test.
Instant Message	You know that your best friend is online and you want to talk to her without having your older brother hear your conversation.
Phone Call	You are planning on visiting your family in another state over the summer. You need to contact them and find out if and when would be a good time for you to visit.

Communication	Situation
Face-to-Face	You and your older sister go shopping for new shoes and school supplies and stop to get lunch on the way home.
E-mail	You read about a student leadership opportunity offered through a government Web site and you want to find out more information about it.
Social Networking	You moved schools recently and don't have contact information for many of your old friends you left behind, but you really want to keep in touch.

ONLINE INSTRUCTIONS

Create a blog, wiki, or Google group in which students in your class can access and contribute to the content of the site. If you do not have a Google Apps for Education account with your school, you will want to set more strict parameters in place regarding content approval. For example, you may wish to have the content go to your e-mail first so that you can view it and approve or deny it before it goes on the Web. This will ensure that your students are practicing safe and appropriate online behavior. Once you have set up and created a blog, wiki, or Google group to use with your class, post the directions, scenario, and writing prompt below onto your blog, wiki, or Google group discussion area.

DIRECTIONS

Read the scenario below. Then, read the writing prompt. Post your response below the prompt. Make sure you do not include any personal information, or do not include your last name. The information on this site is public, which means that anyone in the world can see it. Practice safe and responsible behavior as you communicate positively and effectively with one another using this valuable communication tool. After your classmates have made their posts, read through each one. Think about their comments, questions, and concerns, and then respond to two of your classmates and provide them with thoughtful and insightful feedback.

SCENARIO

Janna loves music and thankfully her mom has allowed her to be in the band at school. She made a lot of new friends in the band and is now on a social networking site to keep up with all of her new friends. Just so she doesn't lose touch with anyone, she has her e-mail address publicly posted on her social networking profile page. Among her networks are her school name and the town and state where she lives. She remembered that she shouldn't post her photo as public, so she has limited her profile pictures to only be shown to her friends and friends of friends. She has multiple e-mail accounts and instant messaging accounts and has trouble keeping track of all of her incoming messages.

PROMPT

If you were Janna's friend, what advice would you give to her about social networking? Is there a more effective method of communication you could suggest for her to use? Explain your answer.

MUDDLED MESSAGES

Name: _____

Directions: Take a look at the text messages below. Decipher and rewrite the text messages into grammatically correct sentences, which would be appropriate to include in a formal letter. Check for spelling, proper capitalization and punctuation, and grammar usage.

1. hw r u? wnt 2 go 2 the mvies?

   _____

2. WUD this w/e? mayB we cn gt 2gthr n hng out? I got a QL nu vid gme we cld play.

   _____

3. DY knw w@ r hmwrk asynmnt S 4 2nite!?!?!?! I lst myn!!!!!

   _____

4. i got a nu pup! shes so cute!!!! Im gona snd u a pic of her

   _____

5. i thnk i jst saw rachel @ th mall. Wznt she ot sick frm skool 2day!?!?!?!!?

   _____

6. I wsh I cld trade my bro 4 a sis.He cn B sucha pain sumtyms. 2day he red my diary!!
   UGH!!!!!!

   _____

   How do you think you did? _____

   Was this task harder or easier than you thought it would be?

   _____

   Why?

   _____

   _____

MUDDLED MESSAGES KEY

Name: _____

Directions: Take a look at the text messages below. Decipher and rewrite the text messages into grammatically correct sentences, which would be appropriate to include in a formal letter. Check for spelling, proper capitalization and punctuation, and grammar usage.

1. hw r u? wnt 2 go 2 the mvies?

   How are you? Do you want to go to the movies?

2. WUD this w/e? mayB we cn gt 2gthr n hng out? I got a QL nu vid gme we cld play.

   What are you doing this weekend? Maybe we can get together and hang out? I got a cool new video game we could play.

3. DY knw w@ r hmwrk asynmnt S 4 2nite!?!?!?! I lst myn!!!!!

   Do you know what our homework assignment is for tonight? I lost mine!

4. i got a nu pup! shes so cute!!!! Im gona snd u a pic of her

   I got a new puppy! She is so cute! I'm going to send you a picture of her.

5. i thnk i jst saw rachel @ th mall. Wznt she ot sick frm skool 2day!?!?!?!!?

   I think I just saw Rachel at the mall. Wasn't she out sick from school today?

6. I wsh I cld trade my bro 4 a sis.He cn B sucha pain sumtyms. 2day he red my diary!! UGH!!!!!!

   I wish I could trade my brother for a sister. He can be such a pain sometimes. Today he read my diary! UGH!

   How do you think you did? _____

   Was this task harder or easier than you thought it would be?

   _____

   Why?

   _____

   _____

Working in Collaboration

Collaborate! True collaboration requires both the library media specialist and the classroom teacher to share in the design of integrated instruction. Collaboration provides you with an excellent opportunity to design inquiry-based learning activities. Here are some ideas for collaborating with the classroom teachers.

5th Grade: Social Studies

Essential Question: How has technology changed the way we communicate with one another?

- Students can research ways communication methods have changed over the years, from writing instruments to the invention of the telephone, the invention of the Internet, and so forth. Another possible activity would be to design a project in which students can discuss and share how communication methods have changed our society.

For further information, please visit
www.destinationcollaboration.com

Bibliography
Work Cited

Lenhart, Amanda. "Teens and Social Media: An Overview." *PEW Internet.* 10 Apr. 2009. Web. 18 Jan. 2010. <http://www.pewinternet.org/Presentations/2009/17-Teens-and-Social-Media-An-Overview.aspx>.

Suggested Print Resource

Cuyler, Margery. *That's Good! That's Bad!* New York: Henry Holt, 1993. Print.

Suggested Web Resources

Carter, Lori. "Internet Safety for Kids." *Internet Safety Custom Search Engine.* Google, 16 Jan. 2010. Web. 24 Jan. 2010. <http://www.google.com/cse/home?cx=006210179467973393198:kqmasc-8dus>.

Cybersmart. Commonwealth of Australia, 19 Aug. 2009. Web. 12 Dec. 2009. <http://www.cybersmart.gov.au/Kids/Tips%20to%20stay%20safe%20and%20cybersmart/Your%20digital%20footprint.aspx>.

"Digital Footprints." *KidSmart.* Childnet International. 2009. Web. 12 Dec. 2009. <http://www.kidsmart.org.uk/digitalfootprints/>.

DuPuis, Danielle, and Lori Carter. *Internet Scavenger Hunt.* Google. 2010. Web. 24 Jan. 2010. <http://sites.google.com/site/dcinternetscavengerhunt/>.

"Google apps." *Google.* Google. 2010. Web. 18 Jan. 2010. <http://www.google.com/a/edu>.

"NETS for Teachers." *ISTE.* ISTE. 2010. Web. 18 Jan. 2010. <http://www.iste.org/Content/NavigationMenu/NETS/ForTeachers/NETS_for_Teachers.htm>.

"Profile Publisher." *ReadWriteThink.* IRA/NCTE. 2010. Web. 24 Jan. 2010. <http://www.readwritethink.org/classroom-resources/student-interactives/profile-publisher-30067.html>.

Shook, Jim. *Unabridged Instant Text Message Dictionary.* 2005. Web. 24 Jan. 2010. <http://www.net-comber.com/acronyms.html>.

"Text Message Translator." *Lingo2Word.* The Great Service Company, 2010. Web. 24 Jan. 2010. <http://www.lingo2word.com/index.php>.

Warner, Mark. *Welcome to the Web.* Teaching Ideas, 2009. Web. 24 Jan. 2010. <http://www.teachingideas.co.uk/welcome/>.

"Wikispaces." *Wikispaces.* Tangient LLC, 2009. Web. 18 Jan. 2010. <http://www.wikispaces.com/>.

Zapato, Lyle. *Save the Pacific Northwest Tree Octopus.* ZPi, 11 Nov. 2009. Web. 24 Jan. 2010. <http://zapatopi.net/treeoctopus/>.

Appendix A

Let's Collaborate!

1. At the end of our unit, we would like for our students to be able to

_____
_____
_____

2. What curriculum standards will we include?

Content

_____
_____
_____
_____
_____
_____
_____
_____
_____

Information Literacy

_____
_____
_____
_____
_____
_____
_____
_____
_____

Technology

_____
_____
_____
_____
_____
_____
_____
_____
_____

3. How will we assess that students have met these standards?

_____
_____
_____
_____
_____

Okay, now let's plan the lessons!

Let's meet again on _____.
We will bring _____
_____.

Appendix B

LET'S PLAN OUR LESSONS

Date: _____

What to bring to the meeting:

- Your personal planning calendar

- Your curriculum documents (use the standards that your school system requires)

  - National standards

  - State standards

  - Local standards

- Lesson plans you have used previously (use these as building blocks for collaboration)

  - Artifacts

  - Exemplary work

- Resources that you would like to use with this unit

  - Books

  - Online databases that your school system has purchased

  - Web sites

  - Other reference materials

  - Manipulatives

THINK ABOUT YOUR COLLABORATIVE UNIT

Think about whether this will be a collaborative unit or a single lesson. How will this unit/ lesson look and be implemented whether taught in the classroom, library media center, or by co-teaching in either location:

- What objectives will we use?
  - Students should be able to use:
    - Bloom's Taxonomy
      - http://www.teachers.ash.org.au/researchskills/dalton.htm
      - http://nerds.unl.edu/pages/preser/sec/articles/blooms.html

- What lessons have I used in the past that may be useful?
  - Lesson ideas
    - _____
    - _____

- How does this lesson require that our students perform an authentic task?
  - Real-life task
    - _____
    - _____

- Could the final product be changed to improve student learning?
  - Final product ideas
    - _____
    - _____

- How can we implement the use of technology into this lesson?
  - Internet
    - _____
  - Online databases
    - _____
  - Hardware
    - _____

- Software
- _____

- Think about current concerns for student achievement in your classroom.
  - Identify concerns
    - Individual Educational Plan (IEP)
    - Student behaviors
    - _____
  - How will these concerns be addressed?
    - _____

- Who will teach the objectives?
  - Library media specialist
    - _____
  - Classroom teacher
    - _____
  - Both
    - _____
  - Other teacher
    - _____

- Where will the learning occur?
  - Classroom
  - Library media center
  - Computer lab
  - Other

- Who will create the materials?
  - New materials
    - _____
  - Adapted materials
    - _____

- We will need to obtain

  - _____

  - _____

- Who will collect and grade students' work?

  - Library media specialist

  - Classroom teacher

  - Both

    - _____

    - _____

  - Other

- Does this lesson/unit remind us of another lesson/unit on which we could collaborate?

  - _____

LESSON PLAN TEMPLATE

Unit Name:

Grade Level:

Lesson Name:

Standards:

Objectives:

Time Required:

Materials List:

Materials We Need To Obtain:

Lesson Procedures:

- Engagement: (The engagement should grab your students' attention and set the stage for what is to follow.)

- Activity: (Explain to students what they will do.)

- Transition: (Give students time to complete a task, or transition them to another are— more than one transition may be required.)

- Activity: (Explain to students what they will continue to do.)

- Closure: (Verify that your students have learned the objectives selected for this lesson.)

- Assessment: (Visual, performance based, or ongoing.)

OUR REFLECTION OF THIS UNIT

Unit Name:

Teachers Involved with this Unit:

Grade Level:

Lesson Names:

What were the strengths of this unit?

What could be improved next time?

- Timing of lessons

- Student considerations

- Collaborative changes

- Other teachers that could be involved

- Changing the final product

- Adding, removing, or changing lessons

- Adding, removing, or changing technology integration

Were additional resources or materials needed? If so, what was needed and why?

Another collaborative idea may be:

Index

About the Authors

DANIELLE N. DUPUIS began her career with libraries as an information specialist for Howard County Library in 2001. After graduating in 2005 from the College of Library and Information Studies program at University of Maryland with her Master of Library Science degree, she was hired as a library media specialist for Howard County Public Schools. Danielle became a Google Certified Teacher in 2009 and received a Master's Certificate from Johns Hopkins University in Instructional Technology for Web-based Professional Development in 2010. Her first book, written with colleague and friend Annette C. H. Nelson, was *The Adventures of Super3: A Teacher's Guide to Information Literacy for Grades K-2*, published in July 2010. Danielle continues to educate students attending Howard County Public Schools.

LORI M. CARTER began her career in education in 1996 as a classroom teacher after graduating from Bowie State University, Bowie, Maryland. In 2000 Lori became an elementary library media specialist after graduating from the College of Library and Information Studies program at the University of Maryland with her Master of Library Science degree. In 2002 she became Nationally Board Certified in Library Media/Early Childhood through Young Adult. Lori holds Master's Certificates in both Administration (2003; McDaniel College in Westminster, MD) and Leadership in Technology Integration (2008; Johns Hopkins University, Baltimore, MD). Currently, Lori is an instructional technology teacher for Howard County Public Schools and serves as the professional development liaison at Forest Ridge Elementary School in Laurel, Maryland. In addition, Lori teaches as an online adjunct faculty member for the Master's of Arts in Teaching Program at National University, La Jolla, California. She lives in Crofton, Maryland, with her husband, Rick, and their family.

Danielle and Lori met at curriculum writing during the summer of 2006. Both discovered that their similar views of education in the library media field could be attributed to the education they received from the College of Library and Information Studies program at University of Maryland. Sharing similar views and beliefs in education gave them the foundation necessary to write the Destination Collaboration books together. However, the drive, determination, passion, and persistence shared between the two was what held them together through edit after edit and rewrite after rewrite during a three-year period of mostly collaboration with a fair amount of coordination and cooperation.